T0369585

# Legislating for Justice

# Legislating for Justice

## *The Making of the 2013 Land Acquisition Law*

JAIRAM RAMESH
MUHAMMAD ALI KHAN

OXFORD
UNIVERSITY PRESS

# OXFORD
UNIVERSITY PRESS

Oxford University Press is a department of the University of Oxford.
It furthers the University's objective of excellence in research, scholarship,
and education by publishing worldwide. Oxford is a registered trademark of
Oxford University Press in the UK and in certain other countries

Published in India by
Oxford University Press
YMCA Library Building, 1 Jai Singh Road, New Delhi 110 001, India

ISBN-13: 978-0-19-945899-8
ISBN-10: 0-19-945899-5

Typeset in Adobe Garamond Pro 11/13
by The Graphics Solution, New Delhi 110 092
Printed in India by Rakmo Press, New Delhi 110 020

# Contents

# Preface

This book is about why and how a truly landmark law that enshrined a new and radically different approach to acquiring land and compensating those affected came into being. In September 2013, Parliament gave its thumping approval, after almost 15 hours of debate in both Houses in which over 60 members took part, to the repeal of the colonial-era Land Acquisition Act, 1894 and bring in its place the Right to Fair Compensation and Transparency in Land Acquisition, Rehabilitation and Resettlement Act, 2013. The very name of the new law signified the momentous change. The repeal followed two years of public debate and extensive consultations with all stakeholders after the introduction of the Bill in the Lok Sabha on 7 September 2011.

There was high drama in the run-up to the passage of the law. Two all-party meetings were held to get all political parties on board and address their concerns. Meetings were held with each of these eleven parties individually as well. The Bill came up in the Lok Sabha on 29 August 2013. Those were the times when Parliament used to meet only to get disrupted. But after some hectic negotiations the Bill was taken up and passed that very night. Six days later it was taken up in the Rajya Sabha again after much uncertainty and last-minute negotiations. The Bill passed but with some amendments suggested by the then principal opposition party. This meant that it had to go back to the Lok Sabha and there was just a day left for the session to get over. Fortunately, the amended Bill passed without any hitch on 5 September 2013. The passage of this law must surely rank as one of the highpoints and major achievements of the Fifteenth Lok Sabha and the 229th Session of the Rajya Sabha. Excerpts from the debates have been included in the book to give the reader a flavour of the thinking across the political spectrum on the new land acquisition law.

The new law evoked different reactions. Civil society groups and social activists felt that it was not progressive enough and retained powers of the government to expropriate land in the name of 'public purpose'. Industry felt that it would make land acquisition for manufacturing, infrastructure, and housing projects expensive and time-consuming. The law was both hailed and criticized but within Parliament there was an overwhelming consensus that it was a huge step forward to ensure justice to land owners and others who are impacted when their lands are being acquired. There was widespread agreement that the new legislation would end the era of protests, agitations, and conflicts that had become ubiquitous because of both the nature of the 1894 law and the manner of its implementation.

The book explains the important provisions of the new law in some detail. It provides the rationale for not only the broad approach adopted but also for the specific formulations incorporated. As the manuscript was in the press, the Government of India issued an Ordinance on 29 December 2014 amending the law in substantial measure. To make the book up-to-date, a chapter has been included analysing these amendments and how they impact on the 'basic structure' of the 2013 law.

# Acknowledgements

This book would not have been possible without the support and encouragement of a very large number of people.

Mr Prabhu Dayal Meena and Mr Charanjeet Mann, both officers of the Ministry of Rural Development were instrumental in the drafting of the law along with Mr K. Raju, then a Joint Secretary in the Government of India.

Mr Salman Khurshid, as the then Minister for Law and Justice, along with Mr V.K. Bhasin, then Secretary of the same Ministry both of whom took a passionate interest in the drafting and helped us out with making the law achieve its final form. Mr Mihir Shah, whose invaluable inputs helped us refine our understanding of acquisition in India.

Our colleagues who encouraged and proofread the drafts with a keen eye—Neelakshi Mann and Jeh Tirodhkar both of whom were there at every step with a kind word and a helping hand.

A word of gratitude also to our young team of advocates and law students who helped in our research on the background—Dhruv Banerji, Divya, and Sparsh.

Thank you all.

# CHAPTER ONE

# Overview

*Statutes on Land Acquisition are an expression of how a nation views the exercise of the sovereign right of eminent domain. This chapter introduces the concept and its evolution in an attempt to explain how it is understood and expressed under the new law.*

## Understanding 'Eminent Domain'

Before embarking upon any legislative revisit, especially one of grand ambition, it is a good idea to acquaint oneself with the first principles upon which the law is to be predicated. Acquisition of property is founded upon the universally recognized principle of 'Eminent Domain'.

All countries enjoy, as a fundamental aspect of their sovereignty, a power over their land resources referred to as Eminent Domain. Eminent domain is the power of the Government, or other body through which the Executive will is expressed, to take over resources for the greater national good. At its most basic Eminent Domain refers to the inherent authority of the Government to acquire private property on the payment of fair compensation for a use that benefits the public at large.

Countries, such as Australia or Hong Kong, also refer to this as 'resumption'—a term founded on the idea that all land belongs to the Government in perpetuity and it is only 'resuming' such ownership when taking over land for a public purpose. The concept enjoys recognition under international law with the caveat that the entities, including citizens of other nations, whose land or property is being acquired, must be justly compensated.[1]

Different nations exercise this power in different ways depending upon how property rights are defined in that nation. In the course of our work on a new law, we found that countries with more evolved legal regimes with a greater emphasis on civil rights provide the greater safeguards.

Most countries see mention of the concept in their Constitutions itself[2] while others have statutes on the subject defining and explaining the use of this power. An illustration can be found in the Constitution of the United States of America where the power of eminent domain is circumscribed by the requirement of due process. The Fifth Amendment to their Constitution states *No person shall... be deprived of life, liberty, or property, without due process of law; nor shall private property be taken for public use, without just compensation.* This is read with the Fourteenth Amendment which states ...*No State shall make or enforce any law which shall abridge the privileges or immunities of citizens of the United States; nor shall any State deprive any person of life, liberty, or property, without due process of law; nor deny to any person within its jurisdiction the equal protection of the laws.*[3]

In the United Kingdom, which does not have a written Constitution, compensation for 'compulsory purchase' is calculated

---

[1] See pages 191–192, Malcolm N. Shaw on International Law (Sixth Edition, 2008) Cambridge University Press , particularly the observations in *Williams & Humbert Ltd vs W & H Trade Marks (Jersey) Ltd* [1986] 1 All ER 129; 75 ILR, p. 312, where the British House of Lords held that 'an English court would recognise a foreign law effecting compulsory acquisition and any change of title to property which came under the control of the foreign state as a result and would accept and enforce the consequences of that compulsory acquisition without considering its merits'. This is an acknowledgment of eminent domain as an element of a nation's sovereignty.

[2] Chile and the United States of America. Article 31 (now repealed) and Article 31A of the Constitution of India. Section 51(xxxi) of the Australian Constitution.

[3] For the background to this interpretation see the decision of the United States Supreme Court in *Chicago, Burlington & Quincy Railroad Co. vs Chicago* [166 U.S. 226 (1897)].

at market value (as it stands at the time of taking over the land) along with compensation for losses caused by the acquisition, including legal fees and loss of profits.[4]

But there is one principle on which there is broad consensus. The process must be subject to a legal method that can withstand judicial review.[5] The Supreme Court of India has long held that *no executive action can interfere with the rights of a citizen unless backed by an existing statutory provision.*[6] Hence, the power of eminent domain has existed, in statutory form, since the enactment of the Land Acquisition Act, 1894. This Act was continued even after the passage of the new Constitution in 1949[7] and it continued in force with amendments. A number of State amendments have also been made to the Act with three prominent amendments being carried out after independence in 1962, 1967 and 1984.

Interestingly, but not surprisingly, Pakistan also has the same Act.[8] Barring a few provincial amendments carried out over the years the principle Act in Pakistan is almost identical to its (now repealed) Indian counterpart. Land Acquisition Awards are passed under Section 11 and objections are heard under Section 5A as under the Land Acquisition Act 1894 for India.

Few countries employ the same unbridled use of acquiring authority that Indian authorities have had. Though the State has been the richer for it the citizenry has suffered.

## WRITING A NEW LAW

Between 2004 and 2009, the Government had made clear that its chosen approach to law making in general was a rights-based one, a

---

[4] *See* Eric Shapiro, Keith Davies and Davind Mackmin, *Modern Methods of Valuation* (10th ed., 2009 EG Books).

[5] Article 300-A, Constitution of India states 'Persons not to be deprived of property save by authority of law: No person shall be deprived of his property save by authority of law.'

[6] See *Bishambhar Dayal Chandra Mohan vs State of U.P.* (1982)1SCC 39; AIR 1982 SC 33.

[7] As a result of the Indian Independence (Adaptation of Central Acts and ordinances) Order 1948.

[8] Also known as the Land Acquisition Act, 1894.

regime premised on the idea that the purpose of laws should be to empower people against the State at large. Laws such as the Right to Education Act, 2009, the Right to Information Act, 2006 and the Mahatma Gandhi National Rural Employment Guarantee Act, 2005 had firmly established this framework. It was to this regime that the exercise of Eminent Domain had to conform as well.

During the course of our consultations, we heard arguments from various quarters suggesting that we ban the very exercise of Eminent Domain. Most notably the Standing Committee of Parliament (the body that reviews all laws placed before Parliament) recommended that the Government impose a limitation upon itself and refuse to acquire land for private parties.[9]

But Eminent Domain is a necessary evil. Without the power of Eminent Domain, the Government could not establish the infrastructure that we rely on—roads, hospitals, airports, public schools, common facilities such as warehouses for farmers, playgrounds for children all are made possible through the use of Eminent Domain. Even the British laws on land acquisition in India (dating back to 1870) were founded on the idea that these Acts are to be 'liberally expounded in favour of the public, and strictly expounded as against the Government or Company taking the land.'[10] It was the adverse manipulation of these concepts over the years that served to make acquisition a cannibalistic and inhuman process.[11]

A law was needed to regulate Eminent Domain so that it would meet the standard that every law seeks to satisfy-serving the greatest good of the greatest number. To achieve this objective, the law would unabashedly have to leave behind conventional practices (no matter how effective), alter the existing balance of power (the beneficiaries of which were the State Administration) and start afresh.

---

[9] See Recommendation in Para 3.19, Report of the Parliamentary Standing Committee on Rural Development, dated 17 May 2012.

[10] See the remarks of Lord Truro in *East and West India Docks and Birmingham Junction Rail. Co. vs Gattlte* (20 L. J., Ch. 217).

[11] A fantastic early history of land acquisition laws in India is provided in *The Land Acquisition Acts* Berverley, Henry (1888). Calcutta: Thacker, Spink And Co. A copy is available at [http://ia600302.us.archive.org/13/items/landacquisitiona00beveuoft/landacquisitiona00beveuoft.pdf].

## WAS THE CENTRAL GOVERNMENT QUALIFIED TO MAKE THE LAW?

Political parties belonging to some states (such as Tamil Nadu and West Bengal) raised objections to the idea of a Central Government law on the subject of land acquisition. Despite an existing legislation (which admittedly claimed primacy as it had come into force before the nation celebrated independence) they argued it was an encroachment into the legislative domain of the States in whom the Constitution vested the law making authority.

Under the Constitution of India, land is a state subject,[12] meaning that only states are empowered to make laws on land and land related matters. The founding fathers of our Constitution laid out a quasi-federal structure which informs all legislative business. Legislative autonomy is an essential part of this structure and barring a few specified circumstances,[13] this scheme must be treated with respect by the Parliament of India and the Executive.

However, the item 'acquisition and requisitioning' of property was placed in the Concurrent List (subjects on which both the Centre and State can make laws).[14] This was a necessity as many national projects are of an inter-state nature particularly those that relate to the construction of highways, railways and atomic energy projects.

But that would suffice to vest the Centre with the legislative power qua land acquisition. How could the Centre justify legislating on rehabilitation and resettlement?

To remedy this, two entries in the Seventh Schedule of the Constitution were relied upon. Specifically Entry 97 in the Union List (or List I) *Any other matter not enumerated in List II or List III*

---

[12] Entry 18, List II, Seventh Schedule to the Constitution of India *18. Land, that is to say, rights in or over land, land tenures including the relation of landlord and tenant, and the collection of rents; transfer and alienation of agricultural land; land improvement and agricultural loans; colonization* and Entry 45, List II, Seventh Schedule to the Constitution of India *45. Land revenue, including the assessment and collection of revenue, the maintenance of land records, survey for revenue purposes and records of rights, and alienation of revenues,* Entry 49, List II, Seventh Schedule to the Constitution of India *49. Taxes on lands and buildings.*

[13] Articles 249, 250 and 252 of the Constitution of India.

[14] Entry 42, List III, Seventh Schedule to the Constitution of India.

*including any tax not mentioned in either of those lists* and Entry 42 of the Concurrent List (List III) *Acquisition and Requisitioning of Property.*

The first item, referred to as the residuary power, allows the Centre to enact laws on any subject not mentioned in either the State List or the Concurrent List. Since Rehabilitation and Resettlement arising out of displacement caused by land acquisition were not found elsewhere it stood to reason that the Central Government could legitimately invoke the residuary power.

As for the latter entry, we relied on the settled law that the power to legislate on a subject carries with it the power to legislate on other related matters. This power has been expressed by the Supreme Court of India in cases such as *Chaturbhai M. Patel vs The Union Of India,*[15] where a bench of the Apex Court, placing reliance on the observations of the Federal Court, held:

> *It must inevitably happen from time to time that legislation, though purporting to deal with a subject in one list, touches also on a subject in another list, and the different provisions of the enactment may be so closely intertwined that blind adherence to a strictly verbal interpretation would result in a large number of statutes being declared invalid because the legislature enacting them may appear to have legislated in a forbidden sphere.*

This interpretation of the Supreme Court has been followed widely. Another bench in a different case held:

> *It is equally well settled that the power to legislate on a topic of legislation carries with it the power to legislate on an ancillary matter which can be said to be reasonably included in the power given.*[16]

Relying on the above precedents, the new law contains provisions on rehabilitation and resettlement (which also extend to private purchase). This is because acquisition has proven to be so inextricably linked to rehabilitation and resettlement that the latter cannot be severed from the former without gross injustice being caused to the affected parties.

---

[15] 1960 AIR 424, 1960 SCR (2) 362.

[16] Justice Hidayatullah in *The State of Rajasthan vs Shri G. Chawla And Dr. Pohumal* 1959 AIR 544, 1959 SCR Supl. (1) 904.

This is also the reason why the rehabilitation and resettlement aspects of the law are confined to such cases where the displacement is a direct result of the acquisition proceedings. It does not seek to go into other cases where say, displacement has been the result of a natural calamity such as a flood or an earthquake.

## WHY A NEW LAW?

The Land Acquisition Act 1894 was a century old when it was repealed and replaced by the new 2013 Act. In that time, the invocation of the Act has come at a very high social cost. From a plain reading of the law, it was evident that it had been drafted to provide as smooth a mechanism as possible for acquisition. It was a fine law if one were to look at it solely from the point of view of the acquiring body.

The Standing Committee of Parliament observed of the amendments made to the Land Acquisition Act in 1984:[17]

> *[They] extinguished any differentiation between acquisition for a State purpose and acquisition for a private enterprise or State enterprise by amending section 4 of the original Act to insert the words 'or for a Company' after any public purpose. The Courts have interpreted this amendment to mean that any notification of acquisition issued under section 4 need not specify whether the acquisition is for a public purpose or for a Company. This opened the floodgates to acquisition of land by the State for Companies. And this in turn has unleashed the tribal and rural backlash that has caused the current decision of the Government to replace the 1894 Act with an altogether new Act.*

Some of the most significant people's movements have revolved around disputed land acquisition—The Narmada Bachao Andolan[18] (a movement seeking redress for families displaced as a result of the Narmada Valley project), the Tarapur agitations (born in the wake of land acquisition for the Tarapur Atomic Project), violence in Nandigram (as a result of forcible acquisition of land from farmers),

---

[17] See Recommendation in Para 3.5, Report of the Parliamentary Standing Committee on Rural Development, dated 17 May 2012.

[18] A summary of which can be found in the accompanying litigation *Narmada Bachao Andolan vs Union of India.* (2000)10SCC674.

the agitations by farmers in the wake of the Yamuna Expressway. All of these represent just a small fraction of cases that received national attention where atrocities committed under the Land Acquisition Act, 1894 were on display.

Courts were reluctant to intervene and very few acquisitions were set aside. This was because the Courts would rarely substitute their discretion for that of the Executive as it would mean an encroachment into the domain of the Executive powers.

In the landmark judgment of *Aflatoon*,[19] an oft relied upon decision of the Supreme Court:

> *The Land Acquisition Act is a pre-Constitution Act. Its provisions are not, therefore, liable to be challenged on the ground that they are not in conformity with the requirement of Article 31(2)[20] of the Constitution. What the appellants and writ petitioners complain is that their properties were acquired by paying them compensation computed with reference to the market value of the land as on the date of the notification under sec. 4 and that sec. 23 is, therefore, bad. This, in substance is nothing but a challenge to the adequacy of compensation. Such a challenge is precluded by reason of Art. 31(5) of the Constitution.* [Emphasis added]

Post 1990, laws had evolved rapidly in India with a strong emphasis on public interest. By contrast the 1894 Act stood out as an anachronism that should have been confined to the century in which it was enacted.

The attitude of the higher judiciary had also begun to change. Justice Ganpat Singhvi, a now retired judge of the Supreme Court of India gave voice to this sentiment saying that the Land Acquisition Act 1894 had *become a fraud* and that it demonstrated a *scant regard for the welfare of the common man.*[21] Another bench of the Hon'ble Supreme Court has echoed this sentiment in its observation that:

[19] *Aflatoon and others vs Lt. Governor of Delhi & others* on 23 August 1974; 1974 AIR 2077, 1975 SCR (1) 802.

[20] Now repealed by the Constitution (Forty Fourth Amendment) Act, 1978.

[21] See, 'Land Acquisition Act is a fraud, ought to be scrapped: SC' *The Indian Express*, 4 August 2011 [http://www.indianexpress.com/news/land-acquisition-act-is-a-fraud-ought-to-be-scrapped-sc/827232/].

*[T]he provisions contained in the Act, of late, have been felt by all concerned, do not adequately protect the interest of the land owners/ persons interested in the land. The Act does not provide for rehabilitation of persons displaced from their land although by such compulsory acquisition, their livelihood gets affected ... To say the least, the Act has become outdated and needs to be replaced at the earliest by fair, reasonable and rational enactment in tune with the constitutional provisions, particularly, Article 300A of the Constitution. We expect the law making process for a comprehensive enactment [sic] with regard to acquisition of land being completed without any unnecessary delay.* [22]

Thus, a clear and persistent sentiment that supported the repeal of the Land Acquisition Act, 1894 was beginning to emerge.

## 1984 AMENDMENTS

The (now repealed) Land Acquisition Act, 1894 was amended several times. The most significant amendments to the Act were carried out, thirty years ago, in 1984. The intention was to close certain loopholes in the process, make it more humane in some regards, and to expand acquisition for the purposes of companies. Twenty one sections were amended, five new sections inserted and one section was omitted, making it the largest set of amendments to the Land Acquisition Act, 1894.[23]

The 1984 Amendment Act is most remembered for its expansion of the State's ability to acquire lands for a public purpose 'or for a private company'.[24] As for compensation, it sought to bring about some measure of relief by providing for the generation and payment of interest, calculated from the day the first notification under Section 4 was made, till the date of award or possession (whichever came first). It also increased the solatium to be paid from 15 per cent to 30 per cent.[25]

---

[22] Justices Lodha and Kehar; order dated 2 November 2011. *Ramji Veerji Patel vs Revenue Divisional officer* (Civil Appeal No. 137 of 2003).

[23] See page 3 of the Document Table Showing 'Effect of Parliamentary Legislation of 1984' published by the Law Ministry of India. The amending Act is at page 647 [http://lawmin.nic.in/legislative/textofcentralacts/1984.pdf].

[24] Section 4(a) of the Land Acquisition (Amendment) Act, 1984.

[25] Section 15 of the Land Acquisition (Amendment) Act, 1984.

The 1984 Amendment Act reduced the period within which a declaration under Section 6 had to be made (following the initial notification under Section 4) to one year (from three).[26] This meant that if the acquiring body did not issue a declaration within one year of announcing its intention to acquire a certain parcel of land, the same would be deemed to have lapsed.

Another provision in the 1984 Amendment Act went one step further and put a two year deadline within which time an award had to be issued after a Section 6 declaration. Prior to this amendment the process could languish *ad nauseum* leaving the land owner in a perpetual state of limbo.

The Amendments also included a provision which directed the publication of the Section 4 notice in two local newspapers (one of which was to be a regional language paper). This publication was in addition to the public notice of the 'substance of such notification' which has to be made by the Collector at convenient places in the locality where the land was situated.[27]

However, the 1984 Act stopped just short of prescribing a time frame for taking possession once the award has been made or for enhancing compensation to be paid.

## WHAT ARE THE KEY DIFFERENCES BETWEEN THE 1894 ACT AND THE 2013 ACT?

The idea that the law on land acquisition needed further modification was mooted by political parties across ideological lines.[28] Draft

---

[26] This three year period had been inserted by the Land Acquisition (Amendment and Validation) ordinance of 1967 (later an Act).

[27] See deliberations of the Law Commission of India in its One Hundred Eighty Second Report on Amendment of Section 6 of the Land Acquisition Act, 1894 dated May, 2002 [http://lawcommissionofindia.nic.in/reports/182rpt.pdf].

[28] During the Parliamentary Debates on the new law, the president of the BJP Rajnath Singh indicated that an attempt had also been made under the Government between 1999 and 2004 but could not reach fruition [Parliament Speech on 29 August 2013, available at http://164.100.47.132/newdebate/15/14/29082013/Fullday.pdf].

work on a fresh set of amendments began in earnest around 2007. However instead of one law, two separate legislations were prepared-the Land Acquisition (Amendment) Bill and the Rehabilitation and Resettlement Bill. Both were laid before Parliament.

In 2011, upon a thorough review of both these legislations two things became evident: *One*, amending the law for a fourth time would be a meaningless exercise with limited impact; *Two*, unless we disregarded the mountain of experiences that had accompanied acquisition in the last two decades, it was imperative to enact a combined law addressing displacement.

Therefore, in lieu of carrying out amendments to the Land Acquisition Act 1894, the Government chose to bring in a new legislation: The Right to Fair Compensation and Transparency in Land Acquisition, Rehabilitation and Resettlement Act, 2013. This revisit has resulted in a complete rewriting of the law thereby pointing to the intention of the Government to depart almost entirely from any association with the 1894 Act.

The 1894 Act was a comparatively short legislation that left much to the discretion of the acquiring authorities with limited room for creative interpretation. The new Act, 2013 is founded upon five pillars-fairer compensation, consensual acquisition for a clear public purpose, rehabilitation and resettlement for displaced families, a marked reduction in the powers of the Collector and an effective appellate mechanism.

## FAIRER COMPENSATION

In theory, the 1894 Act envisaged the compensation of land owners at market rates. This may sound fair but in practice was actually the cause of enormous injustice to the owners. Reporting of land values has been notoriously inaccurate over the years. Due to poor land record management and under reporting by purchasing parties, land values are grossly distorted. Market Value, if taken as it appeared on the books, would therefore be a fraction of the total value.

The new Act, as we shall see later, puts in place a comprehensive formula for the calculation of compensation that completely removed the discretion of authorities.

## CONSENT AND PUBLIC PURPOSE

Acquisition by its very nature is forceful. However, the 1894 Act took this 'compulsory' nature to grotesque extremes. Consent was simply not a factor. Section 5A of the Land Acquisition Act, 1894 allowed for a hearing of objections to be made but put no responsibility on the Collector to take those claims into consideration. In reality the claims were inconsequential as they were not justiciable. There was no other process by which the law could guarantee meaningful consultation. No discussion or negotiation was required by law to accompany the acquisition process.

What compounded this lack of consent was the 'urgency clause'.[29] Leaving the definition of what constituted an 'urgency' to the authority carrying out the acquisition, it allows the acquiring authority to do away with the already flimsy procedure defined under the parent (1894) Act.

'Public Purpose' which was the raison d'etre for any acquisition initiated was drafted in such wide terms that essentially any activity could be construed as public purpose, so long as the Collector felt it did. Courts would generally refrain from substituting their judgment for that of the Executive and therefore 'public purpose' became whatever the Government or acquiring authority defined it to include.

The new law has special provisions to establish the consent of a clear majority (70–80 per cent of affected families). Often times this process has to be carried out twice. The urgency clause has been restricted to only cases of national defence and cases where relief work for natural disasters has to take place—a marked departure from the 'catch all' provision that was applied earlier. The definition of public purpose has been circumscribed to activities that can legitimately be construed to be of a public nature.

## REHABILITATION AND RESETTLEMENT

The issue of rehabilitation was never addressed in the Land Acquisition Act, 1894. This resulted in situations where families

---

[29] Section 17 of the Land Acquisition Act, 1894 *Special Powers in case of Urgency.*

would be dispossessed without any alternatives being provided either for their accommodation or for the livelihoods lost. Millions of families were displaced demonstrating a remarkable lack of concern on the part of the Government for these marginalised communities.

The new law links land acquisition, particularly the taking of possession, to the satisfactory discharge of the rehabilitation and resettlement provisions.

## REDUCTION IN THE POWERS OF THE COLLECTOR

One of the most far reaching features of this new law is the significant reduction of powers of the District Collector. These officers who are the representatives of the Executive at the district level of Governance had almost unbridled authority to determine compensation, define 'public purpose', take possession and even do away with prescribed processes if they felt they 'urgently' needed the land.

In a departure from the 1894 Act, the Collector's authority to decide what activity constitutes 'public purpose' has been completely curtailed. Public purpose must fall strictly within the parameters prescribed under the new law. The Collector cannot add or subtract to the list given.

Under the 1894 Act, the Collector could decide what quantum of compensation could be paid to those displaced. Under the new law, there is a formula that does not require the Collector to exercise any discretion. All he has to do is make sure that the rate is calculated as directed.

Under the old law, the Collector also had the power to decide when to take possession. He could dispossess any family by giving a moment's notice. Now possession can only be taken once all the requirements under the law relating to the payment of compensation, rehabilitation and resettlement have been discharged.

Above all of this, the old 1894 Act also empowered the Collector with sweeping powers to invoke the urgency clause. What constituted an urgent situation was solely a function of the Collector's interpretation. This loophole has been plugged conclusively by limiting urgency to only two cases—natural disasters and national defence. The Collector can no longer acquire land citing 'urgent' reasons.

## APPELLATE MECHANISMS

A law should be able to enforce that which it commands. To ensure that transparent and effective appeals against State decisions can be filed, it was decided that appropriate and functional mechanisms should be provided (in detail) under the law.

If an individual is not satisfied with the award that is prescribed under this new Law, they may ask for the same to be modified or increased by moving a reference before the Land Acquisition Rehabilitation and Resettlement Authority (established under the new Act). This body is required to give its decision within a period not exceeding six months.

If a family continues to be aggrieved or upset with the amount of compensation received they can file an appeal with the High Court in the state where the acquisition is taking place.

## A NEW DIRECTION

This law marks the end of unchecked acquisition by an overenthusiastic State machinery. The policy of accepting displacement and destitution of some as a necessary precondition to development is sought to be rectified.

Like all laws it enjoys its fair share of shortcomings. Some of what was hoped to be achieved was sacrificed to the process of political compromise. Others, to lack of legislative jurisdiction. These challenges are discussed at length in this book.

Already the Supreme Court and the various High Courts have interpreted the provisions of the new law with a wisdom and zeal strongly in favour of those aggrieved by the now repealed law.

It is our hope that these trends continue and give life to the intentions with which the law was passed.

# CHAPTER TWO

# Social Impact Assessment

*The Right to Fair Compensation and Transparency in Land Acquisition, Rehabilitation and Resettlement Act, 2013 introduces and places great reliance on the conduct of a Social Impact Assessment. This chapter explains and deconstructs the process by explaining how it was arrived at and how it is to be implemented.*

## WHAT MAKES A SOCIAL IMPACT ASSESSMENT?

It was decided at the very beginning that a concrete legal process needed to be put in place whenever land was sought to be acquired. Acquisition, as previously defined under the Land Acquisition Act, 1894 followed an inconsistent, arbitrary and haphazard process that differed from project to project with discretion guiding the discharge of authority.

Social Impact Assessment studies are broad notions that often defy conventional characterization. Social Impact Assessments have been carried out to determine the impact of war in conflict zones, Social Impact Analyses have been carried out by agencies such as the World Bank to determine the impact of their poverty reduction schemes and agencies such as the World Health Organization have been known to use Social Impact Assessment to identify environmental concerns.

The encouraging lesson the drafting committee took from these illustrations was that Social Impact Assessment could be anything we wanted it to be.

A Study on the subject of Social Impact Assessments had been commissioned by the Ministry of Rural Development to be undertaken by the Council for Social Development.[1] This study helped introduce the draftsmen to the salient features of Social Impact Assessments and associated best practices. It undertook an evaluation and enquiry into the challenges faced in the implementation of Impact Assessment Studies across five states.[2] It was a good starting point to understand what one could hope to accomplish through such a process and how to go about it.

But given the peculiarities of land acquisition the process as it existed in other areas of practice had to be adapted before it could be used with some expectation of success.

'*What are the fundamental questions an acquiring body must answer before it presumes to take over another party's land?*' became the guiding philosophy behind our version of the Social Impact Assessment. Utilizing a group discussion process that involved officers familiar with land acquisition and members of civil society who had witnessed displacement first hand, a list was drawn up. This list sought to collate and compile data to determine the following:[3]

- Assessment as to whether the proposed acquisition serves public purpose
- Estimation of affected families and the number of families among them likely to be displaced
- Extent of lands, public and private, houses, settlements and other common properties likely to be affected by the proposed acquisition
- Whether the extent of land proposed for acquisition is the absolute bare minimum extent needed for the project
- Whether land acquisition at an alternate place has been considered and found not feasible

---

[1] Sanctioned by the Department of Land Resources, Ministry of Rural Development, vide Sanction letter No 18012/03/2009-LRD dated 25 August 2009. The Report is titled '*Social Impact Assessment: Report of a Research Project on Social Impact Assessment of R&R Policies and Packages in India*', Council for Social Development, New Delhi, August 2010.

[2] Haryana, Rajasthan, Andhra Pradesh, Uttar Pradesh, and Orissa.

[3] Section 4(2) of the Act, 2013.

- Study of social impacts of the project, and the nature and cost of addressing them and the impact of these costs on the overall costs of the project *vis-à-vis* the benefits of the project.

The last item is the most important. It imposes an obligation on the acquiring body to demonstrate the object sought to be achieved justifies the cost of displacement. No other such standard had ever been formally required to be applied in past legal instruments—either of the Centre or States.

In addition to these six questions, the Assessment is also required to determine the 'impact that the project is likely to have on various components such as livelihood of affected families, public and community properties, assets and infrastructure particularly roads, public transport, drainage, sanitation, sources of drinking water, sources of water for cattle, community ponds, grazing land, plantations, public utilities such as post offices, fair price shops, food storage godowns, electricity supply, health care facilities, schools and educational or training facilities, anganwadis, children parks, places of worship, land for traditional tribal institutions and burial and cremation grounds'.[4]

How this impact is to be countered, mitigated, ameliorated and addressed is required to be explained in detail in a document referred to as the Social Impact Management Plan.[5]

---

[4] See Sections 4(3) and 4(4) of the Act, 2013. The underlying sentiment behind this ambitious process are expressed most eloquently in a paper by Usha Ramanathan on Eminent Domain. *There are whole segments of persons who are displaced but who, it would seem, can be pushed to the margins of the State's concerns because of the limited mandate imposed on the State by the eminent domain doctrine. Since only landowners have any direct right to be considered during the exercise of the eminent domain power, those who possess no legal title or interest stand automatically excluded. The landless constitute one such segment. Women, who have at best been subsidiary constitutional subjects in the matter of landholding and ownership, and who, the laws of succession, the notion of 'family' and the presumption of dependency, especially, have disabled from holding legally defined interest in land, constitute a significant group among the excluded*—http://www.ielrc.org/content/a0902.pdf

[5] See Section 4(6) of the Act, 2013.

The answers to these questions are of vital importance as they dictate the entire process that follows. The very consent (of the affected parties) is to be obtained on the basis of answers to the above questions. The Assessment so carried out is scrutinised by the public at large and informs the entirety of the remaining process. Sharing the information is essential to its legitimacy.

Most importantly, it is through this exercise does one truly gauge the purpose of acquisition as being authentically a public one.

The idea behind doing so was to put the onus on the acquiring authority to demonstrate the acquisition was genuine and that the use of 'eminent domain' was confined to the rarest of cases.

## Concerns and Rebuttal

This section faced moderate opposition from some quarters who argued that it added another layer of bureaucracy to an already long list of clearances required from other Government agencies and would delay acquisition. To support their concern they drew attention to the National Rehabilitation and Resettlement Policy of 2007 which also provides for Social Impact Assessment studies but only if four hundred or more families are displaced.[6]

To accommodate these concerns an earlier draft of the new law limited the conduct of Social Impact Assessment to cases where more than a certain amount of land was to be acquired. However, one of our colleagues and a key member of the drafting committee, Mr K. Raju made an insightful observation. An officer of the Indian Administrative Service with vast experience in the field of land acquisition, he remarked that the nature of the questions was such that if the land identified for acquisition was smaller in size then obtaining the answers to those questions would take proportionately less time. In other words, the number of affected families on a one acre plot could be easily and quickly determined as opposed to acquisition of a hundred acres. The process thus had an inbuilt flexibility.

Upon weighing this argument it was felt that there should be no bar for the conduct of Social Impact Assessment. This was also in line with the philosophy of the law to make it as far reaching as possible.

---

[6] See Chapter IV, Para 4.1 of the National Rehabilitation and Resettlement Policy, 2007.

**Key Parameters**

To ensure a balanced and workable process, three directions were added:

*Firstly,* an open ended Social Impact Assessment would indeed allow scope for bureaucratic delay. To avoid a protracted and lengthy process a moratorium was imposed on the preparation of the study. It would have to be completed within six months.[7] To enforce this further a requirement was included that the study would lapse[8] within one year of its appraisal if it was not acted upon. If the land in question was still needed for acquisition then a fresh study would have to be carried out. This would ensure that the threat of acquisition would not hang over the heads of the affected families in perpetuity.

*Secondly,* the very first draft uploaded onto the website of the Ministry of Rural Development contained a three tier process –Social Impact Assessment followed by an Appraisal by the Expert Group with a final vetting by a Committed headed by a senior bureaucrat (Chief Secretary).

To accommodate the concern that the system of checks and balances was growing cumbersome we deleted the third tier and limited it to only the first two measures. This was done after ensuring that the integrity of the process was not being compromised in any manner by such deletion.

*Thirdly,* another clause was drafted to state that the Environmental Impact Assessment as required by law could be completed separately and would not be contingent upon the process. Concerns had been raised by some sections of industry that Environmental Impact Assessment studies would become contingent upon the completion of land acquisition thereby encumbering the process of project clearance with even more delays.

---

[7]  Second Proviso to Section 4(2) of the Act, 2013.

[8]  Section 14 of the Act, 2013. The proviso to the section empowers the Government to extend this period but the reasons for doing so must be recorded in writing and shared on the website of the acquiring authority. The idea behind this 'publication' was that if the extension was made on specious grounds then it should be available for challenge and judicial scrutiny.

During the Parliamentary debates on the law, another exemption was added to say that in the case of irrigation projects, where the Environmental Impact Assessment had been carried out the Social Impact Assessment would not be required.[9]

Social Impact Assessments are mandatory in all cases of land acquisition except when the land is being acquired under the urgency clause or where it is being acquired for an irrigation project where an Environmental Impact Assessment has already been carried out.[10]

## CONSULTATION AND PUBLIC HEARINGS

The Social Impact Assessment relies profoundly, for its legitimacy, upon the participation of other local communities at the level of the Panchayat and the Gram Sabha (representative bodies that operate at the village level).

The law requires two sets of public hearings—the first (under Section 5 of the Act, 2013) as a part of the Social Impact Assessment at the affected area, 'after giving adequate publicity about the date, time and venue for the public hearing, to ascertain the views of the affected families to be recorded and included in the Social Impact Assessment Report'. The second hearing takes place (under Section 16(5) of the Act, 2013) when the Rehabilitation and Resettlement Scheme is being prepared by the Administrator in charge of Rehabilitation and Resettlement.

Technically, under Section 5A of the now repealed Land Acquisition Act, 1894, an aggrieved party could, within thirty days of the preliminary notification (issued under Section 4 of that Act) file an objection with the Collector. The onus was on the aggrieved party to complain or take issue.

Even the Supreme Court held that if the persons have not filed any objections under Section 5A then, in principle, it must be concluded that they had to objection to the original notification.[11] Silence was taken as acquiescence. Public hearings were also a part of the Environmental Impact Assessment process but they needed to be strengthened so as to avoid manipulation.

[9] Proviso to Section 6 of the Act, 2013.
[10] Section 9 of the Act, 2013.
[11] See *Delhi Administration vs Gurdip Singh* AIR 1999 SC 3822.

We had had the privilege to work in the Ministry of Environment and Forests from 2009 to 2011 where we learnt some critical lessons from experiences with a process that shared a similar objective—the Environment Impact Assessment.[12] The 'EIA' process had certain severe shortcomings that we had attempted to address (which included a proposal to create a National Environmental Assessment and Management Agency), and we were keen not to see those same flaws contaminate the proposed system.

## REVIEW BY EXPERT GROUP

Once the Social Impact Assessment report is prepared it requires independent evaluation by unbiased and neutral parties who possess knowledge of the subject matter. To do this an independent multi-disciplinary Expert Group was constituted under the new law.[13] This group would consist of:

• Two non-official social scientists
• Two representatives of Panchayat, Gram Sabha, Municipality or Municipal Corporation, as the case may be
• Two experts on rehabilitation
• A technical expert in the subject relating to the project.

Upon their evaluation if the Group concludes that no real public purpose is served or the social costs and impacts outweigh the benefits then it has the power to reject the project. If it so concludes, then it must give a written appraisal to that effect in writing.[14]

If, however, the Group finds the answers to the above queries in the affirmative and recommends proceeding with the project then it shall give a written appraisal to the effect. In this appraisal it must also state that the land identified for acquisition is the bare minimum required and no other less-placing alternatives are available.[15]

---

[12] Environment Impact Assessment Notification, 2006 – A subordinate legislation under the Environment Protection Act, 1986.

[13] Section 7 of the Act, 2013.

[14] Section 7(4) of the Act, 2013.

[15] Section 7(5) of the Act, 2013.

If the Expert Group finds in the negative and rejects the proposal then it must be abandoned immediately. However the Government still has the power to proceed with the acquisition if it so desires but the reasons for this disregard of the Expert Group's recommendations must be reduced to writing so they may be scrutinised and reviewed by the public at large.[16]

## Review by the Expert Group Report

Once the Expert Group submits its Appraisal report (which it has to do in no less than two months) the Government carrying out the acquisition can give the sanction to proceed with the acquisition. However it must do so after having satisfied itself of the following:[17]

- There is a legitimate and bona fide public purpose which necessitates the acquisition of the land identified.
- The potential benefits and the public purpose outweigh the social costs and adverse social impacts.
- Only the minimum area of land required for the project is proposed to be acquired.
- There is no unutilized land which has been previously acquired in the area.
- The land, if any, acquired earlier remained unutilized, is used for such public purpose and make recommendations in respect thereof.

The Government must also ensure that the consent of the affected families has been obtained in a manner not vitiated by any form of duress or coercion. This step is in effect a final attestation by the Government that they can vouch for the information that is being used to sanction the acquisition.

## Criticism and Response

Some members of civil society questioned this approach. They argued that allowing the Government to proceed in defiance of the

---

[16] Section 7(4) of the Act, 2013.
[17] Section 8(1) of the Act, 2013.

Expert Group's recommendations rendered the process meaningless. However, this criticism failed to take into account the consequences of such a proposition.

The reason for the introduction of that clause was founded in the idea of administrative accountability. Giving a body staffed with unelected, non-executive members the power to approve or disapprove administrative decisions is excessive.

As for fears that the report will be disregarded it was felt that only very reckless officials would proceed against an 'Expert' report and if the reasons (which were to be recorded) are found wanting then the officials can, of course, be held accountable.

## Public Purpose

Next came the task of defining public purpose. This was a challenge because seldom has a term existed that has caused so much persistent confusion as a result of its obscurity. The Land Acquisition Act, 1894 abdicated the task of definition, leaving it to the imagination of the acquiring authority. The observations of a Constitution Bench of the Supreme Court sum up the scenario well:[18]

> *The incident of deprivation of property within the meaning of Article 300A of the Constitution normally occurred mostly in the context of public purpose. Clearly, any law, which deprives a person of his private property for private interest, will be amenable to judicial review. In last sixty years, though the concept of public purpose has been given quite wide interpretation, nevertheless, the 'public purpose' remains the most important condition in order to invoke Article 300A of the Constitution.*

The idea was that you would know it when you see it. But the problem was, technically anything, unless deeply perverse in nature, would have some modicum of public benefit. This was not a solid measure to hang a statute by.

Despite being called upon time and again to adjudge the nature of these so called 'public purpose' driven projects, courts would seldom intervene.

[18] See *Rajiv Sarin vs State of Uttarakhand* on 9 August 2011, Civil Appeal No. 4772 of 1998.

*Typically the State's central role in these projects provided the demarcation line (justifiable or not) between public interest and private profit: if the State was undertaking the project, it was in the public interest. As the Narmada decision showed, the Supreme Court has been unwilling to question the government's prerogative in setting development priorities and defining the public interest.*[19] [Emphasis Added]

A Constitution Bench of the Supreme Court held that the declaration made by the Government (in the notification under Section 4 of the now repealed Land Acquisition Act, 1894), that the land was required for a public purpose, was conclusive and that it was not open to a court to go behind it and try to satisfy itself whether in fact the acquisition was for a public purpose.[20]

*Whether in a particular case the purpose for which land was needed was a public purpose or not was for the Government to be satisfied about and the declaration of the Government would be final subject to one exception, namely that where there was a colourable exercise of the power the declaration would be open to challenge at the instance of the aggrieved party.*

The Ministry of Rural Development had from the very outset made all drafts, as and when they were prepared, available for public scrutiny. This was done in the hope that the comments received would contribute to our own understanding and help enrich the law further. A very large number of comments were dedicated to what would constitute public purpose.

But laws do not exist in a vacuum. There is an entire department in the Law Ministry–Legal Affairs–whose job it is to ensure that there laws are drafted in harmony with other existing laws and to avoid conflicts of interpretation and definition. Attention was drawn by a senior member of Cabinet to a circular issued by the Finance Ministry[21] which laid out what in the eyes of the Government

---

[19] Michael Levien, 'Rationalising Dispossession: The Land Acquisition and Resettlement Bills', 12 March, Vol. XLVI, No. 11, p. 66, (2011) *Economic and Political Weekly.*

[20] *Somavanti vs State of Punjab* 1963 AIR 151, 1963 SCR (3) 774.

[21] Notification of the Government of India in the Department of Economic Affairs (Infrastructure Section) number 13/6/2009-INF, dated 27 March 2012, excluding private hospitals, private educational institutions and private hotels.

constituted 'infrastructure'. We incorporated this definition by referencing it in the section.

In the end, the definition that was felt to be a fair representation of activities that were undeniably public spirited and hence constituted 'public purpose' was prepared. These included:

- **National Defence and Security**: Strategic purposes relating to naval, military, air force, and armed forces of the Union, including central paramilitary forces or any work vital to national security or defence of India or State police, safety of the people; or
- **Infrastructure Projects**:
  o All activities or items listed in the notification of the Government of India in the Department of Economic Affairs (Infrastructure Section) number 13/6/2009-INF, dated 27 March 2012[22], excluding private hospitals, private educational institutions and private hotels;
  o **Agriculture**: Projects involving agro-processing, supply of inputs to agriculture, warehousing, cold storage facilities, marketing infrastructure for agriculture and allied activities such as dairy, fisheries, and meat processing, set up or owned by the appropriate Government or by a farmers' cooperative or by an institution set up under a statute;

---

[22] This list includes the following: **Transport**: Roads and bridges, Ports, Inland waterways, Airports, Railway tracks, Tunnels, Viaducts, Urban Public Transport; **Energy**: Electricity generation, Electricity transmission, Electricity distribution, Oil pipelines, Oil/Gas/Liquefied Natural Gas storage facilities, gas pipelines; **Water & Sanitation**: Solid Waste Management, Water supply pipelines, Water treatment plants, Sewage collection, Treatment and disposal systems, Irrigation (dams, channels, embankments etc.), Storm water drainage system; **Communication**: Telecommunication (fixed network), Telecommunication towers; **Social and Commercial Infrastructure**: Education institutions (capital stock), hospitals (capital stock), Three-star or higher category classified hotels located outside cities with population of more than one million, common infrastructure for industrial parks, SEZ, Tourism facilities and agriculture markets, fertilizer (capital investment), Post-harvest storage infrastructure for agriculture and horticulture produce including cold storage, Terminal markets, Soil-testing laboratories, Cold chain.

- o **Industry**: Project for industrial corridors or mining activities, national investment and manufacturing zones, as designated in the National Manufacturing Policy;
- o **Water and Sanitation**: Project for water harvesting and water conservation structures, sanitation;
- o **Educational Purposes**: Project for Government administered, Government aided educational and research schemes or institutions;
- o **Sports, Tourism, and Transportation**: Project for sports, heath care, tourism, transportation or space programme;
- o **Any infrastructure facility** as may be notified in this regard by the Central Government and after tabling of such notification in Parliament;
- **Relief Development**: Project for project affected families;
- **Planned Housing**: Project for housing, or such income groups, as may be specified from time to time by the appropriate Government;
- **Planned Development**: Project for planned development or the improvement of village sites or any site in the urban areas or provision of land for residential purposes for the weaker sections in rural and urban areas;
- **Housing for Displaced Persons**: Project for residential purposes to the poor or landless or to persons residing in areas affected by natural calamities, or to persons displaced or affected by reason of the implementation of any scheme undertaken by the Government, any local authority or a corporation owned or controlled by the State.

The above definition was reviewed word for word by a high ranking Group of Ministers, a body comprised of senior Cabinet Ministers who deliberated at length on the law before it was introduced in Parliament.

At the same time a view was pressed, from some quarters, asking if acquisition of land for private companies could actually constitute 'public purpose'. Here the Indian courts had applied a more liberal interpretation than say, their American counterparts.[23]

---

[23] As recently as 4 September 2012, this position was followed by the Chhattisgarh High Court in *Gayatri Prasad vs Shri Kishore Bhaduri* [Writ

In the context of public purpose, acquisition for private companies for economic development had become the norm since the Land Acquisition Act, 1894 had been amended in 1984 to include 'companies' under its purview. In this context, it is worth mentioning the decision of the United States Supreme Court in *Kelo vs State of New London*.[24] Kelo involves a lengthy debate on whether public purposes (such as economic development) can justify the acquisition of land for transfer to private third parties. The US Supreme Court (in a 5-4 decision) upheld the right of the Government to carry out such acquisitions. A landmark decision in the history of acquisition it served as a helpful benchmark from an outside perspective and was relevant to our understanding of the law as it provided compelling arguments for why acquisition for private parties (particularly companies) was an overreach on the part of the Government (per the minority opinion).

### Criticism and Response

A frequent criticism we received was that in our zeal to be thorough we had broadened the definition of public purpose to include a very large number of non-public spirited activities.

Our response to this charge would be that it was important to list out everything in the definition because only those items that were listed would, in the final reckoning, be considered in furtherance of public purpose. They could not be added to without the approval of Parliament nor could they be interpreted liberally.

### CONSENT

The term used in the first draft of the new law placed before Parliament was 'prior informed consent'. It had been adopted from

---

Petition No. 279 of 2012] where it held *Public purpose does not cease to be so merely because the acquisition facilitates the setting up of industry by a private enterprise and benefits it to that extent; nor the existence or otherwise of public purpose be judged by the lead and initiative taken by the entrepreneurs desirous of setting up the industry and the measure of coordination between them and various State agencies.*

[24]   545 U.S. 469 (2005).

the Indigenous and Tribal Peoples Convention, 1989 and others conventions which employed such a term.[25]

During the course of discussions on the new law, a unique term evolved—'prior consent'. The objective was not to dilute the idea (as the requirement for information forms a very large part of the Statute) but to render it clear—consent has to be prior to the undertaking. Consent should also be obtained in such clear and unequivocal terms that no doubt can be raised as to its independence. Consent, to be meaningful, should never be the product of coercion.

on the basis of the information collected through the various processes listed under the new Act and the public hearings held, consent is to be sought from the affected parties.

Consent is sought from 70 per cent of the project affected families in the case of public private partnership projects and 80 per cent in case the land is being acquired for a private company.

No consent is required if the Government is acquiring lands for its own, use, hold and control (meaning it does not intend to sell the land or develop it to benefit specific private parties). An example of such a case would be when the Government acquires land to build a playground and uses its own agencies to do so.[26]

These percentages, given above, were not based on the whimsy of select individuals but were rather the product of careful consideration. Three ideas lay behind these numbers:

Firstly, the consent required should be sufficiently high so that it could not be easily manipulated.

Secondly, it should convey the willingness of a sufficiently large number of the people who were to be immediately affected thereby demonstrating that the project involved them in the developmental process.

Thirdly, another law had successfully demonstrated that obtaining written consent from a large majority was indeed workable. The Development Control Regulations for Greater Bombay, 1991 (which

---

[25] See the International Labour Organisations Convention—C169—Indigenous and Tribal Peoples Convention, 1989 (No. 169); See also the Paper on the proceedings of the United Nations Workshop on Free, Prior and Informed Consent (PFII/2004/WS.2/8 dated 17–19 January 2005) organized by the Department of Economic and Social Affairs.

[26] See proviso to Section 2(2) of the Act, 2013.

operate under the Maharashtra Housing and Area Development Act 1976) also prescribe a 70 per cent consent requirement.[27]

It must be added here that we were advised by no less an authority than the then leader of the opposition in the Rajya Sabha, Mr Arun Jaitely a stellar lawyer, to pay heed to the challenges faced in the implementation of the Maharashtra law. As a result an attempt was made to ensure the establishment of mechanisms which would document the process at every step to ensure that the consent given was free and informed.

## Who should Consent?

Next we come to whose consent should be sought. In the very first draft the consent was required to be sought solely from the individuals who owned the land. In the process of our consultations, our attention was drawn by leaders of the Communist Party of India to the notion that in India a tract of land may have stakeholders who may not necessarily enjoy legal titles but who depend upon that area for their livelihood.

Consequentially, a second category of parties was added to the consent section—those working on government assigned lands. It seemed only fair that a law which purported to uphold just and humane ideals should give them some say in a process that would have a profound bearing on their livelihood.

It must be mentioned here that all reporting that is required to take place, all studies that are required to be published, and all documentation that is to accompany processes is to be made available to the public at large in all languages and through far-reaching and easily accessible mediums (such as newspapers and websites).

## SPECIAL CHAPTER TO SAFEGUARD FOOD SECURITY

The years when the law on land acquisition was being drafted also saw the almost simultaneous progress of an equally seminal legislation—The National Food Security Act, 2013. Passed by the

---

[27] Rule 33(7) Development Control Regulations for Greater Bombay, 1991. As amended on 6 December 2008.

Parliament within days of one another, both laws were key pillars of the Government's legislative Agenda.

As a result, it was felt that we would be remiss in our duties if we did not address the concerns of food security (as affected by land acquisition) in a separate chapter.[28]

The new law therefore provides that no irrigated multi-cropped land shall be acquired under this Act except under exceptional circumstances and as a demonstrable last resort. Furthermore, the acquisition of the multi-crop land should not exceed such limits as may be notified by the appropriate Government considering the relevant State specific factors and circumstances.[29]

To counterbalance any multi-crop arable land which has been diverted for acquisition, an equivalent area of 'culturable wasteland' has to be developed for agricultural purposes or an amount equivalent to the value of the land acquired is to be deposited with the appropriate Government for investment in agriculture for enhancing food-security.[30]

The acquisition of all other types of agriculture land is also bound by similar strictures. In a district or State acquisition of other agricultural land should not exceed such limits 'of the total net sown area of that district or State', as may be notified by the appropriate Government.[31]

The only exception to the above stipulations are projects that are linear in nature (meaning they must follow the ordained path and cannot be diverted) such as railways, highways, major district roads, irrigation canals, power lines and the like.[32]

## Criticism and Response

The original draft law had imposed uniform fixed percentage ceilings on the acquisition of such land by States. This was met with almost universal criticism from State Governments. The Government

---

[28] Chapter III, Section 10 of the Act, 2013.
[29] Sections 10(1) and 10(2) of the Act, 2013.
[30] Section 10(3) of the Act, 2013.
[31] Section 10(4) of the Act, 2013.
[32] Proviso to Section 10 of the Act, 2013.

of Madhya Pradesh argued before the Standing Committee of Parliament:[33]

> *This slams the doors of any development of a non-agricultural nature in districts like Hoshangabad and Harda and State like Punjab and Haryana or Western U.P. This will prove a great disincentive for irrigating the land.*

The Government of Chhattisgarh added:[34]

> *[The section] would be impractical as it will be impossible to set up food processing industry or agricultural based industry in the appropriate area. It would also mean that areas which are well irrigated will be deprived of industrialization, urbanization or even better infrastructure. There would also be disputes over definition of 'multi-crop' land.*

The State of Bihar also said that this would result in a ban on '*all land acquisition in a State like Bihar, which abounds in irrigated, multi-crop areas.*'

The challenges of law making in a quasi-federal structure become apparent in this section. Given that decisions related to land use (such as earmarking for agriculture) are to be left to the States under the Constitution,[35] the law makers could not impose a total ban on the acquisition of multi-crop and arable land.

States argued that they should be assumed to be the best judges of their own interests and they should be allowed the right to manage their land resources as they see fit. As a result, and on the recommendation of the Standing Committee of Parliament,[36] this section was amended to leave the ceiling for acquisition to the State Governments themselves.

## PRIVATE PURCHASE

When land is purchased privately from one consenting party by another, the rehabilitation and resettlement provisions will also apply.

---

[33] See Concerns raised by State Governments in Para 3.56, Report of the Parliamentary Standing Committee on Rural Development, dated 17 May 2012.

[34] Ibid.

[35] Entry 14, List II of the Constitution of India.

[36] See Paras 3.59 and 3.60, Report of the Parliamentary Standing Committee on Rural Development, dated 17 May 2012.

However, unlike other cases where rehabilitation and resettlement is mandatory, in this case it is conditional.

States are required to prescribe limits for private purchase. When these limits are crossed by an act of purchase then the buyer has to ensure the rehabilitation and resettlement of all the parties affected by such a purchase.

The original draft of the law laid before Parliament prescribed these limits at 50 acres in urban areas and 100 acres in rural areas. However following intense debate on the subject (and deliberations by the Standing Committee), it was decided that the limits would be left to the discretion of the State Governments. This is discussed in greater detail in Chapter 10.

## RULES

To avoid over-prescription, a decision was taken to leave other less pressing operational details to the Rules. The Rules prescribe the details of the operational procedure to be followed but the law is not dependent upon them for its functioning. This is consonant with the 'design philosophy' followed throughout the drafting process that the Act should be able to operate without conflict or further prescription as and when it came into force.

The law was thus drafted to be self-contained.

# CHAPTER THREE

# Procedure for Acquiring Land

*This chapter lays out the procedure for the acquisition of land in the chronological order in which it should occur. Unfortunately, given the constraints of legal drafting, the Act does not lend itself to a linear narration. Here we have sought to present the process as it is intended to be followed.*

Parties affected by land acquisition are now entitled to a comprehensive process that puts their concerns foremost. Punctuated by deadlines and detailed checks and balances on the discretion to be exercised by officials, this process is clear and cannot be subverted. Let us proceed to analyse this in the form in which it is to be invoked.

## PRELIMINARY NOTIFICATION

Once the pre-acquisition processes listed in the preceding chapter have been executed satisfactorily, the proceedings to acquire the identified land can begin.

A 'Preliminary Notification' is issued (under Section 11 of the Act, 2013).[1] This is an initial notice to the public at large that a certain parcel of land is to be acquired along with details relating to the area. The Notification is required to be widely disseminated so no party suffers for want of information.[2]

The notification is different from its 1894 counterpart inasmuch it must contain a statement on the nature of the public purpose involved along with the reasons necessitating the displacement of

---

[1] This corresponds to the requirement of a preliminary notification given under Section 4 of the Land Acquisition Act, 1894.

[2] See Section 11(1) of the Act, 2013.

the affected persons. This has also to be accompanied by a summary of the Social Impact Assessment Report and particulars of the Administrator appointed for the purposes of rehabilitation and resettlement.[3]

This seems like an obvious step, one that should be the norm for any administrative decision. However, the experiences with the same requirement under the now repealed Land Acquisition Act, 1894 compel us to be cautious.

During the course of consultation, many farmers (from across States such as Haryana, Uttar Pradesh and Karnataka) would complain that they had been caught completely unawares by the process wholly ignorant of whether any 'preliminary' intimation had been given about the project in question. This process was inherently hostile to the person whose land was being acquired and needed to be sanitized completely.

The standard of due diligence required under Section 6 ('Declaration that Land is required for a Public Purpose') of the now repealed 1894 Act was not very high either. The detail required was of a highly *prima facie* nature. In the case of *Delhi Administration vs Gurdip Singh*,[4] the Supreme Court interpreted the requirement for initial detail as follows:

> It was held[5] that it was not necessary that the [Section 6] notification should even refer to the 'satisfaction'. If the satisfaction was challenged, it would be sufficient if such satisfaction is proved by producing the record on the basis of which the Section 6 declaration was issued. Therefore, the argument that Section 6 declaration must contain reasons or refer to the objections for every particular land, is not correct. [Emphasis added]

Mindful and wary of these vulnerabilities, all the requirements of publication are clearly listed within the law itself. The Preliminary Notification is required to be published in the following manner, namely:[6]

---

[3] Section 11(3) of the Act, 2013.

[4] *Delhi Administration vs Gurdip Singh* AIR 1999 SC 3822.

[5] The Court was placing reliance upon an earlier decision of the Supreme Court in *Rai Bahadur Ganga Bishnu Swaika vs Calcutta Pinjrapole Society* 1968 AIR 615, 1968 SCR (2) 117.

[6] Ibid.

- In the Official Gazette[7]
- In two daily newspapers circulating in the locality of such area of which one shall be in the regional language
- In the local language in the Panchayat, Municipality or Municipal Corporation, as the case may be and in the offices of the District Collector, the Sub-divisional Magistrate and the Tehsil
- Uploaded on the website of the appropriate Government
- In the affected areas, in such manner as may be prescribed (under Rules published by the Central or State Governments)

In addition to the above, once the Preliminary Notification has been issued it must 'immediately' be shared with the concerned people's representative bodies.[8] A meeting must be called for this purpose and the members must be proactively informed of the contents of the notification.

To prevent motivated or insalubrious parties from taking advantage of the persons whose land is sought to be acquired, the law prohibits any person from carrying out any transaction with regard to the land (such as sale, lease or mortgages). In other words, no party should be allowed to create any encumbrances on the land from the date of publication of the Preliminary Notification till such time as the proceedings are concluded.[9] This is being done to reduce the potential for 'gaming' the system.

[7] *See Collector (District Magistrate)*, Allahabad vs Raja Ram Jaiswal (AIR 1985 SC 1622) '*Assuming that a notification in the Official Gazette is a formal expression of the decision of the Government, the decision of the Government is hardly relevant unless it takes the concrete shape and form by publication in the Official Gazette. Where a decision of the Government to be effective and valid has to notified in the Government Gazette, the decision itself does not become effective unless a notification in the Official Gazette follows. Therefore, assuming that notification is a formal expression of a decision of the Government to acquire land, unless the decision is notified in the Government Gazette by an appropriate Government notification, the proceedings for acquisition cannot be said to have been initiated and the decision would remain a paper decision*'. [Emphasis added]

[8] Gram Sabha or Sabhas at the village level, municipalities in case of municipal areas and the Autonomous Councils in case of the areas referred to in the Sixth Schedule to the Constitution. See Section 11(2) of the Act, 2013.

[9] The proviso to Section 11 does allow the Collector to exempt cases where special extenuating circumstances exist.

This preliminary notification has to be issued within twelve months from the date of appraisal of the Social Impact Assessment report submitted by the Expert Group.

If the notification is not issued within this time frame then the appraisal report is treated as having lapsed. This means that if the Government wants to proceed with the acquisition then it shall have to carry out the Social Impact Assessment afresh.[10]

## UPDATING RECORDS AND SURVEY

Following the issue of the Preliminary Notification, the Collector is entrusted with updating the land records within two months, so that no beneficiary who is rightfully entitled is left out of the law's purview, and before the final declaration for acquisition is issued.

The Collector is during this time, authorised to enter the premises to undertake a survey and carry out certain activities required to ascertain whether the land is fit for the public purpose envisaged (this can include structural adjustments like boring holes, taking samples and laying down boundaries). This is not a new provision. It has been taken almost verbatim from the now repealed Land Acquisition Act, 1894.[11] A related provision is Section 20 of the new law which also allows the Collector to carry our measurements and make markings as necessary.

One of the salient departures comes from the idea that the declaration as to the purpose being public is not 'conclusive' as it was in the Land Acquisition Act, 1894.[12] The term 'conclusive' meant that the process ended at the level of the Collector with no mechanism for administrative appeal. The only recourse was an expensive and protracted legal review before a court of competent jurisdiction. A modified administrative mechanism had to be put in place. One that does not simply indulge the conveniences of the bureaucracy but also gave primacy the people who pay the final cost.

Of course, there will be genuine cases where there exist genuine circumstances which result in a delay in issuing the notification. If

---

[10] Section 14 of the Act, 2013.
[11] Section 4(2) of the Land Acquisition Act, 1894.
[12] Section 6 of the Land Acquisition Act, 1894.

legitimate justifications exist then an extension is allowed but it must be recorded in writing and it must be made available on the website of the acquiring authority. This is done to encourage judicial review, to fix the accountability of the authority directing the extension and to prevent spurious extensions.

## RAISING OBJECTIONS AFTER THE PRELIMINARY NOTIFICATION

Thereafter, once the preliminary notification has been issued, any person interested in any land which has been notified for acquisition may within sixty days from the date of the publication of the preliminary notification, raise objections under Section 15 of the Act with regard to 'the area and suitability of land proposed to be acquired, the justification offered for public purpose or the findings of the Social Impact Assessment report'. It must be noted that this is the second time in the law that the affected parties have a right to raise their concerns (the first is the public hearing conducted as part of the Social Impact Assessment).

The Collector has to record these objections and he has to give a hearing to the person concerned. After hearing all such objections and after making such further inquiries as may be required, he must make a report containing his recommendations on the objections, 'together with the record of the proceedings held by him along with a separate report giving therein the approximate cost of land acquisition, particulars as to the number of affected families likely to be resettled, for the decision of that Government'.[13]

To a casual observer, this would look like an exercise in autocratic obstructionism. But it must be read in light of the widespread abuses the old law engendered.

## PREPARATION OF THE REHABILITATION AND RESETTLEMENT SCHEME BY ADMINISTRATOR

Following the above, the work on planning for rehabilitation and resettlement begins. Once the preliminary notification has been published by the Collector, the Administrator for Rehabilitation and

[13] Section 15 of the Act, 2013.

Resettlement is required to conduct a survey and undertake a census of the affected families.[14] This survey should include:

- Particulars of lands and immovable properties being acquired of each affected family;
- Livelihoods lost in respect of land losers and landless whose livelihoods are primarily dependent on the lands being acquired;
- A list of public utilities and Government buildings which are affected or likely to be affected, where resettlement of affected families is involved;
- Details of the amenities and infrastructural facilities which are affected or likely to be affected, where resettlement of affected families is involved; and
- Details of any common property resources being acquired.

The Administrator shall, based on this survey and census, prepare a draft Rehabilitation and Resettlement Scheme.

This draft is required to include particulars of the rehabilitation and resettlement entitlements of each land owner and landless individuals (whose livelihoods are primarily dependent on the lands being acquired) and where resettlement of affected families is involved along with a list of Government buildings to be provided in the Resettlement area as well as details of the public amenities and infrastructural facilities which are to be provided in the resettlement area.

The draft Scheme is also required to prescribe a time limit for implementation of the Rehabilitation and Resettlement Scheme.[15]

As is the requirement with all processes and declarations under the law, the draft Rehabilitation and Resettlement scheme shall be disseminated 'by wide publicity in the affected area and discussed in the concerned Gram Sabhas or Municipalities'.

### Second Public Hearing

A second public hearing (the third such opportunity to record concerns) has to be conducted at the affected area. This should be preceded by a process of dissemination where adequate publicity

---

[14] Section 16 of the Act, 2013.
[15] Section 16(3) of the Act, 2013.

about the date, time and venue for the public hearing has been carried out at the affected area.[16]

Where the consultation with the Gram Sabha is to take place in Scheduled Areas then it has to be in accordance with the provisions of the Provisions of the Panchayats (Extension to the Scheduled Areas) Act, 1996. This is important to mitigate the sense of being left out that is traditionally suffered by these groups.

The Administrator after completing this public hearing must submit two documents to the Collector. These are the draft Scheme for Rehabilitation and Resettlement and a specific report on the claims and objections raised in this public hearing.

This draft Scheme has to be reviewed by the Collector along with the body known as the Rehabilitation and Resettlement Committee at the Project level (constituted under Section 45 of the Act but only if the acquisition area is a 100 acres or more).[17] The Collector shall then submit the draft Rehabilitation and Resettlement Scheme with his suggestions to the Commissioner Rehabilitation and Resettlement for approval.[18]

## DECLARATION FOR ACQUISITION AND SUMMARY OF REHABILITATION AND RESETTLEMENT REPORT

The declaration for acquisition of land is then issued under Section 19 of the Act, 2013. The section provides:

[16] *Provided that in case where an affected area involves more than one Gram Panchayat or Municipality, public hearings shall be conducted in every Gram Sabha and Municipality where more than twenty-five per cent of land belonging to that Gram Sabha or Municipality is being acquired.* First Proviso to Section 16(5) of the Act, 2013.

[17] Section 17 of the Act, 2013. This must be followed by public distribution under Section 18 of the Act, 2013, 'The Commissioner shall also cause the approved Rehabilitation and Resettlement Scheme to be made available in the local language to the Panchayat, Municipality or Municipal Corporation, as the case may be, and the offices of the District Collector, the Sub-Divisional Magistrate and the Tehsil, and shall be published in the affected areas, in such manner as may be prescribed, and uploaded on the website of the appropriate Government'.

[18] Section 17 of the Act, 2013.

*(1) When the appropriate Government is satisfied, after considering the report, if any, made under sub-section (2) of Section 15, that any particular land is needed for a public purpose, a declaration shall be made to that effect, along with a declaration of an area identified as the 'resettlement area' for the purposes of rehabilitation and resettlement of the affected families, under the hand and seal of a Secretary to such Government or of any other officer duly authorised to certify its orders and different declarations may be made from time to time in respect of different parcels of any land covered by the same preliminary notification irrespective of whether one report or different reports has or have been made (wherever required).*

This declaration must be accompanied by a summary of the Rehabilitation and Resettlement Scheme.

The two documents—Declaration and Summary—must be published together. This declaration can only be made if the Requiring Body (the body for whom the acquisition is being carried out) has deposited an amount, in full or part, as may be prescribed by the appropriate Government toward the cost of acquisition of the land.

One other thing that must be kept in mind with regard to the declaration under Section 19 is that if it is not issued within twelve months of the Preliminary notification then the same will be deemed to have lapsed.[19] To calculate or compute the period of twelve months, any period or periods during which the proceedings for the acquisition of the land were held up on account of any stay or injunction by the order of any Court shall be excluded.[20] This is necessary so that the process is not allowed to languish in perpetuity.

In large projects where land is acquired in stages, the application for acquisition itself can specify different stages for the rehabilitation and resettlement, and all declarations shall be made according to the stages so specified.

Every declaration under Section 19 shall be published in the Official Gazette, in two daily newspapers being circulated in the locality (of which one shall be in the regional language), in the local language in the Panchayat, Municipality or Municipal Corporation,

---

[19] Section 19(7). However this period can be extended if legitimate reasons exists. The reasons for such an extension must be reduced to writing and must be uploaded on the authority's website.

[20] Proviso to Section 19(7) of the Act, 2013.

as the case may be, and in the offices of the District Collector, the Sub-Divisional Magistrate and the Tehsil, uploaded on the website of the appropriate Government, in the affected areas.

The following essential items must be provided for in the Section 19 declaration:[21]

- The district or other territorial division in which the land is situated
- The purpose for which it is needed, its approximate area
- Where a plan shall have been made for the land, the place at which such plan may be inspected without any cost.

## AWARD

The Land Acquisition Award (which includes a separate and distinct Rehabilitation and Resettlement Award) is passed under Section 23 of the new Act. On any day so fixed by the Collector he has to make an award under his hand which shall contain the following details:

- The true area of the land;
- The compensation as determined (See Chapter 4 for a more detailed discussion on how compensation is arrived at);
- The Rehabilitation and Resettlement award as determined and which in his opinion should be allowed for the land; and
- The apportionment of the said compensation among all the individuals who have an interest in the land (through claims filed or otherwise) whether or not they have appeared before him.

The equivalent section under the now repealed Land Acquisition Act, 1894 was Section 11. This award represented a conclusion of the land acquisition proceedings and would allow the Government to lay claim to the area under acquisition.

The new law does not conclude the proceedings with the Award. The Award merely represents the agreement between the acquiring authority and the person whose land is sought to be acquired. As we shall see, before possession can be taken other processes need to be satisfied.

---

[21] Section 19(5) of the Act, 2013.

## REHABILITATION AND RESETTLEMENT AWARD

The Rehabilitation and Resettlement award seeks to lay out a fair apportionment of the entitlements that an affected individual or family may receive as given in the Second Schedule of the Right to Fair Compensation and Transparency in Land Acquisition, Rehabilitation and Resettlement Act, 2013. A more detailed discussion of the substantive portions is given in Chapter 5. Here, we shall look at the procedure for determining such an award.

The Collector is the authority charged with the responsibility of passing Rehabilitation and Resettlement Awards.[22] He is required to prepare an award for each affected family. The Rehabilitation and Resettlement Award has to include the following elements:[23]

- Rehabilitation and resettlement amount payable to the family
- Bank account number of the person to which the rehabilitation and resettlement award amount is to be transferred
- Particulars of house site and house to be allotted, in case of displaced families
- Particulars of land allotted to the displaced families
- Particulars of one time subsistence allowance and transportation allowance in case of displaced families
- Particulars of payment for cattle shed and petty shops
- Particulars of one-time amount to artisans and small traders
- Details of mandatory employment to be provided to the members of the affected families
- Particulars of any fishing rights that may be involved
- Particulars of annuity and other entitlements to be provided
- Particulars of special provisions for the Scheduled Castes and the Scheduled Tribes to be provided.

The appropriate Government also enjoys the power to increase the rate of rehabilitation and resettlement amount payable to the affected families to better account for any inflation that might have occurred.

In every resettlement area (the area where the affected and displaced families are proposed to be resettled), the Collector has to

---

[22] Section 31 of the Act, 2013.
[23] Ibid.

ensure the provision of all infrastructural facilities and basic minimum amenities specified in the Third Schedule. This is discussed in
greater detail in Chapter 5.

The Collector can rectify any errors which may have inadvertently
crept in to the award (say with regard to amounts calculated or typo-
graphical errors). If the correction is likely to hurt or prejudice an
affected party (by reducing or denying an entitlement) then a hearing
shall be given to the person or family so affected. However, he cannot
make corrections once six months have lapsed after the passage of the
order.[24]

Before the rehabilitation and resettlement award is made, the
Government carrying out the acquisition can call for any record of
any proceedings for the purpose of satisfying itself as to the legality
or propriety of any findings or order passed. In furtherance of this
inquiry it may also issue directions with regard to the process as may be
required. However, if these directions are detrimental to the interests
of an affected person or family then the directions shall be preceded by
giving an opportunity to the said individuals to be heard.[25]

The law also requires the Collector to keep a summary of the entire
land acquisition proceedings at his office including the amount of
compensation awarded to each individual along with details of the
land finally acquired under this Act. This summary of events shall
be made accessible to the public and shall be published on a website
created expressly for this purpose.[26]

## POSSESSION

This is a central safeguard under the new law. Under the old Act
possession would be taken without satisfactorily compensating or
resettling the families. This resulted in enormous injustice being
meted out to the families who had been stripped of their land by the
very Government responsible for their well-being.

The Collector can now take possession of the land only after ensuring the full payment of compensation including the rehabilitation

---

[24] Section 33 of the Act, 2013.
[25] Section 36 of the Act, 2013.
[26] Section 37 of the Act, 2013.

and resettlement entitlements to the entitled persons. Section 38 of the law lays down the conditions that need to be satisfied:

- The financial compensation for the land shall be paid within **three months** of the Rehabilitation and Resettlement Award being made (under Section 31 of the Act).
- The parts of Rehabilitation and Resettlement package that are monetary in nature or have to be paid in the form of cash payments shall be disbursed within a period of **six months** from the date of the Rehabilitation and Resettlement award.
- The components of the Rehabilitation and Resettlement Package that relate to infrastructural entitlements and other long term arrangements (such as on site jobs) shall be provided within a period of **eighteen months** from the date of the award.

In keeping with the directions of the Supreme Court,[27] the proviso to this section states that in case of acquisition of land for irrigation or hydel project, the rehabilitation and resettlement shall be completed six months prior to submergence of the lands acquired.

However, the Collector cannot displace the affected families before ensuring that the rehabilitation and resettlement process is completed in all its aspects.

The law also provides additional safeguards against double displacement.[28] Allowed only as a last resort, the Collector must pay an additional compensation equivalent to that of the compensation determined under this Act for the second or successive displacements. This means double the compensation must be paid if an individual or a family are displaced twice as the result of the same acquisition.

### One Time Payment by Requiring Body

If the requiring body (say a company or a Public-Sector Undertaking) feels that it can quantify, in monetary terms, what it owes to the affected families as the full and final amount (including compensation

---

[27] See *B.D.Sharma vs Union of India* Writ Petition No. 1201 of 1990, the Supreme Court has directed the completion of all relevant rehabilitation activities six months prior to submergence.

[28] Section 39 of the Act, 2013.

and towards discharging its rehabilitation and resettlement amounts) then it is allowed to deposit, subject to the satisfaction of the Collector, the entire amount into an account in complete satisfaction of their responsibilities under the law. This account shall then be the responsibility of the Administrator for Rehabilitation and Resettlement.[29]

This clause was included to accommodate the concern of industry that they would be held liable *ad nauseum* (some amounts such as annuity are long term payments) under the law. This would leave them vulnerable to constant litigation and would in turn, severely handicap the running of the project.

## OFFICERS TASKED WITH REHABILITATION AND RESETTLEMENT

The Act recognises that acquisition needs a proper administrative machinery if the process is to be carried out efficiently, fairly and transparently. To this end, it authorises the Government to appoint officers who are responsible for the rehabilitation and resettlement activities in addition to the Collector. These include the Administrator for Rehabilitation and Resettlement and the Commissioner, Rehabilitation and Resettlement.

The idea for the creation of both these offices comes from the National Rehabilitation and Resettlement Policy, 2007.[30] However, they have been modified to better serve the symbiotic relationship of the land acquisition and rehabilitation/resettlement procedures given under the new law.

### Office of the Administrator Rehabilitation and Resettlement

An Administrator Rehabilitation and Resettlement is required to be appointed where the appropriate Government is satisfied that there is likely to be involuntary displacement of persons due to acquisition of land.[31]

---

[29] Section 47 of the Act, 2013.

[30] Chapter V, Para 5 of the National Rehabilitation and Resettlement Policy, 2007.

[31] *An officer not below the rank of Joint Collector or Additional Collector or Deputy Collector or equivalent official of Revenue Department.* Section 43 of the Act, 2013.

The Administrator carries out his duties subject to the superintendence, directions and control of the appropriate Government and the Commissioner for Rehabilitation and Resettlement. The formulation, execution and monitoring of the Rehabilitation and Resettlement Scheme are the responsibility of the Administrator.[32]

## Office of the Commissioner Rehabilitation and Resettlement

The State Government, of the state where the acquisition is being carried out, shall appoint an officer[33] for rehabilitation and resettlement of affected families to be called the Commissioner for Rehabilitation and Resettlement. The Commissioner is responsible for supervising the formulation of rehabilitation and resettlement schemes or plans. He is also responsible for the proper implementation of these schemes or plans.[34]

In addition to these duties, the Commission is responsible for the post-implementation social audit that is to be carried out in consultation with the representative bodies (Gram Sabha in rural areas and municipality in urban areas).[35]

## Rehabilitation and Resettlement Committee

Where the area under acquisition is a hundred acres or more in size then the government carrying out the acquisition must constitute a Rehabilitation and Resettlement Committee to be chaired by the Collector.

This Committee has to monitor and review the progress of implementation of the Rehabilitation and Resettlement scheme. The Committee also has to carry out a post-implementation social audit in consultation with representative bodies (Gram Sabha in rural areas and municipality in urban areas).[36] This Rehabilitation and Resettlement Committee shall include, apart from officers of the appropriate Government, the following members:

[32] Section 43(3) of the Act, 2013.
[33] *'of the rank of Commissioner or Secretary of that Government'*. Section 44 of the Act, 2013.
[34] Section 44(2) of the Act, 2013.
[35] Section 44(3) of the Act, 2013.
[36] Section 45 of the Act, 2013.

- A representative of women residing in the affected area
- A representative each of the Scheduled Castes and the Scheduled Tribes residing in the affected area
- A representative of a voluntary organisation working in the area
- A representative of a nationalised bank
- The Land Acquisition Officer of the project
- The Chairpersons of the panchayats or municipalities located in the affected area or their nominees
- The Chairperson of the District Planning Committee or his nominee
- The Member of Parliament and Member of the Legislative Assembly of the concerned area or their nominees
- A representative of the Requiring Body
- Administrator for Rehabilitation and Resettlement as the Member-Convenor.

## NATIONAL MONITORING COMMITTEE AND STATE MONITORING COMMITTEE FOR REHABILITATION AND RESETTLEMENT

Two more stand-alone Committees—The National Monitoring Committee for Rehabilitation and Resettlement and State Monitoring Committee for Rehabilitation and Resettlement can be established by the respective Governments wherever necessary. [37]

These bodies are not confined to a particular project but can review and monitor the implementation of any project across the country or in the State respectively. The Committees have to be staffed by representatives of the concerned Ministries and Departments of the Central and State Governments and also eminent experts from the relevant fields.

The States and Union territories have to provide all the relevant information on the matters covered under the new law to the National Monitoring Committee in 'a regular, timely manner and when asked to provide such information'.[38] This is to ensure that a fair and accurate record of all proceedings is maintained to provide guidance and aid in the implementation of future projects.

[37] See Chapter VII (Sections 48 & 50) of the Act, 2013.
[38] Section 49 of the Act, 2013.

# CHAPTER FOUR

# Compensation

*Compensation is at the heart of land acquisition. The amount being paid must be sufficiently fair so as to ameliorate the forcible and involuntary nature of acquisition. Courts have long recognized the act of paying compensation as a necessary condition in the taking over of the land.[1] In India the problem arises with regard to the quantum that officers often award to affected families in the name of 'market value'. This Chapter discusses how the new law attempts to achieve fairness in the payment of compensation.*

Under the Land Acquisition Act, 1894, compensation was required to be paid at market value.[2] This seems to be a sensible idea in theory but is actually responsible for widespread injustices and the cause of action for a litany of legal disputes.

As anyone who has purchased property in India can attest, land values are grossly underquoted in land records. If, for example, a property is listed at 'x' value, then chances are, in urban areas particularly, the property will be sold for at least four times that value (that is, 4x). One reason for this gaping inconsistency is that land records are updated very infrequently.

One of the questions we often got asked was why not take the opportunity that a new law on land acquisition offers and put in a

---

[1] Acquisition is violative of Article 14 (of the Constitution of India) without payment. See *Ram Jiyawan vs State of Uttar Pradesh* AIR 1994 All 38.

[2] As it existed in the land records on the date when the Preliminary Notification under Section 4 of the now repealed Land Acquisition Act, 1894 was issued. See also Section 23 of the now repealed Land Acquisition Act, 1894.

chapter requiring the modernising of land records. Though tempting this was never an option on the table. The law takes advantage of, and owes its existence-primarily to a single entry in the concurrent list of the Constitution—Entry 42, 'Acquisition and Requisitioning of Property'.

'Land' as a subject of governance *per se* falls within the States' legislative domain. The law walks a fine line often risking going into the legislative domain of the State Governments, as was evidenced by the outcry of some states (led by the Governments of Tamil Nadu and West Bengal).

Despite the most acute instincts of the draftsmen to fix land records the law simply could not dictate terms to the States. It focuses instead on devising an approach that adjusts the final compensation to be paid taking into account the inherent shortcomings that affect land records and hence land values.

## ARRIVING AT A 'FAIR COMPENSATION'

One of the key points of distinction between the now repealed 1894 Act and the new law is the manner in which the latter seeks to achieve a fairer degree of financial restitution for the affected parties. It attempts a solution to a system mired in deep rooted flaws and seeks to put in place a measure that brings about greater if not absolute fairness vis-à-vis the compensation paid.

In fact, the idea of compensation was the very first issue to be addressed in a meeting attended by the Minister for Rural Development, officers of the department of land resources and members of the National Advisory Council. It was mutually agreed that existing values fell far short of being considered fair. This gave rise to the question of what would indeed be a fair value.

Once again we went back to first principles. How had market value come to be defined?

*The market value is the price which an ordinary private purchaser might be expected to give for the property, were the owner desirous of parting with it. There are ordinarily three circumstances which may serve to indicate this market value-*

- *The price at which the land was taken, or any part of it, has sold on previous occasions.*

- *The present rental of the property which may be capitalized at so many years' purchase; and*
- *The price at which similar land in the neighbourhood has been sold.*

The above foundations were taken as accepted even a century ago.[3]

This is reflected in the case of *Premchand Burral vs The Collector of Calcutta*,[4] one of the first judicial proceedings on record where the principle of fair and most favourable compensation was discussed:

> *What is the market-value of the property, not according to its present disposition, but laid out in the most lucrative and advantageous way in which the owners could dispose of it.*
>
> *When Government takes property from private persons under statutory powers, it is only right that those persons should obtain such a measure of compensation as is warranted by the price of similar property in the neighbourhood, without any special reference to the uses to which it may be applied at the time when it is taken by the Government, or to the price which its owners may previously have given for it.*[5] [Emphasis added]

After the initial round of consultations in July–August of 2011, it was also acknowledged that land values are, on an average, a sixth of their represented or book value as drawn out in the circle rate. As one moved away from urban centres the disparity became more striking with land records not having been updated for decades in some parts of the country.

This hypothesis was arrived at by studying centres such as Gujarat, Delhi, Haryana, Maharashtra, and Karnataka. In fact, the original draft first uploaded on the website of the Ministry of Rural Development, fixed compensation at three times the market value in urban areas and up to six times the market value in rural areas.

## Criticism and Response

Many groups argued that this was not a fair proposition espe-cially considering all the entitlements to be provided as part of

---

[3] See pages 36–37, *The Land Acquisition Acts* Berverley, Henry (1888). Calcutta: Thacker, Spink And Co.

[4] I. L. R, 2 Cal. 103.

[5] Garth, CJ, (MacPherson, J., concurring).

the rehabilitation and resettlement package (from jobs or twenty year monthly payments) formed a sizeable and perhaps non-viable amount.

Some ministries of the Government of India (Ministry of Urban Development most notably) argued that the high package (particularly in urban areas) would hamper municipal bodies from carrying out development projects such as public parks or low cost housing. As many of these bodies already operated on a limited budget and the project envisaged seldom generates significant revenue (if at all) the body would have no choice but to abandon the project.

In the face of these concerns which were undoubtedly legitimate, the target amount was reduced so as to be effectively twice in urban areas and up to four times in rural areas.

## WHY IS THE FINAL AMOUNT EITHER TWICE OR FOUR TIMES THE MARKET VALUE?

The conclusion regarding the degree of under reporting of land values was strengthened after a meeting with district collectors who possessed actual experience in the acquisition of land. Based on collective insights a formula was devised. The intention was to leave as little as possible to the discretion or guidance of the officer carrying out the process. By reducing human error, we could focus on delivering a value closer (if not equal) to the actual value.

We were mindful that this would still fall short of the fair value in some parts of the country. But a central rule of policy making is that the best should not be made the enemy of the good. If we could arrive at a workable formula that provided a fair value for most, then the law would have achieved a key objective.

At its most fundamental representation, the formula basically seeks to fix the deficiencies of market value by multiplying the given value with a fixed multiplier and then imposing a solatium on the value so arrived at.

The Collector has to adopt diverse criteria to accurately assess and determine the base amount. These include:[6]

---

[6] Section 26(1) of the Act, 2013.

- The market value, if any, specified in the Indian Stamp Act, 1899 for the registration of sale deeds or agreements to sell, as the case may be, in the area, where the land is situated; or
- The average sale price for similar type of land situated in the nearest village or nearest vicinity area;
- Consented amount of compensation as agreed upon under sub-section (2) of Section 2 in case of acquisition of lands for private companies or for public private partnership projects.

Whichever of the three items listed above is the highest will form the base amount.

The average sale price given in the second item above is to be determined by taking into account the sale deeds or the agreements to sell registered for similar type of area in the near village or near vicinity area during the immediately preceding three years from the date on which such acquisition of land is proposed to be made.[7]

For determining this average sale price, one-half of the total number of sale deeds or the agreements to sell in which the highest sale price has been mentioned shall be taken into account.

The idea of using surrounding areas in the vicinity to determine fair market value actually predates the legislation by over a century. In the case of *The Collector of Poonah vs Kashinath Khasgiwala*,[8] the learned bench held forth on what was the 'most lucrative and advantageous way' for the owner to sell the land:

> *The question then is, what would be its market-value if so laid out; and the most reliable evidence on that question must be the rates per square foot at which similar building sites in the neighbourhood have recently been sold.* [Emphasis added]

It was recently endorsed by the Supreme Court[9] in the following terms:

> *It is the duty of both of the Land Acquisition Officer as also of the Court to determine the actual compensation payable for the land acquired by referring to evidence regarding fair and just compensation near about the*

[7] Explanation 1 to Section 26 of the Act, 2013.
[8] I. L. R., 10 Bom. 585.
[9] *A. Natesam Pillai vs Spl. Tahsildar, Land Acquisition, Tiruchy,* (2010) 9 SCC 118: (2010)8 SCALE 152.

*proximate date or on the date itself of the publication of the notification under Section 4. At times, in order to prove the actual, fair and just compensation for the land acquired, sale deeds of the adjacent land or near about adjacent land are produced to indicate the trend of the value of the land within the near vicinity of the acquired land. Such sale deeds are taken notice of generally when they are prior in point of time to the date of notification, and any sale deed which is post notification dated is generally ignored, unless evidence is led to show that there was no increase in price despite such acquisition.* [Emphasis added]

However, it must be noted that any price paid as compensation for land acquired under the provisions of the new Act on an earlier occasion in the district shall not be taken into consideration as a base for any subsequent acquisitions in the area.[10] This is a very important and necessary safeguard. If the amount paid for land acquisition was taken as the base then it would lead to an inflated price spiral.[11]

To illustrate: say four times the market value was paid for a parcel of land in an area to arrive at the final compensation award. If this award were to become the new base then the new acquisition would theoretically be required to pay up to four times this base amount. This would lead to a situation where the new acquisition would end up getting up to sixteen times the original base value ($4X \times 4X = 16X$).

When legislating for a land mass as large and diverse as India, one must be mindful of the capacity of certain sections of the populace to work or 'fix' a system to their advantage (and hence to the disadvantage of others). This qualification becomes necessary to prevent unscrupulous parties from using the system to the detriment of land owners living in an area identified for land acquisition.

While calculating the base, the Collector also has the power to discount any price paid for any property in the vicinity which in his opinion 'is not indicative of actual prevailing market value'.[12]

If the market value cannot be determined for any of the followings reasons:

- The land is situated in such area where the transactions in land are restricted by or under any other law for the time being in force

---

[10] Explanation 3 to Section 26 of the Act, 2013.

[11] Explanation 4 to Section 26 of the Act, 2013.

[12] Proviso to Section 26.

in that area (such as a stay order or an order preventing the sale of lands belonging to specific communities as had been passed in Rajasthan circa 2011–2012); or

- The registered sale deeds or agreements to sell for similar land are not available for the immediately preceding three years (the ill-maintenance of land records and the presumptive nature of titles in India makes this a common source of disputes); or
- The market value has not been specified under the Indian Stamp Act, 1899 by the appropriate authority (the area is so remote that the State Government has not updated or even notified the records).

The State Government concerned shall specify the floor price or minimum price per unit area of the said land based on the price calculated in the manner specified in respect of similar types of land situated in the immediate adjoining areas.

## OPTION OF SHARES

In a case where the Requiring Body offers its shares to the owners of the lands (whose lands have been acquired) as a part compensation, for acquisition of land, the total shares offered should not exceed 25 per cent of the value so calculated.

The Requiring Body is cautioned by the law not to compel or influence any owner of the land (whose land has been acquired) to take its shares. If the entitled beneficiary opts for the shares then the value of the same is to be deducted from value of the land calculated under the Act.

## OTHER ADDITIONS WHILE CALCULATING THE AWARD

Once a final market value has been determined by the Collector then he is required to calculate the total amount of compensation to be paid to the land owner (whose land has been acquired) by including all assets attached to the land.[13] In sum, to arrive at the final

---

[13] Section 27 of the Act, 2013.

compensation amount for the land to be acquired, the Collector has to take into consideration the following items:[14]

- The market value as determined under the Act and the award amount in accordance with the First and Second Schedules
- The damage sustained by the affected person if any standing crops and trees may have been damaged by the Collector while taking possession
- Any damage sustained by the affected person, at the time of the Collector's taking possession of the land, by reason of severing such land from his other land
- Any damage sustained by the affected person, at the time of the Collector's taking possession of the land, by reason of the acquisition injuriously affecting his other property, movable or immovable, in any other manner, or his earnings
- If the affected person is compelled to change his residence or place of business as a direct result of the acquisition of the land, the reasonable expenses incidental to such change
- Any *bona fide* damage resulting from diminution of the profits of the land between the time of the publication of the final declaration under Section 19 and the time of the Collector's taking possession of the land
- Any other ground which may be in the interest of equity, justice and beneficial to the affected families.

The Collector can also use the services of a competent engineer or a specialist (if required) to determine the market value of the building and other immovable property or assets attached to the land or building which are to be acquired.

For the purpose of determining the value of trees and plants attached to the land acquired, use the services of experienced persons

---

[14] Section 28 of the Act, 2013. It must be pointed out that this section is an adaptation of Section 23 of the Land Acquisition Act, 1894 which in turn had adapted it from the Land Acquisition Act, 1870 (Act X of 1870). See *The Land Acquisition Acts* Berverley, Henry (1888), Calcutta: Thacker, Spink and Co.

in the field of agriculture, forestry, horticulture, sericulture, or any other field may also be employed.

To assess the value of the standing crops damaged during the process of land acquisition, the Collector may use the services of experienced persons in the field of agriculture.

## SOLATIUM

Solatium is not a new concept. It had already existed under the now repealed Land Acquisition Act, 1894. Since 1984, following an amendment to the Act, affected individuals were required to be paid an additional 30 per cent of the market value 'in consideration of the compulsory nature of the acquisition'.[15] We simply increased this to a 100 per cent as it was agreed by all (civil society, government officers and members of industry)[16] that 30 per cent was too low a figure to acknowledge the compulsory nature of the acquisition.

The amount (or 'market value') shall accrue interest at the rate of 12 per cent per year until it is actually paid. This is to ensure any erosion in the prevailing market value does not diminish the amount to be paid to the affected individual. The period from which this interest begins to accrue commences from the date of the publication of the notification of the Social Impact Assessment study (under Section 4(2) of the Act), till the date of the award of the Collector or the date of taking possession of the land, whichever happens first.[17]

## USING THE MULTIPLIER

### Urban Areas

In urban areas, the market value has to be taken and then multiplied by the multiplier given in the First Schedule (currently fixed at 'one'). It would then have a 'solatium' imposed upon it which would be equal to a 100 per cent of the amount.

[15] Section 23(2) of the Land Acquisition Act, 1894.
[16] KOTAK finance and ICICI Bank also published internal studies on compensation for land acquisition.
[17] Section 30 of the Act, 2013.

*To illustrate:*

If the market value is determined to be 'X'

Then we first multiply X with the given multiplier in the First Schedule (which is currently fixed at 1): X x 1 = X

Then we take a solatium equal to a 100 per cent of the amount and add it to the principle:
X + X

Thereby getting the final amount:
X + X = 2X

## Rural Areas

In rural areas, calculation varies depending upon the multiplier fixed by the State Government. The market value is taken and then multiplied by the multiplier given in the First Schedule (which can be fixed at a number between 'one to two'). It would then have a 'solatium' imposed upon it which would be equal to a 100 per cent of the amount.

*To illustrate:*

If the market value is determined to be 'X'

Then we first multiply X with the multiplier fixed by the State Government (let us assume it to be 2): X x 2 = 2X

Then we take a solatium equal to a 100 per cent of the amount and add it to the principle:
2X + 2X

Thereby getting the final amount:
2X + 2X = 4X

Therefore, the amount comes out to roughly four times the original value.

(Using the above calculation we can see that if the State fixes the multiplier at say 1.5 then the final amount will be three times the market value).

## CRITICISM AND RESPONSE

Some individuals argued that having a uniform multiplier across the country actually penalises states that are better performing in the maintenance of land records.[18] In some states, the land value may actually be closer to the market value at which the property would be traded. Therefore paying compensation of up to four times in rural areas, in those states would ensure that the State Government (which would be the acquiring authority in most cases) would be better served by keeping the circle rates low.

To address this, a sliding scale was inserted. This scale is founded upon a multiplier (1 to 2) being linked to radial distance from the urban centre. The multiplier in the urban centre or municipality could be one but as one moves farther and farther away it increases until it reaches the maximum of two. How states wish to fix this multiplier is entirely at their discretion. A state could even simply fix the multiplier in urban areas at one and in rural areas at two.

To be fair, this idea has not been received very warmly by farmers' groups as it assumes a magnanimity and largesse on the part of State authorities that might not be entirely justified.

This is one clause that will provide different States ample opportunity to demonstrate how public spirited they are in their attitude towards their residents.

## OTHER CONSIDERATIONS

This market value has also to be calculated keeping in mind the 'building potential' of the area. This is actually a more complex standard than it appears at first glance. The Supreme Court has elaborated upon it in the following terms:

> However, the fact that the acquired land had been acquired for building purposes, cannot be sufficient circumstance to regard it as a land with building potentiality, in that, under clause (4) of section 24 of the LA Act that any increase to the value of land likely to accrue from the use to which it will be put when acquired, is required to be excluded.[19]

[18]  A summary of the best performing states is given on the website of the land records modernization programme.

[19]  *P. Ram Reddy vs Land Acquisition Officer* 1995 SCC (2) 305, JT 1995 (1) 593.

This concept is a matter of interpretation to be drawn based on an appreciation of the facts and materials on record. These materials should include:[20]

* The situation of the acquired land *vis-à-vis*, the city of the town or village which had been growing in size because of its commercial, industrial, educational, religious or any other kind of importance or because of its explosive population;
* The suitability of the acquired land for putting up the buildings, be they residential, commercial or industrial, as the case may be;
* Possibility of obtaining water and electric supply for occupants of buildings to be put up on that land;
* Absence of statutory impediments or the like for using the acquired land for building purposes;
* Existence of highways, public roads, layouts of building plots or developed residential extensions in the vicinity or close proximity of the acquired land;
* Benefits or advantages of educational institutions, health care centres, or the like in the surrounding areas of the acquired land which may become available to the occupiers of buildings, if built on the acquired land; and
* Lands around the acquired land or the acquired land itself being in demand for building purposes, to specify a few.

This concept is important as otherwise, the Collector can evaluate the land based on past agricultural value which is far lower than the comparable commercial value of the estate.

## WHO WOULD BE COMPENSATED?

When the law was first drafted, it provided compensation to be paid only to the person who owned the land. Those who depended upon the land for their livelihood but did not own the land were entitled to benefits provided under the head of rehabilitation and resettlement.

Following consultations with leaders of other national political parties, most specifically upon the suggestion of the Communist Party of India, it was decided that all individuals who counted as

---

[20] *P. Ram Reddy vs Land Acquisition Officer* 1995 SCC (2) 305, JT 1995 (1) 593.

'affected families', should be given compensation (in addition to rehabilitation and resettlement benefits). This includes:[21]

- First and foremost, a family whose land or other immovable property has been acquired
- A family which does not own any land but whose members may be agricultural labourers, tenants (including any form of tenancy or holding of usufruct right), share-croppers or artisans or who may be working in the affected area for *three years prior to the acquisition of the land, whose primary source of livelihood stands affected* by the acquisition of land
- Members of Scheduled Tribes and other traditional forest dwellers who have lost any of their forest rights recognised under the Scheduled Tribes and Other Traditional Forest Dwellers (Recognition of Forest Rights) Act, 2006 due to acquisition of the land in question
- Family *whose primary source of livelihood for three years* prior to the acquisition of the land is dependent on forests or water bodies and includes gatherers of forest produce, hunters, fisher folk and boatmen and such livelihood is affected due to acquisition of land
- A member of the family who has been assigned land by the State Government or the Central Government under any of its schemes and such land is under acquisition
- A family *residing on any land in the urban areas for preceding three years or more* prior to the acquisition of the land *or whose primary source of livelihood for three years prior to the acquisition of the land* is affected by the acquisition of such land.

While the land owner will get the full compensation as calculated, the compensation paid to the other affected families is meant to be in proportion to their claims and with regard to their degree of dependence on the land. This is why the law allows the concerned Government to determine this 'proportion'.[22]

As a more permanent fix, the new law requires the Collector to update land records[23] within two months of the Preliminary

---

[21] Section 3(c) of the Act, 2013.
[22] First Recital to the First Schedule of the Act, 2013.
[23] Section 11 and Section 26 of the Act, 2013.

Notification being issued. This is intended to have two benefits. Firstly, the beneficiaries are accurately identified. Secondly, the land values are closer to the current and prevailing market price.

CHAPTER FIVE

# Rehabilitation and Resettlement

*For the first time in India's legislative history, a new law has tied land acquisition with the necessity to carry out rehabilitation and resettlement. The provisions relating to rehabilitation and resettlement are mandatory and far reaching. This chapter discusses the thinking that went into identifying what benefits should be non-negotiable and the infrastructural amenities that have to be provided in cases of displacement.*

## THE IMPORTANCE OF 'REHABILITATION AND RESETTLEMENT'

'Rehabilitation and Resettlement' represent an idea that has been the subject of impassioned debate for almost three decades in India. Entire movements for effective rehabilitation and resettlement have been spawned in the wake of coercive acquisitions. While there is no comprehensive record of how many individuals have actually been displaced by land acquisition post-independence, estimates put forth by credible studies find that close to 60 million individuals have been displaced since independence. Worse still, only about a third of these have actually seen some measure of resettlement and rehabilitation.[1]

It is therefore remarkable that it received recognition as a policy priority of the Government of India in the form of the National Rehabilitation and Resettlement Policy as late as 2003.[2] The

---

[1] See Chapter titled 'Pawns in the "Development"', by Walter Fernandes in S. Parasuraman and P.V. Unnikrishnan (eds), *India Disasters Report* (2000); See also Walter Fernandes (2004), March, 'Rehabilitation Policy for the Displaced', in *Economic and Political Weekly*, Vol. 39, Issue 12, pp. 1191–3.

[2] See the National Policy on Resettlement and Rehabilitation for Project Affected Families 2003 (Published in the Gazette of India, Extraordinary

Government of India had for the first time, through this measure, acknowledged the need for Rehabilitation and Resettlement of families displaced by the acquisition of land. The policy was prepared in the wake of widespread displacements that had taken place after the Narmada Valley project acquisitions.[3]

Prior to this, States also had their own policies on the subject. The Maharashtra Resettlement of Project Displaced Persons Act, 1976 is a fine example of a state law on the subject with a complete list of amenities being provided. Public Sector Enterprises such as Coal India[4] and the National Thermal Power Corporation also have policies on Rehabilitation and Resettlement which function as guidelines on a project to project basis. In fact, officers of the latter concern, helped with inputs to the Rehabilitation and Resettlement chapters based on the experiences under their policy.

Following the 2003 Policy on Rehabilitation and Resettlement, the Government of India drafted the National Rehabilitation and Resettlement Policy, 2007.[5] It was in this policy that many of the ideas which we are now familiar with (such as Social Impact Assessment) were linked to the proper implementation of the procedure.

However, the problem with a Policy is that it is, in essence, soft law. It does require the approval of Parliament and can be dispensed

Part-I, Section 1, No-46, dated 17 February 2004). Available at: http://www.dolr.nic.in/hyperlink/lrc-status/nprr_2003.htm.

[3] *In the late eighties, the Narmada Bachao Andolan opened discussions around a coherent R&R policy. This was followed by a number of propositions, by both civil society organisations and successive governments. However, none of them were made into law. Finally, in 2011, the National Advisory Council (NAC) called for a law linking land acquisition and R&R law linking land acquisition and R&R* Oxfam India Policy Brief on The proposed Land Acquisition Bill, 2 October 2012.

[4] Coal India's Policy was Issued in May 2008, available at: http://www.coalindia.in/Documents/Policies/PolicyOnCILRR17062008.pdf. The National Thermal Power Corporation's Policy was revised in 2005 and is available at http://www.ntpc.co.in/images/content/corporate_citizenship/NTPC_R&R_Policy_2005.pdf.

[5] The National Rehabilitation and Resettlement Policy, 2007 dated 31 October 2007, available at http://www.dolr.nic.in/NRRP2007.pdf.

with a simple reference to Cabinet.[6] In other cases that requirement too is waived. The contents of the policy are then regarded as guidelines or suggestions that may offer clarity in cases of doubt on the part of the implementing agency. Worse still, the recommendations are to be adopted at the discretion of the implementing authority.

Thus, there is no guaranteed legal mechanism to implement a policy. No remedy which will enforce compliance other than the good graces of judicial whim. In the year 2012, the Supreme Court of India took the National Forest Policy of 1988 and used it to lay down directions as part of a landmark judgment on forest clearances.[7]

> *The principles/guidelines mentioned in the National Forest Policy, 1988 should be read as part of the provisions of the Environment (Protection) Act, 1986 read together with the Forest (Conservation) Act, 1980.*

This was a rare instance where a policy transcended the realm of soft law and actually became an implementable instrument.

In light of growing public sentiment on the issue, a draft law on the subject of Rehabilitation and Resettlement was prepared. It was passed by the Lok Sabha on 25 February 2009 but it lapsed as Parliament dissolved for fresh elections.

However, the principles on which it was premised seemed exclusionary. To begin with the law would only apply to projects where 400 or more families were being displaced en masse in the plains. The requirement was reduced to 200 families if they were being displaced from hilly or scheduled areas. This meant that essential processes such as Social Impact Assessment would not be carried out unless these thresholds were crossed.[8]

Also the idea of separating the law from one on land acquisition seemed specious since the two were inextricably linked. On

---

[6] An Example is the National Forest Policy of the Ministry of Environment and Forests issued in 1988.

[7] Judgment dated 6 July 2011 in *T.N. Godavarman Thirumulpad vs Union Of India & Ors* (I.A. NOS. 1868, 2091, 2225–2227, 2380, 2568 and 2937 in Writ Petition (C) No. 202 OF 1995—Lafarge Umiam Mining Pvt. Ltd.-Applicant).

[8] Section 4(1) Rehabilitation and Resettlement Bill 2009. A copy is available at [http://dolr.nic.in/Acts&Rules/RehabilitationAndResettlement Bill2009%20as%20passed%20by%20Lok%20Sabha.pdf].

the contrary, two laws on a subject would create greater confusion instead of providing the clarity the process desperately needed.

Given the richness of research and legal theory on the subject, it was simply an exercise in sifting through excellent ideas to find which ones could be mainstreamed in the law. The chapter on Rehabilitation and Resettlement draws heavily from the Rehabilitation and Resettlement Policy of 2007 as well as from the research of scholars and political scientists. However, it is not a verbatim reproduction. Many features have been tweaked and adapted to reflect the consensus around the process.

As a result of the Narmada Valley projects, 'tens of thousands of families in Madhya Pradesh, Maharashtra and Gujarat' were displaced.[9] The fact that this displacement was carried out with rehabilitation and resettlement being treated as secondary concerns demonstrated how very dangerous it is to split the process.

## ELEMENTS OF REHABILITATION AND RESETTLEMENT ENTITLEMENTS

The new law lays down uniform and clear entitlements that must be provided to all the affected families regardless of whether they were land owners or individuals whose livelihood was primarily dependent on the land acquired. This is in addition to the compensation to be paid for the land itself.[10]

### House

If a family loses a house in a rural area as a result of the acquisition, then the law requires a constructed house to be provided to them as per the specifications given in the Indira Awas Yojana scheme of the Government of India. If a house is lost in urban areas, a constructed house shall be provided, the size of which will be not less than 50 square metres (in plinth area).

If an affected family does not own the land which is acquired then they too shall be given a house if they can prove that they have been residing in the area continuously for a period of not less than three years prior to the commencement of the acquisition.

---

[9] 'Trampled on Forever' Editorial in the *Economic and Political Weekly*. Vol-XLI No. 14, 8 April 2006.

[10] Second Schedule to the Act, 2013.

Families are also free to take a financial package equal to one lakh fifty thousand rupees in lieu of the house. One house per family is the limit.

## Land

In the case of irrigation project, each affected family which has lost agricultural land (as a result of the acquisition) is to be allotted (in the name of each title holder), a minimum of one acre of land in the command area of the project. However, if the land has been from individuals who belong to the Scheduled Castes or Scheduled Tribes, then land equivalent to the land acquired or two and half acres, whichever is lower will be given.

Stamp duty, registration fees and any other amounts due on the land and house so provided must be borne by the Requiring Body. The land or house allotted may be in the joint names of wife and husband.

House and Land are the very basis of rehabilitation and resettlement. During the course of consultation, some states suggested that the State would simply be unable to find so much land to distribute as part of the rehabilitation and resettlement package. It was decided to stick with this requirement as it would act as a disincentive for wanton acquisition. It would also put pressure on State Governments to utilise their existing land banks more effectively.

However, one concession that was allowed was that in the case of 'irrigation projects', families would either receive compensation or land but not both. Furthermore 'Land' would be offered as an option only if available.

## Offer for Developed Land

In case the land is acquired for urbanisation purposes, 20 per cent of the developed land will be reserved and offered to land owning project affected families, in proportion to the area of their land acquired and at a price equal to the cost of acquisition and the cost of development. If the families opt for this developed land then an equivalent amount will be deducted from the compensation package paid.

## Choice of Annuity or Government Employment

Affected individuals have three options to choose from:

- If jobs are created as a result of the project then the affected individuals (at least one per family) must be given employment at rates not lower than the minimum wages applicable in the project or arrange for a job in such other project as may be required. Where the job requires a certain degree of skill and training, the acquiring authority must provide the individuals with the basic skills and training needed.
- A one-time payment of five lakhs rupees per affected family.
- Annuity payments that shall pay not less than two thousand rupees per month (per family) for 20 years. These will be adjusted annually to take inflation into account.

## Miscellaneous Financial Payments

The law requires the payment of various financial grants to each affected family in addition to the compensation.

- A monthly 'Subsistence grant' shall be paid to each affected family of three thousand rupees per month for a period of one year from the date of award. Individuals belonging to Scheduled Castes and the Scheduled Tribes that are displaced from Scheduled Areas shall receive an additional amount equivalent to fifty thousand rupees.
- 'Transportation cost' shall be paid at fifty thousand rupees as a one-time grant to each affected family which is displaced as transportation cost for shifting of the family, building materials, belongings and cattle.
- Each affected family which owns cattle or has a small shop shall be given a one-time financial assistance of a minimum of twenty-five thousand rupees for construction of cattle shed or petty shop.
- A one-time grant of a minimum of twenty-five thousand rupees shall be paid to artisans, small traders or self-employed persons or to affected families which owned non-agricultural land or a commercial, industrial or institutional structure in the affected area.

- One-time Resettlement Allowance of fifty thousand rupees shall be paid to all affected families.

## RELOCATION AND MISCELLANEOUS

One of the biggest casualties of displacement is that families which have cultural ties to an area are left broken and disoriented. The new law provides, as part of its rehabilitation and resettlement requirements, that if the displacement occurs in a Scheduled Areas then, as far as possible, 'the affected families shall be relocated in a similar ecological zone, so as to preserve the economic opportunities, language, culture and community life of the tribal communities'.

Fishing rights shall be provided to affected families in the reservoirs so created, in cases of irrigation or hydel projects.

## INFRASTRUCTURAL AMENITIES

When an entire population is moved to a new area, it is facile to suggest that they have been rehabilitated. For resettlement and rehabilitation in the true sense, certain basic infrastructural facilities have to be provided at the proposed site. These have to be constructed at the cost of the Authority at whose behest the acquisition is taking place. The Third Schedule to the law lays down the following amenities as the base minimum:

- Roads within the resettled villages and an all-weather road link to the nearest pucca road, passages and easement rights for all the resettled families
- Proper drainage as well as sanitation plans executed before physical resettlement
- Assured sources of safe drinking water for each family as per the norms prescribed by the Government of India
- Provision of drinking water for cattle
- Grazing land as per proportion acceptable in the State
- A reasonable number of Fair Price Shops
- Panchayat Ghars, as appropriate
- Village level Post Offices, as appropriate, with facilities for opening saving accounts

- Appropriate seed-cum-fertilizer storage facility if needed
- Basic irrigation facilities for the agricultural land allocated to the resettled families
- All new villages established for resettlement of the displaced persons shall be provided with suitable transport facility which must include public transport facilities through local bus services with the nearby growth centres/urban localities
- Burial or cremation ground, depending on the caste communities at the site and their practices
- Facilities for sanitation, including individual toilet points
- Individual single electric connections (or connection through non-conventional sources of energy like solar energy), for each household and for public lighting
- Anganwadi's providing child and mother supplemental nutritional services
- School as per the provisions of the Right of Children to Free and Compulsory Education Act, 2009
- Sub-health centre within two kilometres range (of the site)
- Primary Health Centre as prescribed by the Government of India.
- Playground for children
- One community centre for every hundred families
- Places of worship and chowpal/tree platform for every fifty families for community assembly
- Separate land for traditional tribal institutions
- The forest dweller families must be provided, where possible, with their forest rights on non-timber forest produce and common property resources, if available close to the new place of settlement and, in case any such family can continue their access or entry to such forest or common property in the area close to the place of eviction, they must continue to enjoy their earlier rights to the aforesaid sources of livelihood
- Appropriate security arrangements, if needed
- Veterinary service centre as per norms.

## Is this Excessive?

Many quarters argued that the sheer number and scale of rehabilitation and resettlement entitlements is so great that it would render the acquisition impossible to complete (as taking possession of land is predicated on the complete satisfaction of the rehabilitation and resettlement entitlements following payment of compensation).

The law was drafted with the intention to discourage land acquisition. It was drafted so that land acquisition would become a route of last resort. However, when the cost of doing business involves displacement then the business must account for alternatives for those families so uprooted.

The reason for making the provision of the rehabilitation and resettlement benefits mandatory before possession could be taken over was the experiences in past large scale projects such as the Narmada Dam. Despite the orders of the Supreme Court, the displaced families were never resettled and their original lands ended up submerged. A statutory requirement had to be put in place to ensure that these people were indeed taken care of.

To put it simply, the absence of such conditions in the face of overwhelming experience, would have bordered on the irresponsible.

# CHAPTER SIX

# Retrospective Operation

*The most invoked and litigated section of the new law relates to the retrospective operation, that is, Section 24. This chapter goes into the legislative intent that lay behind the drafting and inclusion of such a clause. The chapter also discusses the substantial interpretations offered by the Supreme Court in the implementation of this section.*

No clause has been the subject of such varied and intense debate as Section 24 of the Right to Fair Compensation and Transparency in Land Acquisition, Rehabilitation and Resettlement Act, 2013. Referred to colloquially as the 'Retrospective Clause' this section essentially extended the application of the law to cases that had already been initiated under the Land Acquisition Act, 1894.

Retrospective clauses are very tricky to draft. Often they are causes for litigation as they seek to alter previously existing situations on the basis of legal principles that did not exist at the time of their occurrence. However certain situations may occur where the observance of the law has resulted in such an egregious breach of the principles of natural justice that a revisit is justified to remedy that breach.

Keeping this in mind, the retrospective clause was drafted only in light of the very high number of wrongs that held the promise of being corrected by its service. Given that the impact of land acquisition is felt across many years and sometimes even across generations the law would be incomplete if it denied justice to a larger class of people than it intended to serve.

Even after being drafted, the formulation was subject to repeated scrutiny and review by stakeholders and their representatives in meetings of the Group of Ministers, in the All Party Meetings and especially by farmers' rights organisations. Only in the face of almost universal consensus was the clause adopted and retained in the final draft.

## WHY RETROSPECTIVE OPERATION

A few months before work began on a new law on land acquisition, widespread rioting and carnage had been witnessed in certain villages of Western Uttar Pradesh directly as a consequence of ill thought out land acquisition proceedings.[1] Land had been acquired by the State Government for the construction of the 'Yamuna Expressway'. Land was acquired and sold to private parties for multiple times the price that had been paid to the farmers from whom the land had been taken. This had resulted in farmers carrying out protests across the length of the proposed project. Problems occurred when these protests turned violent, lives were lost and a curfew had to be imposed.

Cases were filed before the Supreme Court of India and the State High Court at Allahabad. However, not much was achieved through this avenue and the matter continues to remain pending before the Court. The project has since been completed thereby effectively rendering some of the matters infructuous.

The Uttar Pradesh Government did in fact come out with a new land acquisition policy (which was referred to by former Chief Minister Ms Mayawati in Parliament during the debates on the new law as a source of inspiration).[2] The Policy had requirements for consensual acquisition, enhanced compensation and long term annuity payments.[3] However, given that it was only prospective in nature it had little impact towards alleviating the atrocities that had been visited upon the victims of the land acquisition. This was also compounded by the fact the land acquisition policy was, in fact, a

---

[1] Bhatta, Parsaul, Acheypur, Tappal and Motaina; See the Report of the National Human Rights Commission at [http://nhrc.nic.in/disparchive. asp?fno=2379], See also the Press Release issued by the National Commission for Women [http://ncw.nic.in/PressReleasePDF/PR10052011.pdf].

[2] Parliamentary Debates in the Rajya Sabha, 5 September 2013.

[3] The Uttar Pradesh Land Acquisition Policy dated 2 June, 2011. [http://awas.up.nic.in/policies/New%20L.A.%20Policy%2002.06.11. pdf].

policy and hence it fell in the realm of soft law (not enjoying the backing of a statute).

In many ways, this case brought to light some of the most apparent flaws with the prevalent system of land acquisition. The events also acted as the catalyst for starting the work on a new draft law. But above all, it made one thing very clear: A new law would necessarily have to take steps to address the historical injustices that had been perpetuated and continued to perpetuate under the Land Acquisition Act, 1894.

## ELEMENTS OF THE CLAUSE

The clause can be broken down into the following elements:[4]

Condition I: If an award has been passed under the Land Acquisition Act, 1894 then the proceedings will be considered beyond the purview of the new law and the land acquisition will proceed as per the provisions of the Land Acquisition Act, 1894.

Condition II: If the acquisition has been initiated under the Land Acquisition Act, 1894 (in other words a preliminary notification has been issued under Section 4 of that Act) but the award under Section 11 of that Act has not been passed then the provisions of the new law which entitle the affected party to enhanced compensation will apply.

Condition III: Where the award under Section 11 of the Land Acquisition Act, 1894 was passed five or more years ago but compensation has not been accepted or the physical possession of the land has not been taken by the acquiring authority then the acquisition will be treated as having lapsed and a fresh acquisition, if necessary, will be carried out under the new Act.

Condition IV: Where an award has been made under Section 11 of the Land Acquisition Act, 1894 and compensation in respect of a majority of land holdings has not been accepted, then, all beneficiaries or persons who are likely to be affected by the acquisition (as specified in the notification for acquisition under Section 4 of the said Land Acquisition Act), shall be entitled to compensation as per the provisions of the new law.

---

[4] Section 24 of the Act, 2013.

## UNDERSTANDING THE IMPLICATIONS

### Why is Five Years the Qualifying Period for Return of Land?

During the course of research on land acquisition cases, it was found that the average amount of time that a requiring body needs to carry out a land acquisition proceeding was approximately five years. This time period was also sufficient to satisfy the letter of the law, acquire other permits and clearances that might be needed (such as environmental or forest related).

There had to be a time limit within which the acquiring authority could undertake the activity towards the public purpose for which it had acquired the land. If the land remained vacant and unutilised it would stand to reason that it was not serving the public purpose for which it was intended. It certainly was not benefitting those individuals from whom it had been wrested. In this case, a moratorium had to be imposed failing which the land would necessarily be returned to the original owner.

After at least five years, it could safely be assumed that the public purpose for which the land was sought to have been acquired would have been eroded by the passage of time and the acquisition rendered pointless.

Condition I: The consensus of opinion that emerged after the Group of Ministers met and deliberated was that a logical conclusion to the land acquisition proceedings was the issuance of a final Award under Section 11 of the Land Acquisition Act, 1894. If the new law were to reopen those awards which had been concluded then a vast majority of concluded proceedings would be opened up to scrutiny.

The sheer amount of litigation that would be fomented as a result of such reopening would be enormous. This would cause detriment not just to the government bodies that would have already passed the award but also the litigants who would be saddled with the cost of litigation.

Condition II: Where no award had been made, a partial application of the new law is allowed. If the proceedings have not reached the stage of an award then it would be unjust to pay these individuals compensation at old rates when the new law had already come into force. This would breed two different sets of classes (in some cases even on the same land), one set receiving compensation for acquisition at old rates and another at the revised rates.

To fix this where acquisition had begun but no award had been passed then compensation would have to be paid at new rates. The earlier version of this section which was passed by the Lok Sabha also ensured that the affected party would also be entitled to rehabilitation and resettlement benefits as given under the new law. However following the passage in the Lok Sabha, anxious officers from the Government of Madhya Pradesh flew down with a list of concerns. Suddenly having been presented with the very real possibility that the Bill might become law, they sought certain amendments to prevent the law from having a deleterious impact on existing/pending projects.

One of these recommendations suggested that compelling the State to provide rehabilitation and resettlement projects which had partly been completed would unleash a chain of protest and litigation that could derail the entire project. Giving way to this concern (which did seem legitimate) and mindful of the support required from the leading opposition party in the Rajya Sabha, it was agreed to carry out the required amendment.

The acquiring authorities are not required to seek the consent of the affected families nor are they required to carry out a social impact assessment study or any of the related processes required under the new law.

Condition III: Where the land acquisition proceedings have been concluded by way of an Award being made five or more years prior to the commencement of the new Act (which came into force on 1 January 2014) but either compensation has not been accepted or the possession has not physically been taken then the proceedings will lapse and the new 2013 law will apply in its entirety.

Note the use of the word 'physical' before the word 'possession'. This is deliberate and by design. In all other cases where possession is referred to it includes both physical and deemed possession (the latter being where the name of the owner is changed in the records). However under this section, the intention was to refer to those cases where the affected party still held on to the physical possession.

Physical possession was made the necessary standard as 'deemed' possession, or possession in name/papers, can immediately be created by the Collector who has access to the records. Physical possession is a state which is easily verifiable and demonstrates an undeniable form of protest to the acquisition sought to be carried out.

This physical possession could be a result of the individual's refusal to give up the land as a persistent objector or that the land was under litigation for so long that the acquisition had been rendered moot. This could also be due to negligence on the part of the acquiring authority.

Condition IV: Where an award under the 1894 Act has been passed but a majority of land owners under a notified or identified area have not accepted the compensation then all parties (including those who have accepted compensation) will receive compensation as per the requirements of the new law.

This differentiation again finds its reasoning in the doctrine of reasonable classification. Reasonable classification is a doctrine under Article 14 of the Constitution of India which prevents discrimination between two classes of individuals who share the same situations. In this case, it would be a violation of the doctrine of reasonable classification if land was being acquired for the same project but the affected families were being paid differential rates. In such cases the rehabilitation and resettlements entitlements are not attracted.

## JUDGMENTS OF THE SUPREME COURT AND THEIR IMPACT

On 24 January 2014, a three judge bench of the Supreme Court of India pronounced the very first judgment on the Right to Fair Compensation and Transparency in Land Acquisition, Rehabilitation and Resettlement Act, 2013 in a case titled *Pune Municipal Corporation vs Harakchand Solanki.*[5]

This Judgement was of particular significance because it clarified and pronounced upon the operation and interpretation of Section 24(2), the 'retrospective clause'.

This was the very first pronouncement by the Apex Court on the subject with major implications vis-à-vis those affected families who

[5] *Pune Municipal Corporation vs Harakchand Misirimal Solanki* , Civil Appeal No. 877 OF 2014 (Arising out of SLP(C) No. 30283 of 2008). Reported as (2014) 3 SCC 183.

were seeking justice against arbitrary acquisitions that have been carried out over the last decade.

This judgment was welcomed by the Ministry of Rural Development on the grounds that it had aptly given expression to the very intention with which Parliament passed the law. It also settled the contentious issue of the retrospective clause to a great extent while providing clarity on the way forward. Many displaced families would benefit as a result of this solid precedent.

## Background to the Case

Eighteen Appeals had been filed before the Supreme Court of India invoking the application of the retrospective clause. All the applications had one thing in common: a period of five or more years had passed since the land acquisition award had been made under Section 11 of the Land Acquisition Act, 1894 and the applicants/petitioners had refused to accept the compensation.

Given the new rights bestowed by the new law on Land Acquisition which allowed pending litigations to be reviewed and retrospectively annulled, these parties approached the Supreme Court asking for the law to be applied in their favour.

In this litigation, the acquiring authority (the Pune Municipal Corporation) argued that they had deposited the amount in the treasury of the Government in fulfilment of their obligations and therefore satisfied the requirement of paying compensation. It must be mentioned here that this practice is the norm with most acquisitions.

## Judgment

A three judge bench of the Supreme Court (Justices Lodha, Mudan Lokur and Kurian Joseph) held that compensation would only be deemed to have been paid if it had been deposited with the Court and after having been offered to the individual concerned. In this case, the compensation had only been deposited in the treasury.

As a result compensation could not be deemed to have been paid and the acquisition was considered to have lapsed in conformity with Section 24 of the Right to Fair Compensation and Transparency in Land Acquisition, Rehabilitation and Resettlement Act, 2013.

The Judgment was of significance at the time for the following reasons:

- It interpreted and construed the retrospective clause in a harmonious manner and in the interests of those aggrieved by arbitrary acquisition mechanisms.
- It did not resort to artificial limitations to deprive the applicants of the intended benefit. In other words, it did not subtract the period of litigation from the total amount of time that had lapsed nor did it allow the Government to claim satisfaction by simply depositing the money in the treasury.
- By implementing it and placing reliance on it, the Bench approved the validity of the clause itself, which was the subject of enormous debate prior to the passage of the law.
- It reinforced the idea of fair compensation inasmuch the Bench finds the deposited compensation to be inadequate because it does not include the interest that has been accruing on the amount since the deposit.

### Scope of the Pune Municipal Judgment

Though a step forward, the judgment was confined only to defining the import of the term 'compensation has not been paid' as it occurs in Section 24(2) of the 2013 Act. *More importantly* it did not define what constituted physical possession or what needed to be established to invoke the condition of retaining physical possession as defined under Section 24(2) of the Act. The averments of the parties with regard to possession also did not find mention in the judgment.

However, the Court did observe that 'The legal fiction under Section 24(2) comes into operation as soon as conditions stated therein are satisfied'. It would be inferred from this that the law would apply even when the other condition of 'physical possession not being taken' has been satisfied.

The issue of physical possession would be clarified later (and in a harmonious fashion) by the Supreme Court in the case of *Shri Balaji Nagar Residential Association vs the State of Tamil Nadu*.[6]

[6] CA. No. 8700/2013.

## Second Set of Judgments

This interpretation would soon become part of a trend to be followed by the Supreme Court. In the second judgment (*Bharat Kumar vs State of Haryana*[7]) given on 2 February 2014, a two judge bench comprising of Justices Dattu and Bobde of the Supreme Court, pronounced a similar judgment on the new law.

This judgment also related to the operation and interpretation of Section 24(2) the retrospective clause. The learned bench overturned a 2004 judgment of the Punjab and Haryana High Court (which had upheld a long pending acquisition) and quashed the acquisition, returning the land to the original owners.

Following this, on 14 March 2014 a two judge bench (comprising Justices Lodha and Bobde) of the Supreme Court in *Bimla Devi vs State of Haryana*[8] again went into the question of retrospective operation.

In this case, the award had been passed in 1995 and the parties had still not accepted compensation or parted with physical possession. In light of this, the Supreme Court, relying on the retrospective clause, ordered the return of the land to the original owners.

The Ministry for Rural Development was closely following the progress of these cases. A press statement was issued welcoming the judgments of the Hon'ble Supreme Court saying 'this demonstrates the Hon'ble Supreme Court has drawn clear and humane lines for the implementation of a very significant clause in the law. These add to the growing list of important precedents which will have a far-reaching impact on those who have suffered historically from arbitrary acquisitions and give life to the intention behind the new law.'

Both these cases were important because while Pune Municipal Corporation (the first judgment) dealt only with the question of where compensation had been paid or not, these two new judgments also go into the question of where the parties have held on to the physical possession of the land.

In both these cases, the Supreme Court returned the land in acknowledgement of the fact that, in addition to compensation not being

---

[7] (2014) 3 SCALE 393.
[8] Civil Appeal No. 3871-3876 of 2014 decided on 14 March 2014.

accepted, the physical possession of the land had also not been given away. As a result the learned Supreme Court upheld the Retrospective Clause in its entirety viz. compensation and physical possession.

## Three Judge Bench Decision

On 7 May 2014, the fourth and most comprehensive judgment (*Shivraj vs Union of India*[9]) was pronounced.

A landmark judgment (published on Friday, 10 May 2014) a three judge bench of Justices B.S. Chouhan, J. Chelameshwar and M.Y. Eqbal ordered the return of land to its original owners who had been in litigation for over two decades. Invoking the retrospective clause, the three judge bench returned the land and held the acquisition to have lapsed.

Thus, in a relatively short amount of time, a great degree of legislative clarity was achieved with regard to the retrospective clause of the new law as a result of the Supreme Court's positive and constructive interventions.

Over time these judgments opened the door for a greater number of applicants to seek justice. They became the foundation for future decisions on the subject which continue to be pronounced in judicial forums across the country.

*Shivraj's* case was also of particular significance for two reasons:

- It enriched the existing jurisprudence on the subject of retrospective operation of the new law by deciding it in consonance with the judgments pronounced before it by the Supreme Court.
- Most importantly, it relied on and invoked the Opinion of the Solicitor General of India (that had been taken by the Ministry of Rural Development to clarify certain points of doubt on 28 December 2013) thereby fortifying as law, the position given in the Opinion.

## OPINION OF THE SOLICITOR GENERAL OF INDIA

After the law had passed but before it was notified, many doubts were raised as to the implementation of the clauses. While the law

---

[9] [SLP(C) No. 24297-24302 of 2007].

had been drafted with a clear intention to aid individuals against arbitrary acquisitions some of the clauses (particularly the retrospective clause), it was suggested, could be perverted by authorities biased in favour of the state.

To eliminate this possibility, the Ministry of Rural Development wrote to the Solicitor General Mr Mohan Parasaran asking for his opinion on whether the interpretations adopted by the Ministry were valid. The four points regarding 'retrospective operation' on which the opinion was sought were:

| RETROSPECTIVE OPERATION | |
|---|---|
| (1) **Operability:** | The retrospective operation of the Act as prescribed in Section 24 of the Act will be deemed to have come into operation on and from the date on which the new law is notified in the Official Gazette. |
| (2) **Physical Possession:** | Physical possession will be considered to have been taken when the land acquired had been physically demarcated and effective physical and absolute control taken within 5 years of the award. |
| (3) **Interpretation of Five Year Period:** | Where acquisitions have been initiated under the Land Acquisition Act, 1894 and the parties under acquisition have either not accepted compensation or have not released the physical possession of the land but do not qualify for the benefits of the Act as given in sub-section 2 of Section 24 due to the fact that they have remained pending for a period less than five years then the new law shall apply only if the situation of pendency continues unchanged for a period that equals to or exceeds five years; |
| | It is further clarified that in none of the cases the period of 5 years would have elapsed pursuant to an award made under Section 11 from the date of commencement of the Act and that the benefit of Section 24(2) will be available to those cases which are pending and where during pendency, the situation has remained unchanged with physical possession not being handed over or compensation |

| | |
|---|---|
| | not having been accepted and the period equals to or exceeds five years. |
| **(4) Limitation** | Where possession has not been taken or compensation has not been paid due to the fact that the acquisition process has been challenged in a court of law then the period spent under litigation shall also be counted for the purpose of determining whether the period of five years has been crossed or not; |
| | It is clarified that it will apply only to cases where awards were passed under Section 11 of the Land Acquisition Act, 1894 5 years or more prior to 01.01.2014, to avoid any ambiguity as specified in Section 24(2) of the Act. |

In his Opinion dated 28 December 2013, the learned Solicitor General of India upheld the above interpretations concurring with the intention behind the same.[10]

Two portions, the interpretation relating to 'limitation period' and the other relating to the 'interpretation of the Five Year Period' were quoted with approval in the case of *Union of India vs Shivraj*.[11]

The impact of this move is that authorities could not discount the time spent under litigation from the qualifying period of five years to deny the landowner his rightful benefit.

The other impact which shall have salubrious repercussions in cases to come, allows landowners who have not qualified yet (because they fall short of the five year mark but satisfy the other two conditions) to come before the court when the acquisition remains pending for five years (assuming compensation has not been paid and/or physical possession has not been taken).

## WHERE ONLY PHYSICAL POSSESSION IS RETAINED AND THE ROLE OF THE DELHI HIGH COURT

In September 2014, the Supreme Court again upheld the sanctity of Section 24(2) of the new Land Acquisition Act, 2013 in the case

[10] A copy is available at http://rural.nic.in/sites/downloads/NewReleases/SGI.pdf.

[11] [SLP(C) No. 24297-24302 of 2007].

of *Shri Balaji Nagar Residential Association vs State of Tamil Nadu*[12] wherein a two judge bench of the Supreme Court (Justices Shiv Kirti Singh and Kalifullah) held that it can be safely concluded:

> [T]he Legislature has consciously omitted to extend the period of five years indicated in Section 24(2) even if the proceedings had been delayed on account of an order of stay or injunction granted by a court of law or for any reason. Such casus omissus cannot be supplied by the court in view of law on the subject elaborately discussed by this Court in the case of Padma Sundara Rao (Dead) & Ors. vs State of T.N. & Ors. (2002) 3 SCC 533.

The two judge bench decision also relied on the abovementioned case of *Union of India vs Shivraj* and the now landmark case of *Pune Municipal Corporation.*

It is also important to note the noble role the Delhi High Court has played in the implementation of the Act. The High Court pronounced some of the most detailed and insightful judgments of any High Court on the subject to release land that had been held up by a laconic bureaucracy.

In the now historic case of *Jagjit Singh and Ors vs Union of India and Ors.*[13] Justice Badr Durrez Ahmed and Justice Sidharth Mridul of the Hon'ble High Court of Delhi quashed a number of pending acquisitions by the DDA as it was found the parties had satisfied the terms of Section 24(2) of the 2013 Act. In that case the learned judges held that

> …it is obvious that the deeming provision of Section 24(2) is a legal fiction which is a created and an imagined situation. We ought not to be concerned with the inevitable corollaries that may flow out of it unless there is a clear prohibition in the statute itself. Once the state of affairs is imagined as real, the consequences and instances would also have to be imagined as real. Therefore, the fact that the possession could not have been taken by the respondents because of interim orders of the Court, would not in any way prevent this Court from imagining the state of affairs stipulated in Section 24(2) of the new Act. The only conditions that are required for the deeming provisions to be triggered are that the award must have been made five years or more prior to the commencement of the new Act and that either physical possession of the land has not been

[12] Civil Appeal No.8700 Of 2013 decided on 10 September 2014.
[13] Decided on 27.05.2014 being WP(C) No. 2806/2004.

*taken or that the compensation has not been paid. In fact in these writ petitions all the conditions stand satisfied. Therefore, the contention of the learned counsel for the respondent cannot be accepted.*

The respondent in this case was the Delhi Development Authority. Thereafter the learned judges of the Delhi High Court in the cases of *Surender Singh vs Union of India*[14], *Girish Chabra vs Lt. Governor of Delhi*[15], in *Raman Grover vs Union of India*[16] and prior to that in *Ashwal Vaderaa vs Union of India*[17] continued to add to the growing jurisprudence on the interpretation and application of Section 24(2) strengthening the harmonious interpretations laid down in the preceding judgments. Judgments along similar lines have also been pronounced by the High Courts of other states.

These judgments vindicated the legislative intent that went into the clause being inserted. The ultimate test of a legislation is that it must withstand the scrutiny of judicial review. After the emergence of this rich consensus as a result of these judicial pronouncements and the number of affected families who have had their land returned, the members of the Cabinet who had a key role in the authoring of this clause can be assured of the worth of their decision.

## ORDINANCE

The Government of India promulgated an Ordinance on 31 December 2014. Among other amendments carried out by this Ordinance the Government also sought to curtail the application of the Retrospective Clause by increasing the qualifications required to invoke the benefits under Section 24(2) of the Act. The impact of this Ordinance is discussed in detail in Chapter 11.

---

[14] W.P.(C) 2294/2014 and CM No. 4815/2014, judgment delivered on 12 September 2014.

[15] W.P.(C) 2759/2014 and CM Nos. 10673/2014, 14840/2014, also decided on 12 September 2014.

[16] W.P.(C) 13814/2009, decided on 22 August 2014.

[17] W.P.(C) 1897/2014, decided on 30 July 2014.

CHAPTER SEVEN

# Urgency Clause

*Section 17 of the Land Acquisition Act, 1894 was used to forcibly dispossess people of their land in a frequent and brutal fashion by suspending the requirement for due process. An anachronism in this day and age this clause was widely regarded as draconian. This chapter explains the debate that went into diminishing this clause and explains the current form.*

The severity of the Land Acquisition Act, 1894 stemmed from the fact that it was a tool specifically designed to facilitate the process of taking over land with least resistance. Nowhere was this spirit more evident than in the drafting and use of the urgency clause. Its exercise was a slave to the will and discretion of the Collector who could decide what circumstances necessitated its invocation. It has been suggested that this high degree of autonomy and the lack of accompanying safeguards had a corrupting influence which diminished a flawed legislation even further.

## THE ORIGINAL SECTION IN THE 1894 ACT

Section 17 of the now repealed Land Acquisition Act, 1894 gave the State and its agencies 'Special powers in case of urgency'. The broad and curious elements of this section were:[1]

- **Nature of Emergency:** Emergencies could include natural disasters, emergencies of the railways, maintenance of any structure or system pertaining to irrigation, water supply, drainage, road communication or electricity etc.

---

[1] Section 17, Land Acquisition Act, 1894.

- **Notice:** If the appropriate Government felt an urgent need existed then it could direct the Collector, even though no award may have been made, to take possession of the land within fifteen days of giving notice. Such land would then vest absolutely in the Government, free from all encumbrances.

- *Possession:* The Collector could take possession of any building or part of a building but he had to give the owner or occupier at least forty-eight hours' notice of his intention to do so at the minimum 'as may be reasonably sufficient to enable such occupier to remove his movable property from such building without unnecessary inconvenience'.

- *Additional Damages:* The Collector was also required to pay compensation for the standing crops and trees (if any) on such land and for any other damage sustained by them as a result of sudden dispossession.

- *Immediate Payment:* In situations where the urgency clause was invoked the law required the immediate payment of 80 per cent of the compensation amount for such land (as estimated by the Collector) to the affected person.

- *No Hearings:* The appropriate Government could direct that the provisions related to hearing objections prior to the acquisition[2] need not apply, and, if it did so, then a declaration could be made under Section 6 in respect of the land at any time after the date of the publication of the notification under Section 4 of the 1894 Act.

The frequency with which this section was invoked was alarming. During our consultations with Collectors, we found a number of examples where the urgency clause had been invoked. The Outer Ring Road Project of Hyderabad and the Expressway in Uttar Pradesh are both striking (and recent) examples of acquisitions where large tracts fell prey to the urgency clause. The recourse to the urgency clause seemed to be an opportunity to abandon all reference to not just facts, but also to the very principles of natural justice.

Courts had also been reluctant to intervene to place limits on this power, fearing that such an exercise would be an encroachment into the realm of the Executive.

---

[2] Section 5A, Land Acquisition Act, 1894.

In *First Land Acquisition Collector vs Nirodhi Prakash Gangoli*,[3] a two judge bench of the Supreme Court of India issued the following order on the exercise of power under the urgency clause:

> *The question of urgency of an acquisition under Section 17(1) and (4) of the Act is a matter of subjective satisfaction of the Government and ordinarily it is not open to the Court to make a scrutiny of the propriety of that satisfaction on an objective appraisal of facts.* In this view of the matter when the Government takes a decision, taking all relevant considerations into account and is satisfied that there exists emergency for invoking powers under Section 17 (1) and (4) of the Act, and issues Notification accordingly, *the same should not be interfered with by the Court unless the Court comes to the conclusion that the appropriate authority had not applied its mind to the relevant factors or that the decision has been taken by the appropriate authority mala fide.* Whether in a given situation there existed urgency or not is left to the *discretion and decision of the concerned authorities.* If an order invoking power under Section 17(4) is assailed, the Courts may enquire whether the appropriate authority had all the relevant materials before it or whether the order has been passed by non-application of mind. *Any post Notification delay subsequent to the decision of the State Government dispensing with an enquiry under Section 5(A) by invoking powers under Section 17(1) of the Act would not invalidate the decision itself specially when no mala fides on the part of the government or its officers are alleged. Opinion of the State Government can be challenged in a Court of law if it could be shown that the State Government never applied its mind to the matter or that action of the State Government is mala fide.* Though the satisfaction under Section 17(4) is a subjective one and is not open to challenge before a Court of law, except for the grounds already indicated, but the said satisfaction must be of the Appropriate Government and that the satisfaction must be, as to the existence of an urgency. The conclusion of the Government that there was urgency even though cannot be conclusive but is entitled to great weight, as has been held by this Court in Jage Ram and others vs. The State of Haryana and Others[4]. *Even a mere allegation that power was exercised mala fide would not be enough and in support of such allegation specific materials should be placed before the Court. The burden of establishing mala fides is very heavy on the person who alleges it.* [Emphasis added]

[3] (2002) 4 SCC 160.
[4] AIR 1971 Supreme Court 1033.

Where the courts did intervene, they intervened to the extent that objections had not been satisfactorily heard.

This situation needed drastic amendment.

## THE NEW URGENCY CLAUSE

The disparity of power between the acquirer and the disposed was enormous. The old clause was concerned with disempowering land owners completely, by disinvesting them from having any say in the process. The new law, which adopted a completely different approach to serve a completely different objective of empowering the affected, simply could not afford to do so. The problem arose from the fact that the old law, which itself bordered on draconian, never limited the definition of what could constitute an 'urgency'.

- **The Three Cases of Urgency**: Section 40 of the new Act of 2013 limits the invocation of the urgency powers to cases which genuinely qualify as emergencies. It restricts the powers of the appropriate Government to rely on the power only in the following cases:

  1. The minimum area required for the defence of India or national security, or
  2. Any emergencies arising out of natural calamities, or
  3. Any other emergency with the approval of Parliament

- **Notice:** In cases of such urgency, and on the instructions of the appropriate Government, the Collector even if no award has been made, may, on the expiration of thirty days from the publication of the notice to persons interested, take possession of any land needed for a public purpose and such land shall thereupon vest absolutely in the Government, free from all encumbrances.
- **Possession:** The Collector cannot take possession of any building or part of a building without giving at least forty-eight hours' notice to the occupier of his intention to do so, or such longer notice as may be reasonably sufficient to enable such occupier to remove his movable property from such building without unnecessary inconvenience.
- **Payment:** Before taking possession of any land, the Collector must pay 80 per cent of the compensation for such land to the person interested entitled thereto.

- **Suspension of Social Impact Assessment and Other Procedures:** In the case of any land to which, in the opinion of the appropriate Government, the provisions of urgency are applicable, the appropriate Government may direct that any or all of the provisions related to Social Impact Assessment, public purpose and Rehabilitation and Resettlemnt shall not apply. If such a direction is made then a declaration may be made under Section 19 in respect of the land at any time after the date of the publication of the preliminary notification under Section 11 of the Act, 2013.
- **Additional Compensation:** An additional compensation of 75 per cent of the total compensation as determined under the law, has to be paid by the Collector in respect of land and property for acquisition of which proceedings have been initiated under this section.[5]

The gist and import of the above is that the urgency clause can only be invoked in cases where issues of national defence or (the amelioration of) natural calamities are concerned. The third ground was added after intense discussion in the meetings of the Group of Ministers where it was suggested that there could exist emergencies, sufficiently valid, but with which we have not yet been presented.

It is conceivable that circumstances not yet imagined but of a truly urgent nature could arise and in turn necessitate the acquisition of land. A residuary clause was accordingly drafted to include the term 'any other emergency' but it must be checked by a safeguard. The safeguard was prior parliamentary approval must be sought before expanding the category.

It is our hope that the urgency clause will be used for genuine emergencies, if at all.

---

[5] Provided that no additional compensation will be required to be paid in case the project is one that affects the sovereignty and integrity of India, the security and strategic interests of the State or relations with foreign States.

# CHAPTER EIGHT

# Special Provisions for Scheduled Castes and Scheduled Tribes

*This chapter goes into the special safeguards and benefits provided for Scheduled Castes and Tribes. It also goes into how the law is compatible with the ideology and commitment laid out in other laws passed during the UPA-2's tenure.*

The biggest victims of acquisition have always been those at the bottom end of the stakeholder spectrum. Studies, such as the one by the National Commission for Scheduled Castes and Tribes in 1985[1], have found that tribal communities constituted over 40 per cent of the displaced families. Other credible studies have seconded this observing:

> *While the government never bothered to keep track, the most reliable estimates suggest that at least 60 million Indian citizens were displaced from over 25 million hectares of land between 1947 and 2004, among whom at least 40 per cent were adivasis and 20 per cent dalits…Of the more than 60 million people displaced for development projects since independence, it is estimated that less than 18 per cent were resettled, not to say rehabilitated with alternative livelihoods.*[2]

Due to their inability to organize collectively and a pervasive lack of influence, certain groups have always suffered more than others. And often the suffering has been at the hands of an aggressive state machinery.

[1] Walter Fernandes (2004), 'Rehabilitation Policy for the Displaced', *Economic & Political Weekly*, Vol. 39, Issue 12, p. 1191.

[2] Ibid. See also in Hari Mohan Mathur (ed.), *India: Social Development Report 2008: Development and Displacement* (New Delhi: Oxford University Press).

When drafting a new law on the subject of land acquisition, the principal cause of numerous displacements, the authors would be failing in their commitment to the objectives of the law, if they did not take into account the special needs of those belonging to the Scheduled Castes and the Scheduled Tribes.

## WHY A SEPARATE CHAPTER

To understand the need for putting in place a separate chapter for individuals belonging to the Scheduled Castes and the Scheduled Tribes, it is important to evaluate the legislative and policy history of the Government between 2004 and 2014. During this period, the Government had one clear priority: the putting in place of measures to enhance the status of marginalised communities. Laws were interpreted broadly and then zealously implemented with the objective of fortifying the rights of a historically disadvantaged people.

The Government had adopted a clear agenda during its terms: empower the lowest common denominator through meaningful and far reaching measures. This had been reflected in its approach to legislation by enacting rights based laws that would go beyond abstract aspirational statements. It had been reflected in the stands taken to safeguard the interests of niche backward groups despite nationwide scepticism. It had been made abundantly evident in its refusal, despite rallying and persistent cries by powerful corporate lobbies, to yield this ground.

One such far reaching legislation targeted at members belonging to the Scheduled Tribes is the Forest Rights Act—a six page law passed in 2006 that guarantees tribal populations livelihood rights over their area of habitation. Small but significant, the Act is remarkable because it leapfrogged over the 1996 Panchayat (Extension to Scheduled Areas) Act. The latter law also sought to empower the Gram Sabha insofar as the governance of its own resources was concerned but it never really took off and continues to flounder for a variety of reasons (lack of operational clarity being one).

Though enacted in the first term of the Government, the Forest Rights Act came unto its own during the second tenure that ran from 2009–2014. The Government's commitment to its law went beyond the latter and this became evident through the actions adopted.

When a dispute arose as to its implementation, no less an authority than the Chief Minister of Maharashtra, along with the then Minister for Environment and Forests (along with noted civil society activist Sunita Narain) flew down to Gadchiroli district.[3] The issue in question? Whether bamboo qualified as 'forest produce' which tribals were allowed to sell for their benefit. The government, both Centre and State, quickly and unanimously held in favour of the tribals. But for this attention, such a dispute would have previously been the subject matter of lower courts, provided it reached that far.

Prior to that in yet another historic move, on 3 August 2009, the Ministry of Environment and Forests issued a circular directing and declaring that before any forest clearances could even be considered, the process of settlement of rights as laid down under the Forest Rights Act would first have to be discharged.[4] This one circular changed the very order of clearances to be obtained and gave primacy to settling the rights of tribal groups well before any other steps for diversion of forest land could be taken. In other words, forest rights went from being an administrative formality to being a mandatory prerequisite.

Now these could have been dismissed as small concessions to fringe groups. But the extent of the Government's resolve was demonstrated in two decisions that left no doubt about the clarity of its agenda.

In the first case, various complaints alleging violations of tribal rights in the Niyamgiri region of Orissa in the process of obtaining forest clearance for a bauxite mine were received by the Government. The Government chose to reopen the case and finally, having reason to believe that violations had occurred, chose to deny forest clearance to the project.[5] This decision has been hailed both nationally and in international forums as a landmark in administrative decision

---

[3] Meena Menon 'Bamboo is Liberated', *The Hindu*, 29 April 2011, http://www.hindu.com/2011/04/29/stories/2011042965731000.htm.

[4] Though still valid this has been modified by a letter dated 5 February 2013 which exempts certain linear projects from this requirement. It is available at http://www.moef.nic.in/assets/Diversion%20of%20forest%20land05022013.pdf.

[5] The Order of Jairam Ramesh, the Minister for Environment and Forests, Government of India, dated 24 August 2010, http://moef.nic.in/sites/default/files/Vedanta-24082010.pdf.

making. The Order has been challenged at both the High Court and the Supreme Court, both having upheld the sanctity of the same.

Note that this was at the outset of the second tenure, barely a year into 2009. No electoral considerations could have been alleged as the next election was a good four years away. Furthermore, the number of people affected barely numbered 1,500 in total. Sweeping electoral gains were simply not a justifiable concern. It was a rare sight: a stand on political principle.

The Niyamgiri decision alone would have been enough to remove any doubts with regard to the Government's commitment to marginalised groups. But these decisions also set precedents which had to be upheld. Another example of placing tribal rights above private concerns is the case of a steel plant in Jagatsinghpur in Odisha. Here the Government, following investigation by an expert committee ordered all acquisition processes to be stopped until the issues relating to settlement of tirbals were resolved. It was not until these were satisfactorily addressed that clearance was finally given.

Schemes such as the Prime Minister's Rural Development Fellows programmes were launched to tap the services of bright young professionals to work in tribal regions. Administrative relaxations were made under the Pradhan Mantri Gram Sadak Yojana (to build rural roads) for areas identified as 'Integrated Action Plan' districts where the majority of the population is tribal and which are under threat from naxalite groups. Scholarships for tribal children saw an exponential and marked increase as well.

The Mines and Minerals (Development and Regulation) Bill 2011 (being debated at that time) also proposes the payment of a type of royalty to local parties. The law proposes that a District Mineral Fund be established in each district where mining occurs. Since these mineral reserves are concentrated mostly in tribal areas the principle beneficiaries will be members of the tribal communities.

In 2013, a Group of Ministers also approved the establishment of the Bharat Rural Livelihoods Foundation, an autonomous body that shall provide financial and technical support to civil society organisations to bolster the work they are doing in tribal dominated districts.

In other words, unprecedented attention was given to the rights of those belonging to the Scheduled Castes, the Scheduled Tribes and those living in forest areas. A genuine and enduring sensitivity to tribal concerns was sought to be fostered.

## SPECIAL PROVISIONS FOR SCHEDULED CASTES AND SCHEDULED TRIBES

It was in this context that a separate chapter was included on benefits that shall accrue to individuals belonging to the Scheduled Castes and the Scheduled Tribes under the Right to Fair Compensation and Transparency in Land Acquisition, Rehabilitation and Resettlement Act, 2013.

This is in addition to a number of other provisions which have been crafted to specifically ensure the primacy that should be accorded to the special rights of the marginalised sections. Some of the key features are given below.

## SEPARATE DEFINED CLASS

In the very definition of 'affected persons' under Section 3 of the Act, a separate sub-category has been included viz.:

> *the Scheduled Tribes and other traditional forest dwellers who have lost any of their forest rights recognised under the Scheduled Tribes and Other Traditional Forest Dwellers (Recognition of Forest Rights) Act, 2006 due to acquisition of land.*

Furthermore, the definition of 'Land owner' includes any person who is granted forest rights under the Scheduled Tribes and Other Traditional Forest Dwellers (Recognition of Forest Rights) Act, 2006 or under any other law for the time being in force.

## NO ACQUISITION IN PROTECTED AREAS

Land acquisition itself in tribal areas is strongly discouraged under the new law and is to be done only in the rarest of circumstances where no alternatives are available. The operative section begins with the following caveat:

> *Section 41: (1) As far as possible,* **no acquisition of land shall be made in the Scheduled Areas.**

*(2) Where such acquisition does take place it shall be done only as a* **demonstrable last resort.** [Emphasis added]

Recognising that acquisition could not be banned outright in these protected areas, it was decided to limit the cases in which acquisition could be carried out.

## ADDITIONAL REQUIREMENT TO GAUGE 'CONSENT'

In case of acquisition or alienation of any land in the Scheduled Areas (as given under the Fifth Schedule to the Constitution), the prior consent of the concerned Gram Sabha or the Panchayats or the autonomous District Councils, at the appropriate level in Scheduled Areas, has to be obtained, in all cases of land acquisition. This includes acquisitions carried out in cases of urgency. This process of consent has to be discharged before a notification for acquisition is issued either under a Central or State legislation.[6]

If the Gram Sabha does not exist or has not been constituted then the consent of the Panchayats or the Autonomous Districts Councils shall be obtained.

## DEVELOPMENT PLAN

In case of a project involving land acquisition which involves involuntary displacement of the Scheduled Castes or the Scheduled Tribes families, a Development Plan shall be prepared, laying down the details of procedure for settling land rights due, but not settled and restoring titles of the Scheduled Tribes as well as the Scheduled Castes on the alienated land by undertaking a special drive together with land acquisition. The form/template of this Development Plan can be defined by the various State Governments for themselves.

The Development Plan must also contain a programme for the development of alternate fuel, fodder and, non-timber forest produce resources on non-forest lands within a period of five years, sufficient to meet the requirements of tribal communities as well as the Scheduled Castes.

---

[6] Section 41 of the Act, 2013.

## ADVANCE PAYMENT OF COMPENSATION

In case of land being acquired from members of the Scheduled Castes or the Scheduled Tribes, at least one-third of the compensation amount due shall be paid to the affected families initially as a first instalment and the rest shall be paid after taking over of the possession of the land.

## RESETTLEMENT IN SAME/SIMILAR AREA

The Act enjoins upon the acquiring authority the responsibility to resettle the affected families preferably in the same Scheduled Area in a compact block. The goal is to prevent the erosion of the ethnic, linguistic and cultural identities of these groups.

Where the affected families belonging to the Scheduled Castes and the Scheduled Tribes are relocated outside of the district, then, they shall be paid an additional 25 per cent, rehabilitation and resettlement benefits to which they are entitled in monetary terms along with a one-time entitlement of 50,000 rupees.

## ADDITIONAL LAND FOR COMMUNITY PURPOSES

The resettlement areas predominantly inhabited by the Scheduled Castes and the Scheduled Tribes shall get land, free of cost for community and social gatherings. The extent of such land has been led to the discretion of the Government concerned.

The affected Scheduled Tribes, other traditional forest dwellers and the Scheduled Castes that enjoyed fishing rights in a river or pond or dam in the affected area prior to the acquisition shall be given fishing rights in the reservoir area of the irrigation or hydel projects.

## ACQUISITION IN CONTRAVENTION, VOID

Any alienation of tribal lands or lands belonging to members of the Scheduled Castes in disregard of the laws and regulations for the time being in force shall be treated as null and void, and in the case of acquisition of such lands, the rehabilitation and resettlement benefits shall be made available to the original tribal land owners or land owners belonging to the Scheduled Castes.

It must be noted that all benefits, including the reservation benefits available to the Scheduled Tribes and the Scheduled Castes in the affected areas shall continue in the resettlement area. The Act provides:

> *Whenever the affected families belonging to the Scheduled Tribes who are residing in the Scheduled Areas referred to in the Fifth Scheduled or the tribal areas referred to in the Sixth Scheduled to the Constitution are relocated outside those areas, than, all the statutory safeguards, entitlements and benefits being enjoyed by them under this Act shall be extended to the area to which they are resettled regardless of whether the resettlement area is a Scheduled Area referred to in the said Fifth Scheduled, or a tribal area referred to in the said Sixth Schedule, or not.*

## MONETARY SETTLEMENT OF FOREST RIGHTS

Where the community rights have been settled under the provisions of the Scheduled Tribes and Other Traditional Forest Dwellers (Recognition of Forest Rights) Act, 2006, the acquiring authority shall calculate the total value of the community rights so settled in monetary terms. This amount shall then be paid to the individual concerned who has been displaced due to the acquisition of land in proportion with his or her share in such community rights.

# CHAPTER NINE

# The Land Acquisition Rehabilitation and Resettlement Authority

*Review by way of appeal is necessary. Flaws are corrected, awards are ensured to be just, and the process is judicially demarcated. An expeditious mechanism for the resolution of disputes is provided in the form of the Land Acquisition Rehabilitation and Resettlement Authority. This chapter explains the process of appeals and hearings.*

Land Acquisition litigations, given the civil nature of the proceedings, tend to be long drawn and protracted often running into decades. Also acquisition proceedings almost always tend to become the subject of challenge on the grounds of low compensation, lack of fair and adequate hearings, absence of a genuine public purpose or the arbitrary nature of the acquisition process being itself in violation of due process.

Despite an overarching attempt to minimize litigation borne out of loopholes, it was decided that a special body should be constituted to provide quick and effective resolution of disputes. It was for this reason the 'Land Acquisition, Rehabilitation and Resettlement Authority' was created.

The Act provides that *for the purpose of providing speedy disposal of disputes relating to land acquisition, compensation, rehabilitation and resettlement* the appropriate Government shall establish one or more Authorities to be known as 'the Land Acquisition, Rehabilitation and Resettlement Authority'.[1] The import of this is that there can be multiple bodies exercising the function of this Authority if the Central or State Governments so decide.

---

[1] Chapter VIII, Section 51 of the Act, 2013.

The establishing Notification has to specify certain details with regard to the operation of the body including the areas within which the Authority may exercise jurisdiction for entertaining and deciding the references made to it.[2] However, the Act gives the Authority original jurisdiction to adjudicate upon every reference made to it under Act itself.

## CONSTITUTION OF AUTHORITY

The Authority shall consist of one person—the Presiding Officer— to be appointed, by notification, by the appropriate Government. To qualify for appointment as the Presiding Officer of an Authority an individual must fulfil the following criteria:[3]

• He is or has been a District Judge; or
• He is a qualified legal practitioner for not less than seven years.

The Appropriate Government has to appoint this Presiding Officer in consultation with the Chief Justice of a High Court in whose jurisdiction the Authority is proposed to be established. The Presiding Officer holds office for a term of three years from the date on which he enters upon his office or until he attains the age of 65 years, whichever is earlier.

States are free to prescribe the salary and allowances payable to the Presiding Officer and the other officers (unless Central Rules are enacted which give specific directions on the same) and other terms and conditions of service (including pension, gratuity and other retirement benefits).

The Presiding officer of an Authority shall not be removed from his office except by an order made by the appropriate Government on the ground of proven misbehaviour or incapacity after an inquiry (made by a Judge of a High Court) in which the Presiding Officer concerned has been informed of the charges against him and given a reasonable opportunity of being heard in respect of these charges.

---

[2] References to the Authority are made under Section 64 of the Act.
[3] Section 53 of the Act, 2013.

The member and officers of the Authority are considered to be public servants within the meaning of Section 21 of the Indian Penal Code, 1860.

The appropriate Government under whose jurisdiction the Authority has been established may also authorise the Presiding Officer of one Authority to discharge also the functions of the Presiding Officer of another Authority.

## POWERS OF A CIVIL COURT

The Authority has been empowered with the same powers as are vested in a civil court under the Code of Civil Procedure, 1908. Specifically these powers, given under Section 60 of the 2013 Act, include:

- Summoning and enforcing the attendance of any person and examining him on oath
- Discovery and production of any document or other material object producible as evidence
- Receiving evidence on affidavits
- Requisitioning of any public record
- Issuing commission for the examination of witnesses
- Reviewing its decisions, directions and orders.

It must be noted however, that the Authority has the power to regulate its own procedure. In other words the Authority is not to be bound by the procedure laid down in the Code of Civil Procedure, 1908 but shall be guided by the principles of natural justice and subject to the other provisions of the Act (and any rules made thereunder).

Finally, all proceedings before the Authority are deemed to be judicial proceedings within the meaning of Sections 193 and 228 of the Indian Penal Code, 1860 and the Authority shall be deemed to be a civil court for the purposes of Sections 345 and 346 of the Code of Criminal Procedure, 1973.

## DEADLINE FOR DISPOSAL

To ensure that the proceedings would not run for an inordinate amount of time, the language of the law mandatorily prescribes a deadline to which the Authority must conform.

The Authority shall, after receiving a reference under the Act and after giving notice of such reference to all the parties concerned and after affording opportunity of hearing to all parties, dispose of such reference within a period of six months from the date of receipt of such reference and make an award accordingly. Unlike other laws where authorities are required to endeavour to finish the proceedings within a certain time, Section 60(4) of the law categorically lays down that the proceedings should be concluded within the given time frame.

The Authority shall arrange to deliver copies of the award to the parties concerned within a period of fifteen days from the date of such award.

## PRIMACY OF JURISDICTION

No civil court (other than the High Court exercising writ jurisdiction under Article 226 or Article 227 of the Constitution or the Supreme Court under Article 32 of the Constitution) has the jurisdiction to entertain any dispute relating to land acquisition listed under the law. No injunction, temporary or permanent can be granted by any court in respect of any such matter. This bar ensures that civil courts will not be burdened by additional land acquisition litigation.

## MAKING A COMPLAINT (REFERENCE)

Any person who is qualified to receive compensation and has not accepted the award may, by written application to the Collector, require that the matter be referred by the Collector for the determination of the Authority. The main grounds on which such a reference can be made relate to the measurement of the land, the amount of the compensation, the person to whom it is payable, the rights of Rehabilitation and Resettlement or the apportionment of the compensation among the persons interested.

Once the Collector has received this application, he has to mandatorily refer the same to the Appropriate Authority within 30 days of such receipt.

The reason the Act requires the aggrieved individual to make an application to the Collector (and not the Authority directly) is so that the Collector may have an opportunity of addressing and correcting the grievance himself. If he cannot resolve the grievance then he must refer it to the Authority failing which the aggrieved party is at liberty to apply to the Authority directly.

Every application must state the grounds on which objection to the award is taken. The limitation period (the time frame within which the application must be made) varies depending upon the circumstances. To illustrate:

- If the aggrieved party was present or represented before the Collector at the time when he made his award, then the application must be made within six weeks from the date of the Collector's award.
- In other cases, within six weeks of the receipt of the notice from the Collector regarding the acquisition, or within six months from the date of the Collector's award, whichever period shall first expire.

The above deadlines are not meant to be barriers to a legitimate application. The Collector may entertain an application after the expiry of the said period, within a further period of one year, if he is satisfied that there was sufficient cause for not filing it within the periods specified.[4]

In making the reference, the Collector shall provide the following information in writing:

- The situation and extent of the land, with particulars of any trees, buildings or standing crops thereon
- The names of the persons whom he has reason to think are interested in such land
- The amount awarded for damages and paid or tendered and the amount of compensation awarded under the provisions of this Act
- The amount paid or deposited under any other provisions of this Act
- If the objection be to the amount of the compensation, the grounds on which the amount of compensation was determined.

[4] Proviso to Section 64 of the Act, 2013.

The statement of the applicants shall be attached in a schedule giving the particulars of the notices served upon them.

## PROCEDURE AND SCOPE

The Authority shall upon receipt of a reference/complaint issue a notice specifying the day on which the Authority will proceed to determine the objection. This notice will also contain a direction regarding the appearance of the parties concerned before the Authority on that day. Copies of this notice have to be served on the applicant and on all persons interested in the objection. If, however, some of the parties have accepted the award or compensation then they may be excluded from the proceedings.

The scope of the enquiry in every such proceeding is to be restricted to a consideration of the interest of the persons affected by the objection.

All such proceedings are to take place in public, and all persons entitled to practice in any Civil Court in the State shall be entitled to appear, plead and act (as the case may be) in such proceedings.

In determining the amount of compensation to be awarded for land acquired (including the Rehabilitation and Resettlement entitlements), the Authority shall take into consideration whether the Collector has followed the relevant parameters set out under the law (for calculation of compensation and rehabilitation/resettlement benefits).

## PAYMENT OF INTEREST AND ENHANCED SOLATIUM

In addition to the market value of the land, the Authority shall in every case award an additional amount calculated at the rate of 12 per cent per annum on such market value for the period commencing on and from the date of the publication of the preliminary notification in respect of such land to the date of the award of the Collector or the date of taking possession of the land, whichever is earlier.

In this case, in computing the period referred to in this subsection, any period of time where the acquisition was held up on account of any stay or injunction by the order of any Court shall be excluded.

In addition to the market value of the land as above provided, the Authority shall in every case award a solatium of 100 per cent over the total compensation amount. This is to ensure consistency with the formula laid out for compensation.

## AWARD OF THE AUTHORITY

Every award under this chapter shall be in writing signed by the Presiding Officer of the Authority, and shall specify the amount awarded as compensation, and other amounts (if any).

Every such award shall be deemed to be a decree and the statement of the grounds of every such award a judgment within the meaning of Sections 2(2) and (9) of the Code of Civil Procedure, 1908.

Every such award shall also state the amount of costs (such as stamp fees, lawyers charges etc.) incurred in the proceeding under this Chapter, and by what persons and in what proportions they are to be paid.

When the award of the Collector is not upheld, the cost shall ordinarily be paid by the Collector, unless the Authority concerned is of the opinion that the claim of the applicant was so extravagant or that he was so negligent in putting his case before the Collector that some deduction from his costs should be made or that he should pay a part of the Collector's costs.

If the sum, which in the opinion of the Authority concerned, the Collector ought to have awarded as compensation is in excess of the sum which the Collector did award as compensation, the award of the Authority concerned may direct that the Collector shall pay interest on such excess at the rate of nine per cent per annum from the date on which he took possession of the land to the date of payment of such excess into the Authority's designated account.

The Authority may also direct that where such excess amount is paid to the Authority after the date or expiry of a period of one year from the date on which possession is taken, interest at the rate of 15 per cent per annum shall be payable from the date of expiry of the said period of one year on the amount of such excess which has not been paid into Authority before the date of such expiry.[5]

If the Authority passes an award to enhance the amount of compensation for an aggrieved individual then other individuals whose

[5]  Proviso to Section 72.

land was also acquired but were not parties to the proceedings (and who are otherwise similarly placed) may make an application to the Collector to enhance their compensation as well under Section 73 of the Act, 2013. This must be done within three months of the award which enhances the compensation.

## APPEALS

The Requiring Body or any person aggrieved by the Award passed by a Land Acquisition, Rehabilitation and Resettlement Authority may file an appeal to the High Court within 60 days from the date of Award under Section 74 of the Act, 2013. The High Court that shall have jurisdiction will be the one in the State where the land has been acquired or is proposed to be acquired.

Provided that the High Court may, if it is satisfied that the appellant was prevented by sufficient cause from filing the appeal within the said period, allow it to be filed within a further period not exceeding 60 days.

Every appeal is required to be heard as expeditiously as possible and the law prescribes a time frame of six months within which the High Court must endeavour to dispose of the appeal.

## OFFENCES AND PENALTIES

A salient distinction of the new Act from its 1894 predecessor is the presence of very real penalties to be imposed on officials and others involved in the acquisition process if they fail to comply with the provisions of the Act.

Segments of the higher bureaucracy familiar with acquisition were perturbed by this section as they felt it violates the protection given to officials under the Constitution. Nonetheless Chapter XII of the law was drafted and inserted to ensure compliance not just in letter but also in spirit.

## GENERAL PENALTIES

If a person, in connection with a requirement or direction under this Act, provides any information that is false or misleading, or produces any false document, he shall be liable to be punished with imprisonment of either description for a term which may extend to six months, or with fine which may extend to one lakh rupees, or with both.

Any rehabilitation and resettlement benefit availed of by making a false claim or through fraudulent means shall be liable to be recovered by the appropriate Government in the manner as may be prescribed.

## PENALTIES AGAINST GOVERNMENT SERVANTS

Disciplinary proceedings may be drawn up by the disciplinary authority against a Government servant, who if proved to be guilty of a mala fide action in respect of any provision of this Act, shall be liable to such punishment including a fine as the disciplinary authority may decide.

If any person contravenes any of the provisions relating to payment of compensation or rehabilitation and resettlement, every such person shall be liable to a punishment of six months which may extend to three years or with fine or with both.

Where an offence under this Act has been committed by any department of the Government, the head of the department, shall be deemed to be guilty of the offence and shall be liable to be proceeded against and punished accordingly.

It must be mentioned that the impact of this section has been diminished somewhat by the new Ordinance promulgated on 31 December 2014 which now requires sanction to be taken from the relevant department before an officer can be prosecuted.

## PENALTIES AGAINST COMPANIES

Where an offence under this Act has been committed by a company, every person who at the time the offence was committed was in charge of, and was responsible to, the company for the conduct of the business of the company, shall be deemed to be guilty of the offence and shall be liable to be proceeded against and punished accordingly.

Section 86 of the Act also provides that where an offence under this Act has been committed by a company and it is proved that the offence has been committed with the consent or connivance of, or that the commission of the offence is attributable to any neglect on the part of, any director, manager, secretary or other officer of the company, then they shall also be deemed to be guilty of that offence and shall be liable to be proceeded against and punished accordingly.

## IGNORANCE OF FACT DEFENCE

If an offence was committed without the knowledge of the person being charged or if he had exercised all due diligence to prevent the commission of such offence then the charges may be dropped.

Where any offence under this Act has been committed by a Department of the Government and it is proved that the offence has been committed with the consent or connivance of, or is attributable to any neglect on the part of any officer, other than the head of the department, such officer shall also be deemed to be guilty of that offence and shall be liable to be proceeded against and punished accordingly.

## MISCELLANEOUS

No court inferior to that of a Metropolitan Magistrate or a Judicial Magistrate of the first class shall be competent to try any offence punishable under this Act and every offence under this Act shall be deemed to be non-cognizable.[6]

No court shall take cognizance of any offence under this Act which is alleged to have been committed by a Requiring Body except on a complaint in writing made by the Collector or any other officer authorised by the appropriate Government or any member of the affected family.

---

[6] Sections 88–89 of the Act, 2013.

# CHAPTER TEN

# Miscellaneous Clauses

*The Right to Fair Compensation and Transparency in Land Acquisition, Rehabilitation and Resettlement Act, 2013 seeks to supplement the procedures laid out with other supporting provisions to ensure that the law serves the overarching theme of securing social justice for the greatest possible number. Some of these clauses are discussed in this chapter.*

The provisions of the 2013 law which are most often cited relate to the retrospective operation/release of land, the consent provision, compensation and rehabilitation/resettlement prerequisites and the Social Impact Assessment. These have attracted the most attention because stakeholders find them either the most relevant (particularly long suffering land holders) or because they pose the greatest challenges (to administrators and prospective acquirers). However, the law itself has many other provisions which are deserving of attention and understanding.

This chapter attempts to highlight these clauses and their impact.

## PRIVATE PURCHASE

Can a law on land acquisition contain provisions that regulate the private sale and purchase of land between two individual parties? And assuming it can, then does the Central Government enjoy the legislative power to do so?

The first draft of the law which was presented in Parliament specified the limits of private purchase upon which disbursement of Rehabilitation and Resettlement benefits became mandatory. These limits, which were set at 50 acres for urban areas and 100 acres for rural areas, were objected to by various State Governments (before the Standing Committee of Parliament) as an encroachment by the Union upon the legislative domain of the States.[1] Officers of the State of Madhya Pradesh argued:[2]

> The State Government would like to put on record its strong reservations about the purported assault on the federal principle by this Bill. While it is true that the subject 'Acquisition and Requisitioning of Property' finds mention in the concurrent list of the Constitution (Entry no. 42), it is also true that the subject 'Land' has been included under the 'State List' wherein the State Government has unfettered Constitutional powers to enact laws and make rules to regulate land and land related matters (Entry no. 18). The Entry in the State list makes it abundantly clear that the State Government has sole powers to legislate laws pertaining to Land which includes 'right in or over land, land tenures including the relation of landlord and tenant, and collection of rents, transfer and alienation of agricultural land, land improvement and agricultural loans; colonization. And yet, the Bill as introduced in Lok Sabha has this section 42 which tries to restrict purchase of land. Something that has nothing to do with the Entry no. 42 of the Concurrent List and which comes wholly under Entry no. 18 of the State List. If at all any reasonable restrictions are to be imposed, the job is comprehensively within the purview and domain of the States. Purchase of land property is a statutory right and is a freedom made available to the Indian citizen and it cannot be curtailed'. [Emphasis added]

The Standing Committee expressed agreement with this sentiment but also acknowledged the need for rehabilitation and resettlement measures for those displaced by large scale purchases of land. The Committee recommended that the limits (upon the crossing of which the rehabilitation and resettlement provisions will apply) should be left to the discretion of the State Governments.[3] This section was accordingly amended to reflect this position.

Under the law as passed by Parliament, States are now free to set the limits as they desire. This arrangement, where the central statute

---

[1] See Discussion in Para 3.20, Report of the Parliamentary Standing Committee on Rural Development, dated 17 May 2012.

[2] See Comments in Para 3.21, Report of the Parliamentary Standing Committee on Rural Development, dated 17 May 2012.

[3] See Recommendation in Para 3.30, Report of the Parliamentary Standing Committee on Rural Development, dated 17 May 2012.

proposes the measure but the implementation of the same is left entirely to the discretion and machinery of the state, was a compromise within constitutional limits. It also had the added advantage of allowing states to make policy interventions to strengthen land rights within their territories.

Consequently, States must ensure that once the purchase limit is crossed the displaced individuals have to be taken care of and provided with sufficient support so as not to be devastated by the purchase. Failing to do so will ensure a barrier to their land use change application and can even be declared as void under the law.

Private purchase is regulated by the provisions of Section 46 of the Act. It reads:

> (1) Where any person other than a specified person is purchasing land through private negotiations for an area equal to or more than such limits, as may be notified by the appropriate Government, considering the relevant State specific factors and circumstances, for which the payment of Rehabilitation and Resettlement Costs under this Act is required, he shall file an application with the District Collector notifying him of—
>     (a) intent to purchase;
>     (b) purpose for which such purchase is being made;
>     (c) particulars of lands to be purchased.
> (2) It shall be the duty of the Collector to refer the matter to the Commissioner for the satisfaction of all relevant provisions under this Act related to rehabilitation and resettlement.
> (3) Based upon the Rehabilitation and Resettlement Scheme approved by the Commissioner as per the provisions of this Act, the Collector shall pass individual awards covering Rehabilitation and Resettlement entitlements as per the provisions of this Act.
> (4) No land use change shall be permitted if rehabilitation and resettlement is not complied with in full.
> (5) Any purchase of land by a person other than specified persons without complying with the provisions of Rehabilitation and Resettlement Scheme shall be void ab initio.
>     Provided that the appropriate Government may provide for rehabilitation and resettlement provisions on sale or purchase of land in its State and shall also fix the limits or ceiling for the said purpose.
> (6) If any land has been purchased through private negotiations by a person on or after the 5th day of September, 2011, which is more

*than such limits referred to in sub-section (1) and, if the same land is acquired within three years from the date of commencement of this Act, then, forty per cent of the compensation paid for such land acquired shall be shared with the original landowners.*

*Explanation.*—For the purpose of this section, the expression—

(a) *'original landowner' refers to the owner of the land as on the 5th day of September, 2011;*
(b) *'specified persons' includes any person other than—*
  (i) *appropriate Government;*
  (ii) *Government company;*
  (iii) *association of persons or trust or society as registered under the Societies Registration Act, 1860, wholly or partially aided by the appropriate Government or controlled by the appropriate Government.*

It was never a matter of debate that purchase of land between parties is entirely a private matter.[4] But the genesis of this section lay in our experiences, learned at the Environment Ministry, illustrating first hand that when large scale corporations are pitted against small and marginalised farmers a certain disparity in terms of bargaining power is very likely to contaminate the proceedings. This problem becomes more acute in rural areas where farmers (or other backward groups such as tribal communities) are unable to organize collectively.

The law therefore provides that private purchase will also be regulated to the extent that rehabilitation and resettlement benefits shall mandatorily be provided under the law to the affected families (who are displaced as a result of that purchase). However, this requirement will only be invoked when the party purchasing the land crosses a certain threshold in terms of area. This threshold has been left to the discretion of the State Governments.[5] States such as Punjab and Karnataka have already specified this threshold.[6]

[4] See *MC Chacko vs State of Travancore* (1969 SCC (2) 343) for a discussion on the doctrine of Privity of Contract ('no right may be enforced by a person who is not a party to the contract').
[5] Section 46 of the Act, 2013.
[6] Maharashtra has specified the limit at 2,500 acres while Karnataka has specified 500 acres.

This section does not affect the compensation agreed upon between the parties which is subject to personal negotiations in which the Government does not have the legal standing to intervene.

## SHARE TO ORIGINAL OWNER

During consultations with leaders of the Opposition, attention was drawn to the potential of the law for abuse by motivated parties. The then leader of the Opposition in the Lok Sabha, Ms. Sushma Swaraj, pointed out that the law had been placed in Parliament in September of 2011 and the proceedings related to its passage had stretched to 2013. During this period, the law had been covered in great detail by both the national and regional press and its provisions had been scrutinized by the public at length.

As a result, a class of cases would arise where certain individuals sensing the imminent nature of the law's passage, would have sought to take advantage of its provisions. One particular method which the then learned leader of Opposition pointed out was that unscrupulous individuals would purchase land from poor and illiterate farmers or landowners in areas which were likely to be acquired as part of a State's Master Plan (or other planned projects). The motive for doing so would be to reap the enhanced compensation (and other benefits) if the land was subsequently acquired by the State. Given the chance that the farmers would be unaware of these events, they would sell the land innocently to these parties and would ultimately be left deprived of this benefit if the land stood acquired.

To account for these cases, a clause was drafted to ensure that even those individuals who owned the land on or after 5 September 2011 (the day the law was laid in Parliament) and who had subsequently sold their land to other parties (other than the exempted parties), would get a share of the total compensation package if the land was acquired in the next three years (see sub clause (6) of Section 46 given above). This share will not be less than 40 per cent of the total compensation package.

However, the land purchased must exceed the area which the State has notified as being the limit for private purchase.

## WITHDRAWAL FROM ACQUISITIONS

Wherever acquisition has been initiated but the possession of the land under acquisition has not been taken then the Government may choose to withdraw from the acquisition but the Collector has to compensate the person for any loss suffered.

The Collector is required to calculate the compensation due for the damage suffered by the owner in the wake of the acquisition initiated and shall pay such amount to the person. This payment should also include other costs incurred by the person that he has paid in furtherance of proceedings initiated under the law on land acquisition.[7]

## NO INCOME TAX OR OTHER LEVIES

When the 'All-Party' Meetings on the law took place, a fair observation was raised by the members; considering that the taking of the land is being done for and by the State Authorities (mandatorily for a 'public purpose') the State is already taxing the individual and his property.

It was felt that it would be grossly unfair to levy any taxes in addition to the property already being taken. As a result, all taxes and levies on transactions and agreements arising under the new law would have to be necessarily exempted.

In acknowledgement of this sentiment and recognizing the tensions placed on individuals, the new law has a clause that no income tax or stamp duty shall be levied on any award or agreement made under the new law. This does not apply where the land is being taken for private purchase and the same crosses the State specified threshold.[8]

In addition to this, no individual who is covered by this law to receive an award (or who enters into an agreement in keeping with the provisions of this Act) shall have to pay any fees to receive copies. This clause existed under the now repealed Land Acquisition Act, 1894 as well[9] and it was agreed that it should be incorporated into the new law as well.

[7]  Section 93 of the Act, 2013.
[8]  Section 96 of the Act, 2013.
[9]  Section 51 of the now repealed Land Acquisition Act, 1894.

## REQUEST FOR ACQUISITION BY LANDOWNER

If an affected individual or family are losing part of their land (including a house, building or manufacturing unit) to acquisition but retain the other half they can ask the Government to acquire that remaining portion as well. However, they must demonstrate that the first acquisition has so unchangeably impaired the use of the premises so as to make them redundant for the object or purpose which they were serving earlier.

Section 94 provides:

(1)  *The provisions of this Act shall not be put in force for the purpose of acquiring a part only of any house, manufactory or other building, if the owner desires that the whole of such house, manufactory or building shall be so acquired:*

*Provided that, if any question shall arise as to whether any land proposed to be taken under this Act does or does not form part of a house, manufactory or building within the meaning of this section, the Collector shall refer the determination of such question to the Authority concerned and shall not be taken possession of such land until after the question has been determined.*

(2)  *In deciding on such a reference made under the proviso to sub-section (1), the Authority concerned shall have regard to the question whether the land proposed to be taken, is reasonably required for the full and unimpaired use of the house, manufactory or building.*

(3)  *If, in the case of any claim under this Act, by a person interested, on account of the severing of the land to be acquired from his other land, the appropriate Government is of opinion that the claim is unreasonable or excessive, it may, at any time before the Collector has made his award, order the acquisition of the whole of the land of which the land first sought to be acquired forms a part.*

(4)  *In the case of any acquisition of land so required no fresh declaration or other proceedings under sections 11 to 19, (both inclusive) shall be necessary; but the Collector shall without delay furnish a copy of the order of the appropriate Government to the person interested, and shall thereafter proceed to make his award under Section 23.*

This is to protect individuals whose use of the land on which they were residing or working is so interrupted or the livelihood deprived therefrom is so affected by the acquisition that it makes no sense to continue with the unit, they can invoke Section 94 of the Act.

## EXPENSE OF ACQUISITION

Section 95 reads:

*(1) Where the provisions of this Act are put in force for the purpose of acquiring land at the cost of any fund controlled or managed by a local authority or of any Requiring Body, the charges of land incidental to such acquisition shall be defrayed from or by such fund or Requiring Body.*

*(2) In any proceeding held before a Collector or Authority concerned in such cases the local authority or Requiring Body concerned may appear and adduce evidence for the purpose of determining the amount of compensation:*

*Provided that no such local authority or Requiring Body shall be entitled to demand a reference to the Authority concerned under Section 64.*

This section ensures that the financial burden or the responsibility of bearing the cost of the acquisition shall be borne by the body which has requested the acquisition. The body cannot avoid making such payment nor can it debate its quantum by seeking to approach the Land Acquisition Rehabilitation and Resettlement Authority created to hear disputes under this Act.

## PREVENTION OF POST-ACQUISITION MISUSE OF LAND

### No Change in Public Purpose or Ownership

Section 99 of the Act reads:

*No change from the purpose or related purposes for which the land is originally sought to be acquired shall be allowed:*

*Provided that if the land acquired is rendered unusable for the purpose for which it was acquired due to a fundamental change because of any unforeseen circumstances, then the appropriate Government may use such land for any other public purpose.*

Under the now repealed Land Acquisition Act, 1894, there was no way to prevent the Government from acquiring land for one purpose and then diverting to another purpose. There was also no method to prevent the Government from reselling it to another individual. This unfettered discretion was not subject to judicial review as the land had become the property of the government over which it enjoyed absolute title.

This was not an alarmist view. In 2009, the Uttar Pradesh Government had indeed acquired land as part of a concession agreement and then resold it to the Jaypee/Jaiprash associates group as part of a bundling project for the construction of the Yamuna Expressway. There was no legal bar on doing so under the old law but such a situation where the state was allowed to profit off the land of its citizens could not be tolerated anymore.

The new law prohibits changing the purpose for which the land was acquired to any other purpose.[10] So if land was acquired to build a hospital and consent was obtained on that ground then the land cannot subsequently be used for building a mall or be diverted to another unrelated activity.

The law also does not allow for change of ownership without specific permission to that effect. This prevents property acquired at prices lower than the market rate from undergoing a land use change and being resold at much higher prices.

### Return of Unutilized Land

Section 101 of the Act reads:

> *When any land, acquired under this Act remains unutilised for a period of five years from the date of taking over the possession, the same shall be returned to the original owner or owners or their legal heirs, as the case may be, or to the Land Bank of the appropriate Government by reversion in the manner as may be prescribed by the appropriate Government.*
>
> *Explanation.—For the purpose of this section, 'Land Bank' means a governmental entity that focuses on the conversion of Government owned vacant, abandoned, unutilised acquired lands and tax-delinquent properties into productive use.*

One of the worst abuses of the Land Acquisition Act, 1894 was that once land would be acquired it was at the absolute disposal of the State to dispense with at will. Many States built up substantial land banks resorting to Acquisition for ostensible public purposes

---

[10] Section 100 of the Act reads 'No change of ownership without specific permission from the appropriate Government shall be allowed.'

that never came to be.[11] Land acquisition, when employed in such a fashion ran the risk of resembling a state run, land grabbing scheme.

To ensure that land acquired would be utilized for the purpose it was being sought for, a new safeguard was inserted in the law. When any land, acquired under this Act remains unutilized for a period of five years from the date of taking over the possession, the same shall be returned to the original owner (or the legal heirs), or to the Land Bank of the appropriate Government. The decision of whether it goes to the original owners or the land bank has been left to the Central (in the case of Union Territories) and State Governments.

This means that States shall first consider looking at returning the land. They can also put it in the land bank. However, the decision to do so must be based on sound policy. Ideally the land should be returned (and that is what the very first draft of the law provided) but given the position taken by the States on land being a state subject, the final option had to be left to the States.

### Resale of Acquired Land

Section 102 of the Act reads:

> *Whenever the ownership of any land acquired under this Act is transferred to any person for a consideration, without any development having taken place on such land, forty per cent of the appreciated land value shall be shared amongst the persons from whom the lands were acquired or their heirs, in proportion to the value at which the lands were acquired within a period of five years from the date of acquisition:*
>
> *Provided that benefit shall accrue only on the first sale or transfer that occurs after the conclusion of the acquisition proceedings.*

In 2011, in the State of Uttar Pradesh, land was acquired from farmers at low prices then resold to private individuals for multiple times the acquisition price without carrying out any development to the land. This was considered palpably arbitrary and unconscionable.

To ensure that land acquisition does not become a tool for unjust enrichment of the State, a safeguard has been inserted which requires 40 per cent of the profit on resale to be shared with the original

---

[11] Kerala is one of the few states to have actually published details of its land bank holdings. http://www.kslb.kerala.gov.in/

owner if the same land, without any development (which would add value), is resold at a higher price. This is not a right in perpetuity but is extinguished after the first sale.

## LEASE

The learned leader of the Opposition in the Lok Sabha also suggested that the recourse to acquisition had become the first choice for Government's and their agencies. This approach needed to be discouraged and attention had to be drawn to other better alternatives the consequences of which would not be so absolute.

The Act makes a point of mentioning that the appropriate Government shall wherever possible, be free to exercise the option of taking the land on lease. How this clause is interpreted is for the courts to decide.

As a result Section 104 of the Act was drafted which reads:

*Notwithstanding anything contained in this Act, the appropriate Government shall, wherever possible, be free to exercise the option of taking the land on lease, instead of acquisition, for any public purpose referred to in sub-section (1) of Section 2.*

## AMENDMENT TO SCHEDULES

Though Schedules accompany the Act, they enjoy a different legal footing from the rest of the Statute as they are easier to amend. The Central Government may amend the contents of the Schedules by a simple administrative notification. They can alter or modify any of the Schedules without having to seek parliamentary approval.

However, a special safeguard has been inserted in the body of the main law which prohibits the Government from carrying out such amendments or modifications that have the impact of reducing the compensation or other provisions given in the Schedule relating to rehabilitation and resettlement.[12]

This caveat, that none of the benefits should be reduced was inserted at the recommendation of leaders of the Communist Party of India.

---

[12] Section 106 of the Act, 2013.

A copy of every notification proposed to be issued shall be laid in draft before each House of Parliament, while it is in session, for a total period of 30 days which may be comprised in one session or in two or more successive sessions, and if, before the expiry of the session immediately following the session or the successive sessions aforesaid, both Houses agree in disapproving the issue of the notification or both Houses agree in making any modification in the notification, the notification shall not be issued or as the case may be, shall be issued only in such modified form as may be agreed upon by both the Houses of Parliament.

## STATES CAN INCREMENT BUT NOT SUBTRACT

Nothing in this Act prevents any State from enacting any law to enhance or add to the entitlements enumerated under this Act which confers higher compensation than payable under the Act or to make provisions for rehabilitation and resettlement which are more beneficial than those provided under this Act. The States cannot reduce the entitlements or quantum of compensation so given.[13]

Where a State law or a policy framed by the Government of a State provides for a higher compensation than calculated under this Act for the acquisition of land, the affected persons or his family or member of his family may at their option opt to avail such higher compensation and rehabilitation and resettlement under such State law or such policy of the State. The same option is available to the families if a State offers enhanced rehabilitation and resettlement benefits.[14]

## RULES

Like any sufficiently detailed law, the Act also empowers Governments to come up with rules for the smooth functioning of the Act. Rules, though important, are not essential to the functioning of this Act which was designed to be operational from the date of Notification.

Rules do not need Parliamentary approval in the same sense as a law does. However, every rule made by the Central Government under the Act has to be laid as soon as may be after it is made, before

[13] Section 107 of the Act, 2013.
[14] Section 108 of the Act, 2013.

each House of Parliament while it is in session for a total period of 30 days which may be comprised in one session or two or more successive sessions.

If before the expiry of the session immediately following the session or the successive sessions aforesaid, both Houses agree in making any modification in the rule or both Houses agree that the rule should not be made, the rule shall thereafter have effect only in such modified form. Any such modification or annulment shall be without prejudice to the validity of anything previously done under that rule.[15]

## POWER TO ISSUE CLARIFICATIONS

The Government is further empowered to issue such orders as may be necessary to facilitate the smooth functioning of the Act. This is a power distinct from the Rule making power. If any difficulty arises in giving effect to the provisions of the law, the Central Government is empowered to issue orders making such provisions or giving such directions not inconsistent with the provisions of this Act as may appear to it to be necessary for the removal of the difficulty.

It must be noted that this power was originally time bound in the Act as passed by the Parliament. It could not be exercised after the expiry of a period of two years from the commencement of this Act (that is, it becomes redundant on 31 December 2015). However, the new Ordinance which came into force on 31 December 2014 extends this period from two years to five years. The Ordinance is discussed in the next Chapter.

Every order so made to remove difficulties must be laid, as soon as possible, before each House of Parliament.

## EXEMPTED LAWS

The principle challenge of bringing about a new law on land acquisition, especially one with retrospective operation, was accounting for the impact it would have on existing projects. Many acquisitions cover tracts of land that are very large in size and acquisition must necessarily take place in parcels or stages.

[15] Section 109 of the Act, 2013.

This staggered approach is followed most commonly in cases of a linear nature such as road building, laying of railroads, erection of poles to connect power lines etc. If the law was made to apply to these cases, parts of which have already concluded land acquisition, it would result in a situation of widespread chaos.

Individuals in the same project plan would receive different amounts of compensation depending upon whether their land was acquired before or after the new law came into force. Cases which would have concluded would have to be reopened to avoid charges of bias or arbitrariness. As a result, the entire project would face closure.

In addition to the above, it is also true that there exists a class of projects which are essential for the economic and social growth of the country. Given the sensitive nature of some of these projects and given the very high necessity for their construction it made sense to exempt some of these activities from the operation of the new law, at least for the time being. With the New Ordinance (discussed in the next chapter) even these exempted laws are now bound by the provisions of the 2013 Act insofar as they relate to compensation, rehabilitation and resettlement.

These include:

- **The Ancient Monuments and Archaeological Sites and Remains Act, 1958:** The objective of the statute is to protect monuments of national importance by taking over areas in the vicinity which would erode or harm the existence of the monument. It is unlikely that any fresh acquisitions will be undertaken under this law.
- **The Atomic Energy Act, 1962:** An Act of great national importance, it lays down the law with regard to 'the development, control and use of atomic energy for the welfare of the people of India and for other peaceful purposes'.[16]
- **The Damodar Valley Corporation Act, 1948:** This law provides for the 'establishment and regulation of the Corporation for the development of the Damodar Valley in the Provinces of Bihar and West Bengal'.[17]

[16] Short Title to the Atomic Energy Act, 1962; Sections 10 to 12 deal with acquisition in various forms.

[17] Short Title to the Damodar Valley Corporation Act, 1948; Section 50 deals with acquisition.

- **The Indian Tramways Act, 1886:** This law to 'facilitate construction and regulation of tramways' holds relevance as it is sometimes invoked for the construction of elevated tramways in urban areas.[18]
- **The Land Acquisition (Mines) Act, 1885:** This law provides for cases in which Mines or Minerals are situated under the land for which acquisition is necessary.
- **The Metro Railways (Construction of Works) Act, 1978:** This law provides for the construction of works relating to metro railways in metropolitan cities.[19]
- **The National Highways Act, 1956:** This law provides for the declaration of certain highways to be national highways[20] and the acquisition of land for the same.
- **The Petroleum and Minerals Pipelines (Acquisition of Right of User in Land) Act, 1962:** This law provides for the acquisition of land for laying pipelines for the transport of petroleum and minerals.
- **The Requisitioning and Acquisition of Immovable Property Act, 1952:** This law provides for the requisitioning and acquisition of immovable property for the purposes of the Union. It is mostly confined to temporary requisitioning of property for the purposes of the Central Government.
- **The Resettlement of Displaced Persons (Land Acquisition) Act, 1948:** This law is confined in its operation to acquisition for resettling displaced persons in those territories which immediately before 1 November 1956 were comprised in the States of Delhi and Ajmer.
- **The Coal Bearing Areas Acquisition and Development Act, 1957:** This law, stands apart from the others in this list, as an entire law for the acquisition of land in coal bearing areas. The entire procedure for acquisition, insofar as it covers the subjects of this law, is provided under this law.

---

[18] Short Title to the Indian Tramways Act, 1886; Sections 7(2) and 7(3) deals with acquisition.

[19] Chapter III of this law deals with acquisition.

[20] Section 3 deals with acquisition. Section 3J excluded the application of the Land Acquisition Act, 1894.

- **The Electricity Act, 2003:** This is a comprehensive Act containing provisions relating to generation, transmission, distribution, trading and use of electricity and for taking measures conducive to development of electricity industry.[21]
- **The Railways Act, 1989:** This is the principle law employed by the Indian Railways for activities related to construction and maintenance of railway lines and stations.[22]

The Defence of India Act, the Cantonments Act and the SEZ Act, all of which were exempted in the original draft, were removed from exemption upon the recommendation of the Standing Committee.

As a result the law provides that the provisions of this Act shall not apply to the enactments relating to land acquisition specified in the Fourth Schedule. The Central Government may, by notification, omit or add to any of the enactments specified in the Fourth Schedule.

However, these statutes enjoyed only a limited exemption in terms of time. Within one year (that is, by 31 December 2014) all these laws had to be amended to some degree by bringing in the provisions of the new law as they relate to compensation, rehabilitation and resettlement.

In other words, the provisions of these exempted laws relating to compensation had to be brought in line with that of the new law and separate provisions would have to be made to provide rehabilitation and resettlement benefits as enumerated under the new Act of 2013. The Ordinance promulgated by the Government on 31 December 2014 brought about an amendment to this effect.

---

[21] Short Title to the Electricity Act, 2003. Section 165 relates to acquisition of land and also amends the Land Acquisition Act, 1894.

[22] The Railways Act, 1989. Section 11 deals with acquisition.

CHAPTER ELEVEN

# The Ordinance

*On 31 December 2014, the Government of India came out with a new Ordinance that amended the Act of 2013. This chapter deals with the significance and consequences of this legislative measure.*

Shortly after a new Government was sworn into office, it became clear that changes to the land acquisition law were imminent. Development had been a central theme running through the political campaign and land acquisition was an important part of that discourse.

The authors wrote extensively in the press arguing for an honest attempt at implementation before giving in to imagined or hypothetical challenges. This sentiment was also echoed in the actions of various farmers rights organization who organized rallies with the hope of dissuading the Government from amending the law.

## BACKGROUND AND RUN-UP TO THE AMENDMENTS

On 29 December 2014, a press release was issued by the Press Information Bureau, the official media arm of the Government of India. It declared without substantiation that 'many difficulties are being faced in its [the Act's] implementation'. It went on to state that 'in order to remove them, certain amendments have been made in the Act to further strengthen the provisions to protect the interests of the "affected families"'. This release presented a rather innocuous picture of the amendments that were going to be carried out.[1] It would be two days before the official Ordinance[2] would be shared with the public.

[1] http://pib.nic.in/newsite/PrintRelease.aspx?relid=114190.
[2] Ordinance No. 9 of 2014.

The press release gave the impression that only two amendments were to be carried out. The first related to applying the provisions of compensation and rehabilitation and resettlement to the laws that had been exempted under the Fourth Schedule.

Under the unamended Act, the only exemptions to the consent and the Social Impact Assessment clause were the 13 laws given in the Fourth Schedule to the Act. This exception had been crafted as a temporary measure in view of the fact that some projects were indeed, deserving of greater priority than others. This list included acquisition for the purposes of Railways, National Highways, Atomic Energy, Electricity etc. And even these 13 laws had to be amended within one year, that is, by 31 December 2014 to ensure that compensation, rehabilitation and resettlement clauses were brought at par with the new law (see Section 105 of the unamended law).

Since this requirement of amendment had been built into the law when it had been passed this was not entirely unanticipated. In fact, it was a necessary safeguard that the framers had inserted to ensure parity amongst different statutes prescribing the acquisition route. The Press Release understandably emphasised this, going to the extent of making a virtue out of what was a legislative necessity.

The second amendment related to creating a new category of projects which would be exempt from seeking the consent of the affected families. These projects would also not be required to be tested on parameters laid down in the Social Impact Assessment Process. This new set of categories (inserted by a new Section 10A) included vaguely worded terms such as infrastructure projects (including PPP projects) alongside the more noble public purposes of rural electrification and housing for the poor.

The rationale for creating this category was never presented. The exemptions given in the unamended law were the result of sustained public consultation and were in fact, to some degree a grand compromise. In the case of the Ordinance, exemptions were created without any explanation as why these activities or sectors were being placed in a class of their own.

The Press Release also misguidedly suggested that these measures would ease acquisitions for defence purposes. However, in making this claim the framers overlooked the fact that acquisition for defence and national security had already been protected under the urgency clause. This was a frightening illustration of the *ad hoc* approach with which the amendments had been presented.

For a law that had been founded on consultation with the public, no draft had been shared with public at large. The requirement of inviting comments from the public had been dispensed with and a law was prepared by a group of individuals consisting largely of officials and Ministerial Representatives. Many groups struggled to get their say before the law was amended but few, if any, got the opportunity. It can be argued they simply were not the stakeholders for whom the amendments were being carried out.

The Government had for a variety of reasons been unable to present a Bill on the subject in Parliament. No official document had even been placed before either House of Parliament. It was a surprise to all when the Ordinance was announced and promulgated in the matter of four very long days.

## LIST OF AMENDMENTS CARRIED OUT BY THE LAND ACQUISITION AMENDMENT ORDINANCE, 2014

The following is the list of amendments carried out by the Government which were not envisaged by the Original Law.

- The Ordinance creates a Special Category of Projects (New Section 10A) which are exempt from the consent requirements, the Social Impact Assessment requirements, the review by the Expert Group and the bar placed on acquisition of multi-crop/agricultural land. The five items in the special category include industrial corridors and infrastructure and social infrastructure projects including projects under Public Private Partnership. Since most acquisitions fall in these two categories this has the impact of completely nullifying the safeguards contained under the original 2013 law.
- Significant amendments to Section 24(2), the Retrospective Clause have also been made. The section, the most invoked since the law came into force, has been amended to exclude the time spent under litigation where a stay order has been passed. Furthermore the definition of 'compensation paid' as laid down by the Supreme Court has been nullified. The Supreme Court

had defined compensation paid as an amount deposited in the court. The new section states that any amount paid into any account maintained for that purpose shall be sufficient. Both of these amendments will disqualify a majority of beneficiaries and, It can be deduced, are designed to serve the interests of the State in preserving its land banks.

- Defaulting Civil Servants are now to be prosecuted only after sanction has been obtained for such prosecution. The unamended law had ensured greater accountability for officers working to implement the law by providing for provisions to penalise them in case of violations. However the new Government has amended the relevant section (Section 87) to allow for their prosecution only after taking sanction from the Government. Now officers can proceed to implement the law with limited fear of being held accountable.

- The Provisions for Return of Unutilized Land stand diluted. The period of time after which a piece of acquired land must be returned to its original owner has been diluted. The unamended law stated expressly that the land must be returned after five years (to the original owner or the state land bank) if the land is not utilized. However, the Ordinance amends the clause negating the period of five years by alternatively allowing the acquirer to provide for a 'the period specified for the setting up of any project' whichever might be greater. The impact of this will be that the acquirer can specify an extremely lengthy and generous period for the completion of any project without any accountability. This in effect nullifies the clause.

- The Special Powers retained with the Government to implement the Law have been extended. The Unamended law gave the Government the power to take any action that may be necessary to implement the law for two years after its passage. The time period was an important limitation on potential abuse and was designed to ensure that the Government would only invoke it in bona fide and unanticipated situations. However the current Government has extended the time period to five years. This allows the Government sweeping residual powers to take any action necessary to support their interpretation of the Act.

- The definition of 'private entity' has been expanded to include proprietorships, partnerships, companies, corporations, non-profit organisations and any other entity under any law for the time being in force.

All these amendments represent a violation of the spirit of the Act which focused on empowering the common man and not the State machinery. The objective of the law which was to limit the mechanism of forced acquisition has also been undermined significantly.

## CONSEQUENCES

The authors immediately published an editorial in a leading English daily drawing attention to the consequences of this move.[3] In the Article it was argued that the immediate and likely impact of this amendment is that land can now be acquired for a vast number of projects without having to exhaust the pre-acquisition processes that had been put in place, namely the Social Impact Assessment (SIA) and the determination of prior informed consent from the affected families.

The authors went on to explain the reason for why the consent and Social Impact Assessment process had been hardcoded into the DNA of the law. Acquisition had become a tool for the use of brutal force by the State. Acquisition was almost always forceful leading invariably to riots and protests (often violent in nature). By requiring the state to seek the consent of 70 to 80 per cent of the affected families, the law empowered those who were to be directly impacted against the arbitrary exercise of the power by the State. For the first time in the history of independent India was the citizenry given a say in how the State would deal with their land. Now with this one step the ruling party had returned us to the days of the British enacted law where our citizens enjoyed no say in their development.

Attention was also drawn by the authors to the fact that the unamended law was enacted after unprecedented nation-wide consultations which took place over two years. Two All-Party Meetings were convened. The Bill was subject to 12 hour debates in both Houses in which over 60 members took part. Two key amendments suggested

---

[3] 'Fencing the Farmer Out', Ramesh and Khan, Op-Ed, *The Hindu* (31 December 2014).

by Smt. Sushma Swaraj and Shri Arun Jaitley were also accepted (these related to providing for lease as an option and the share of an original owner in case his land was subsequently acquired). The BJP, then the principal party in opposition, unambiguously supported the law in Parliament and even expressed support for these very provisions it now sought to exclude.

The Minister for Finance in an article circulated by their Party Media Cell defended the Ordinance argued that the law does not dilute the provisions of compensation, rehabilitation and resettlement but instead only makes the process for acquiring the land easier.

What was missing in the defence was the realization or even acknowledgement of the vast gap between the bargaining power of the state and the lowest common denominator. The Social Impact Assessment process gave these people (often farmers) the right to negotiate fairer rates of compensation while determining if the project was truly in the public interest. It had also removed the scope for the subjective use of discretion by the Collector and other representatives of the Government—a key hallmark of the unamended law.

Now with the Social Impact Assessment process being waived the Collector can once again determine what constitutes a public purpose and how soon can land be acquired. It was this unchecked authority that was at the heart of the multiple abuses of the law chronicled over the last 70 years. Discretion had been replaced by verifiable systems and processes to check capricious decision making. Now this safeguard stands eroded.

The Social Impact Assessment was designed to ensure that no acquisition in excess of the bare minimum requirement took place. This was an important objective as most acquisitions were characterised by excess zeal on the part of the state. More land was always acquired than was needed for the project in question. Without the Social Impact Assessment the possibility of arbitrary diversions once again becomes a reality.

Also, the new law did not introduce the concepts of rehabilitation and resettlement. It merely put in place a process that ensured compliance and enforcement. The Supreme Court of India had already mandated Rehabilitation and Resettlement even before the new law was enacted. There was even a national policy that existed on the subject but violations remained rampant. The Social Impact

Assessment process was created to provide a framework that would ensure its implementation.

Another likely impact is that this new ordinance will effectively undo the implicit limits that had been placed on the acquisition of agricultural or multi-crop land by the unamended Act (done to ensure continued food security for our citizens). However, the amendments seem to allow such acquisitions without restrictions.

The authors argued in the press that the Government should have instead used this opportunity to strengthen the legal regime governing land titles in States where they are now in power (since land is primarily a state subject). Knowledge asymmetry and an active land mafia lead to the purchase of land being a risky proposition (and hence making acquisition more attractive). It is a pity that the Government did not take this opportunity given that they are in power in both the Centre and State in key State Governments where acquisition is a burning issue (Maharashtra, Haryana, Rajasthan and Madhya Pradesh).

Despite protests held across the country, the Government passed the Amendments to the Act in the Lok Sabha on 10 March 2015. These amendments varied slightly from the Ordinance that had been promulgated. While all the sections that had been introduced in the Ordinance remained intact, the term 'social infrastructure' (which had been exempted from consent and the application of the Social Impact Assessment) was dropped in the face of the criticism that it was too broad a category and held potential for abuse. However, the remaining items remained exempted.

Another amendment was made to add a provision guaranteeing employment to farm labour. This concession was misleading and not entirely clear, as the 2013 Act had already promised employment to agricultural labourers (or an amount of Rupees five lakhs in lieu thereof). Farmers groups travelled from across the country to the capital to register their protests. The Government remained unmoved.

In the name of economic reforms and development, the Government has taken a significant step backward in India's march to land reforms. Given that the choice of opting for an Ordinance came within eight months of the Government coming to power, this story is also a telling commentary on the weakening of democratic and constitutional institutions.

# Conclusion
## Acknowledging the Real Challenges

Devising laws and regulations on land will always be a contentious topic. Given that we have more people than land, the subject will always give rise to impassioned debate and inflamed opinions on the form and extent of regulation to be employed by the State.

India's very large population is forced to condense itself into a land mass ill fit to accommodate the hopes and aspirations of so many. As a result, land has been the fulcrum for almost every significant political movement in the last seven decades since India became a free nation. In West Bengal, conflicts over land acquisition ended the record breaking reign of the Communist party. In the 1970s, land related movements led to the passage of Ceiling laws which placed a limit on how much land an individual could own and cemented the political legacy of Indira Gandhi.

Some will argue that the State should not interfere with the sale and purchase of land while others will argue for regulation to such extent that laws should be passed dividing available land for homes to all (the proposed Homestead Act, 2013 comes to mind).

Competing ideas on land use have been locked in argument since the idea of land ownership was conceived. However, during the course of our work on this law we found that there exist some deep seated problems which need to be addressed.

The scarcity of land is the single greatest challenge for a leader or policy maker tasked with crafting legislation on the subject. It is his or her job to figure out solutions to India's land problems and to provide sound legal frameworks for doing so. But the catch is that the Constitution of India classifies 'Land' as a state subject. This means, given India's quasi-federal structure, that only States are free to make laws on the subject. So in effect, the Union cannot enforce what it commands.

Upon taking charge of the Ministry of Rural Development (which houses the department of land resources) in July of 2011, three fundamental problems became apparent:

- Land records are poorly and not uniformly maintained, if at all (imagine a big ledger filled in with ink and scratched over to correct entries, not open for scrutiny save by officials and immediate buyers).
- Price reporting is episodic and highly inaccurate especially as one moves away from urban centres and into rural areas (with the rates in some districts not having been updated for decades).
- Titles over land are presumptive and never conclusive. A weakness exploited by an active (and creative) land mafia and one that opens every land transaction up to legal challenge.

The Indian Parliament made history when it passed a new law on land acquisition. As the law's authors, we knew that many of the laws more far reaching objectives with regard to fairer compensation could only be achieved if the above problems were reconciled. The law would only be as good as the mechanics on which it relied. We had to adopt a nuanced approach to the legal framework and the following are what we came up with:

*First*, we knew we did not have the legislative competence to enact a new law on reporting. So we took an existing law, passed before the Constitution came into force, and moved amendments to it: the Indian Registration Act, 1908 (which prescribes the procedure for the registration of documents by local authorities). The purpose of these amendments: mandate the computerization of land records and make them accessible to all at the lowest level, that is, at the block and District. The immediate impact will be that a buyer can see the chain of transactions before he/she purchases the land, leading to more clarity with regard to title. The buyer can also hold the officer accountable for inaccuracies in reporting. However, Parliament was dissolved before these could be taken up.

*Second*, we stepped up the Land Records Modernization Programme. Though unenforceable it seeks to provide States with support to update and modernize their land records to boost transparency. Originally launched in 2008, it had languished until earlier this year with only four States actually following the programme guidelines. The idea of a framework of legal incentives (such as linking land records upgradation to faster release of grants for road construction) could work well and was also mooted. This is an idea that needs further development and one that the existing Government should examine more deeply.

*Third*, and what we desperately need (but have not been able to figure out how, yet) is to enact a law making land titles 'conclusive' instead of 'presumptive'. A draft law exists and is actually available on the website of the Department of Land Resources.[1] It is suggested that since the BJP Government is in power in the Centre and in some key states, they can demonstrate their commitment by moving the law in States which are ruled by them and implement it rapidly to demonstrate its potential. Security and clarity of title have proven to be the single biggest draw for large scale investors over the last few years (as evidenced by Gujarat and Maharashtra). This will force other states, if they want to compete effectively, to draw up similar frameworks. Our experience with state laws on Renewable Energy also provides solid evidence to back up this premise.

The authors have been privileged to have been an intimate part in devising and pushing these solutions. Resistance to some of the above ideas may come from a languorous bureaucracy, but given a mix of legal and political strategies, these ideas may well succeed. The baton, for now, has been passed on.

The new law on land acquisition is seen as a hurdle by many to our continued economic growth. This is a myopic view. Land acquisition was a cruel and inhuman solution to a deeper problem—that of poorly maintained land records and weak land rights. These still exist. The answer lies in finding unique solutions, enabled by technology, to give people better protection over the land that they own. Amending the law on acquisition to assuage the fears of a particular constituency is bad policy making.

Through this law, an attempt has been made to first protect our citizenry against the unlawful advances of the State. It is our hope that the current Government will add to the legacy of legal protection rather than seek to abridge its growth.

[1]  http://dolr.nic.in/landtitlingbill_notice.htm.

# Annexures

## Selected Debates in the Lok Sabha

The Right to Fair Compensation and Transparency in Land Acquisition, Rehabilitation and Resettlement Bill, 2013 was Passed by the Lok Sabha on 30 August 2013. The Following are the Motions Put Forth by Various Members of the House.[1]

[I] Rajnath Singh[2]

**श्री राजनाथ सिंह (गाज़ियाबाद):** अध्यक्ष महोदया, सबसे पहले मैं आपके प्रति आभार व्यक्त करना चाहता हूं कि आपने इस देश के अत्यधिक संवेदनशील सवाल भूमि अधिग्रहण पर अपने विचार व्यक्त करने का अवसर दिया है। लम्बे इंतजार के बाद भूमि अधिग्रहण से संबंधित बिल संसद के समक्ष विचार के लिए आया हुआ है। बहुत ही गौर से पूरे विधेयक का मैंने अध्ययन किया है। सबसे पहले हमारी नजर इस विधेयक के नाम पर पड़ी। नाम में भी संशोधन हुआ है और इस नाम को पढ़ने के बाद मुझे बहुत ही अनुभूति हुई, अच्छा लगा। इस विधेयक का नाम है—The Right to Fair Compensation and Transparency in Land Acquisition, Rehabilitation and Resettlement Bill, 2011. इस विधेयक के नाम को पढ़ने के बाद मुझे लगा कि शायद सरकार ने सोचा होगा कि ऐसा नाम दिया जाए ताकि सारी की सारी विधेयक की जो मंशा है, वह पूरी तरह से इस नाम में ही समाहित हो जाये।

---

[1] The full text is available at http://164.100.47.132/LssNew/psearch/Result15.aspx?dbsl=10604.

[2] English Summaries of all Hindi speeches are available at http://164.100.47.132/synop/15/XIV/2Sup+Sup+Synopsis-29-08-13.pdf.

**श्री राजनाथ सिंह:** हां, कोशिश यह की गई है, इसीलिए विधेयक का नाम इतना प्रभावी रखा गया है। लेकिन जब मैंने विधेयक का विस्तार में जाकर अध्ययन किया तो मैंने देखा कि कई ऐसे महत्वपूर्ण पहलू हैं, जो कि पूरी तरह से अनदेखे रह गये हैं। वैसे यह विधेयक तो ग्रामीण विकास मंत्रालय के द्वारा तैयार किया गया है, लेकिन मुझे लगा कि गांवों में रहने वाले किसानों की, गरीबों की इस विधेयक के माध्यम से जो चिन्ता की जानी चाहिए और जिस गम्भीरता से चिन्ता की जानी चाहिए, उतनी गम्भीरता के साथ चिन्ता नहीं की गई है, बल्कि शहरों और उद्योगों की तरफ विशेष ध्यान दिया गया है। मैं शहरों और उद्योगों का विरोधी नहीं हूं, शहरों में भी सारी सुख-सुविधाएं मिलनी चाहिए, उद्योग भी इस देश में बढ़ने चाहिए, उन्हें आवश्यक सुविधाएं मुहैया कराई जानी चाहिए, इसमें कोई दो मत नहीं हैं। लेकिन गांव, गरीब और किसान से जुड़े हुए सवाल पर, जो कि अत्यधिक संवेदनशील सवाल होता है, यदि सरकार ने उनकी समस्याओं के निराकरण के लिए ध्यान नहीं दिया तो मैं समझता हूं कि जिस प्रकार की विषम स्थिति इस देश में पैदा होगी, उसकी कल्पना नहीं की जा सकती है।

इस बिल के बारे में मैं यह जरूर कहूंगा कि पहले से थोड़ा बेहतर यह बिल बनाने की कोशिश सरकार के द्वारा की गई है, लेकिन पूरे बिल का अध्ययन करने के बाद मैं इस नतीजे पर पहुंचा कि यह बिल अपने मूल उद्देश्य से काफी भटक गया है। जहां तक भूमि का सवाल है, हम भूमि को केवल एक कमोडिटी नहीं मानते हैं और भूमि से हम केवल आर्थिक गतिविधियों को ही जोड़कर नहीं देख सकते हैं। भूमि का जहां तक प्रश्न है, इसके साथ किसान का भावनात्मक रिश्ता भी जुड़ा हुआ है, भूमि के साथ उसका एक सांस्कृतिक रिश्ता भी जुड़ा हुआ है। अध्यक्ष महोदया, आपको भी जानकारी है, आप भी गांव की रहने वाली हैं कि भूमि के छोटे से टुकड़े के लिए अपनी जान देने के लिए भी किसान का पूरा का पूरा परिवार तैयार हो जाता है, इस प्रकार का भावनात्मक रिश्ता होता है। मैं भी किसान परिवार से हूं, मैं जानता हूं कि जिस दिन अपनी ज़मीन दूसरे के हाथों बेचनी पड़ती है, भले ही उसके कारण पैसा हासिल होता है, लेकिन अपने मन को अच्छा नहीं लगता है, यह कदम किसान को मजबूरी में उठाना पड़ता है, इस सीमा तक भावनात्मक रिश्ता उस ज़मीन के साथ होता है। सांस्कृतिक रिश्ता भी...(व्यवधान)

**श्री राजनाथ सिंह:** जहां तक सांस्कृतिक रिश्ते का प्रश्न है, आप जानते हैं कि हम भूमि को एक साधारण ज़मीन का टुकड़ा नहीं मानते हैं, बल्कि इस भूमि को, पृथ्वी को हमने मातातुल्य माना है। इस प्रकार का एक सांस्कृतिक रिश्ता इस भूमि के साथ हम लोगों का है। लेकिन आजादी मिलने के पहले भी और आजादी हासिल होने के बाद भी आर्थिक विकास के नाम पर जिस तरीके से अंधाधुंध भूमि का अधिग्रहण हुआ है, मैं यह कह सकता हूं कि उससे इस देश के किसानों में घोर असंतोष पैदा हुआ है।

इससे लगभग 6.5 करोड़ की संख्या में किसान विस्थापित हुए हैं। यह मेरा आंकड़ा नहीं है, बल्कि यूनाइटिड नेशंस का एक कमीशन है, उस कमीशन ने अपनी रिपोर्ट में यह बात कही है। चूंकि भूमि किसान का एकमात्र सहारा होती है, इसलिए भूमि के प्रश्न को लेकर जब कभी कोई विवाद खड़ा होता है तो स्वाभाविक रूप से किसान एकजुट होकर आन्दोलन करता है, उसके लिए लाठियां खाता है, गोलियां खाता है, लेकिन फिर भी भूमि को बचाने के लिए अपनी तरफ से भरपूर कोशिश करता है, लेकिन विडम्बना यह है कि 1894 में, जब अंग्रेजों की हुकूमत इस हिन्दुस्तान में थी तो भूमि अधिग्रहण से सम्बन्धित एक बिल तैयार किया गया था। उस समय भी यह भूमि का अधिग्रहण थोड़ी बहुत मात्रा में होता था, तब भी किसानों के अन्दर असंतोष पैदा होता था, किसान आन्दोलन करता था, लेकिन जिस निर्ममतापूर्वक ब्रिटिश हुकूमत द्वारा उसके आन्दोलन को दबा दिया जाता था तो फिर ब्रिटिश हुकूमत के सामने वह उफ करने का साहस वह नहीं जुटा पाता था, लेकिन 1894 के बाद आजादी हासिल होने के बाद तीन बार इस बिल में संशोधन हुआ है। 1962, 1967 और 1984, तीन बार इसका संशोधन हुआ, लेकिन फिर भी मंशा इस देश के किसानों की यही थी कि भूमि अधिग्रहण इस तरीके से किया जाना चाहिए, ताकि हमारे परिवार के समक्ष किसी प्रकार का भविष्य में कोई संकट पैदा न हो। इस पर सरकारों को ध्यान देना चाहिए। फिर जो कुछ भी संशोधन हुए, संशोधन के बावजूद वह राहत इस देश के किसानों को नहीं मिल पायी। फिर यहां पर बीजेपी लेड एनडीए गवर्नमेंट आयी, हम लोगों ने इस प्रश्न को अपनी सरकार के जो तत्कालीन प्रधानमंत्री थे, आदरणीय अटल बिहारी वाजपेयी जी के समक्ष रखा। उन्होंने इसकी गंभीरता को स्वीकार किया और यह कहा कि निश्चित रूप से एक ऐसा बिल तैयार किया जाना चाहिए ताकि किसानों को अधिकतम राहत दी जा सके और आनन-फानन में कोई फैसला नहीं किया जाना चाहिए। यह आदरणीय अटल बिहारी वाजपेयी जी ने उस समय भी हिदायत दी थी। तब तक वर्ष 2003 समास होते-होते ही हमारी सरकार चली गयी। अब कांग्रेस लेड यूपीए गवर्नमेंट के आये हुए लगभग साढ़े 9 वर्षों का समय गुजर गया और मैं तब से सुन रहा हूं, जब से वर्ष 2004 में यह कांग्रेस नेतृत्व की यूपीए सरकार बनी है कि भूमि अधिग्रहण के लिए एक संशोधित बिल लाया जा रहा है। लेकिन साढ़े 9 वर्षों का समय गुजर जाने के बाद, इतने संवेदनशील सवाल पर, यह बिल जो लाया गया है, मैं समझता हूं कि यह बिल पूरी तरह से अपने मूल उद्देश्य से भटक गया है।

जहां तक मंत्री जी का सवाल है, मैं जानता हूं कि मंत्री जी निहायत ही एक अच्छे इंसान हैं और जिस समय हमारी बातचीत हुई थी और जो पहला बिल आया था, अपेक्षाकृत इससे वह बेहतर बिल था। मैं यह जानता हूं कि जब कैबिनेट में यह प्रपोजल गया होगा तो निश्चित रूप से मंत्री जी के ऊपर कोई न कोई दबाव आया

होगा, इसलिए यह बिल अपने मूल उद्देश्य से भटक गया है, ऐसा मेरा मानना है। मैं यह कहना चाहता हूं कि कभी भी अधीरता में, जल्दबाजी में भूमि अधिग्रहण से सम्बन्धित किसी मामले पर कोई निर्णय नहीं किया जाना चाहिए। यह हमारी मंशा है।

गहोबणा, इस विधेयक में तो निजी क्षेत्र के लिए भी भूमि अधिग्रहण का एक रास्ता निकाल लिया गया है। वैसे निजी क्षेत्र के लिए भूमि अधिग्रहण अंग्रेजों की हुकूमत में भी होता था। इसके पहले का जो पुराना बिल है, उसमें भी उनके लिए होता था, लेकिन पब्लिक परपज़ एक नया शब्द जो इसमें इंट्रोड्यूज़ किया गया है, यह पब्लिक परपज़ का शब्द उस समय भी था। इस पब्लिक परपज़ की ओर मैं आपका ध्यान आकर्षित करना चाहता हूं कि पब्लिक परपज़ की श्रेणी में एक लम्बी सूची इस बिल में दी गयी है, इस बिल के अन्तर्गत वह मैंशंड है, जिसमें इंफ्रास्ट्रक्चर भी शामिल है। इंफ्रास्ट्रक्चर का जहां तक सवाल है, मैं याद दिलाना चाहता हूं कि 27 मार्च, 2012 को एक गजट जारी किया गया। वह इतना व्यापक है, इतना व्यापक है, इसमें कई व्यावसायिक गतिविधियों को भी शामिल किया गया। अब मैं सारी व्यावसायिक गतिविधियों की यहां चर्चा नहीं करना चाहता हूं जिनको कि इस बिल में मैंशन किया गया, लेकिन मैं स्पेशल इकॉनामिक जोन की ओर ध्यान आकर्षित करना चाहता हूं।

अध्यक्ष महोदया, पूरी संसद इस बात की साक्षी है, स्पेशल इकॉनामिक जोन जिस समय बनाया जा रहा था, उसके पीछे क्या उद्देश्य था, इससे भी हम सभी अच्छी तरह परिचित हैं। हम लोगों को लगता था कि स्पेशल इकॉनामिक जोन से निश्चित रूप से किसानों को राहत मिलेगी। बड़ी संख्या में 700, 800 की संख्या में स्पेशल इकॉनामिक जोंस अंधाधुंध इस देश में बना दिए गए। आज स्पेशल इकॉनामिक जोन का कोई भी काम वहां प्रारंभ नहीं किया गया है। मनमाने तरीके से किसानों की ज़मीन अधिग्रहीत कर ली गयी है। किसान यह आंदोलन कर रहा है कि हमारी ज़मीन को वापस किया जाना चाहिए। लेकिन इस बिल में पब्लिक परपज़ की व्याख्या करते समय एक भ्रम की स्थिति बनी हुयी है। मैं ध्यान आकर्षित करना चाहता हूं इस बिल के क्लॉज 2 के सैक्शन 1 की तरफ, इसमें लिखा है, 'Public purpose and shall include the following purposes.' अभी हमारी समझ में बात नहीं आती है, क्या-क्या पब्लिक परपज़ है या तो उसको आप मैंशन कर देते, लेकिन पब्लिक परपज़ के अतिरिक्त आपने जो कुछ भी परपज़ेज एक सूची में डाले हैं, उस पर हमको कोई आपत्ति नहीं है। लेकिन मैं मंत्री जी से जानना चाहता हूं, अलग से यह पब्लिक परपज़ और उसके बाद अन्य जो कुछ भी आपने सूची मैंशन की है इसमें, उसके पीछे आपकी मंशा क्या है? आप क्या कहना चाहते हैं? इसके संबंध में मैं क्लैरिफिकेशन चाहूंगा। हमारा यह कहना है कि या तो यह होना चाहिए कि 'Public purpose including purposes mentioned below.' पब्लिक परपज़ को अलग

नहीं करना चाहिए था। यदि पब्लिक परपज़ है तो उसमें कहना चाहिए था 'Public purpose including purposes mentioned below.' इस पर मैं मंत्री जी का क्लैरिफिकेशन चाहता हूं कि इसके पीछे मंत्री जी की मंशा क्या रही है? इस बिल के क्लॉज़-2 के सेक्शन-वन में कहा गया है कि प्राइवेट कम्पनीज़ के लिए prior consent of at least 80 per cent of the affected families जरूरी है। यानी जितने प्रभावित परिवार हैं, उनके 80 फीसदी लोगों की यह प्रायर कंसेंट होनी चाहिए कि यह भूमि अधिग्रहीत की जाए या यह भूमि अधिग्रहीत न की जाए। लेकिन पब्लिक प्राइवेट पार्टनरशिप के जो प्रोजैक्ट्स होंगे, उनके लिए यहां पर 70 परसेंट यहां पर रखा गया है। मगर सरकारी प्रोजैक्ट्स के लिए किसी प्रकार की कोई बाध्यता नहीं है। मैं यह कहना चाहता हूं कि आप यह अनइवेन प्लेइंग फील्ड क्यों देना चाहते हैं? देना है तो जो सरकारी प्रोजैक्ट्स हैं, उनके लिए भी, और साथ ही साथ गैरसरकारी जो प्रोजैक्ट्स हैं, उनके लिए भी आपको प्ले फील्ड देनी है, तो आप समान प्ले फील्ड दीजिए। लेकिन यदि आपके समक्ष कोई ऐसी मजबूरी है, तो मंत्री जी प्रायर कंसेंट के जो नॉर्म्स हैं, वह यूनिफार्म रखने में क्या परेशानी थी? इस संबंध में भी मैं क्लैरिफिकेशन चाहूंगा।

क्या इस बिल के बाद भी जबरिया भूमि अधिग्रहण का रास्ता खुला रहेगा? मैं यह जानना चाहता हूं, क्योंकि यह क्लॉज़ पढ़ने के बाद, यह शंका हमारे मन में पैदा हुई है कि अब भी जबरिया किया जाएगा, लेकिन मैं मानता हूं, मैंने भी सरकार चलाई है, कि कुछ विशेष परिस्थितियों में भूमि अधिग्रहण करना अत्यधिक आवश्यक होता है। आपात स्थिति भी कभी ऐसी पैदा हो जाती है कि भूमि अधिग्रहण आवश्यक होता है। मैं अपनी तरफ से इतना ही सुझाव देना चाहूंगा कि ऐसी परिस्थिति कभी पैदा होती है तो कुछ स्पेशल इंसैंटिव्स किसानों को दिए जाने चाहिए। इस बिल में इसकी भी व्यवस्था होनी चाहिए।

इस बिल में प्रावधान किया गया है कि निजी क्षेत्र के अधिग्रहण में 80 प्रतिशत प्रभावित परिवारों की जो कंसेंट ली जाएगी, उसके साथ यह कहा गया है, प्रभावित परिवार किसको माना जाएगा, सोशल इम्पैक्ट असैसमैंट के बाद, इनवायरमेंटल इम्पैक्ट असैसमैंट के बाद, लेकिन सोशल इम्पैक्ट असैसमैंट और इनवायरमेंटल इम्पैक्ट असैसमैंट, यह कब से प्रारंभ करेंगे? आप के बिल से तो ऐसा प्रतीत होता है कि भूमि अधिग्रहण का सिलसिला प्रारंभ होने के बाद यह किया जाएगा। लेकिन यह पहले होना चाहिए। सोशल इम्पैक्ट असैसमैंट भूमि अधिग्रहण का प्रोसेस प्रारंभ होने के पहले होना चाहिए। इनवायरमेंटल इम्पैक्ट असैसमैंट भी भूमि अधिग्रहण का यह सिलसिला प्रारंभ होने के पहले होना चाहिए। इसके पहले यह संभव नहीं है।

मैं लैंड ओनर की जो परिभाषा है, उसके बारे में कुछ कहना चाहता हूं। मंत्री जी, आप को भी जानकारी है कि आज हमारे देश में लैंड टाइटल्स को लेकर लगभग 20 फीसदी मामले उलझे हुए हैं। अदालतों में उनके विवाद चल रहे हैं। ऐसी स्थिति से निपटने के लिए इस बिल में कोई प्रोविजन नहीं है। क्या आपने सोना है ? मैं आगके उत्तर में यह भी जानना चाहूंगा।

साथ-साथ लाल डोरा और एल.एम.सी. इनकी भी समस्या है। गांव में रहने वाला हर व्यक्ति इससे परिचित है। आबादी जिस तेजी के साथ इस समय बढ़ रही है, उस आबादी को रहने के लिए जगह भी तो चाहिए, लेकिन इसमें कहीं पर कोई प्रोविजन नहीं है। लाल डोरा और एल.एम.सी. के बारे में यह बिल कुछ स्पष्ट करे, ऐसा कुछ भी हमको देखने को नहीं मिला है। हमारा यह कहना है कि अधिग्रहण के समय गांवों में भी आबादी के लिए कुछ ज़मीन छोड़ने का एक निर्धारित मानदंड होना चाहिए, और इस बिल के अंदर भी एक ऐसा प्रोविजन होना चाहिए, यह हमारा मानना है।

सोशल इम्पैक्ट असैसमेंट और इनवायरमेंटल इम्पैक्ट असैसमेंट, जब यह सिलसिला प्रारंभ हो तो यह टाइम बाउंड होना चाहिए। कहीं ऐसा नहीं होना चाहिए कि सोशल इम्पैक्ट असैसमेंट और साथ ही इनवायरमेंटल इम्पैक्ट असैसमेंट आपने प्रारंभ कर दिया और साल-डेढ़ साल तक यह असैसमेंट का सिलसिला चलता रहे, तो मैं समझता हूं कि इसका जो परपज़ है, वह परपज़ पूरी तरह से समाप्त हो जाएगा।

अध्यक्ष महोदया, मैं बिल के क्लॉज 9 की तरफ आता हूं - अर्जेन्सी का प्रोविजन आ गया। सबसे खतरनाक प्रोविजन अर्जेन्सी का प्रोविजन है। यह अर्जेन्सी का जो प्रोविजन क्लॉज 9 का है, वह कहता क्या है। एक क्लॉज 38 है। क्लॉज 38 के तहत अर्जेन्सी प्रोविजन के माध्यम से यदि सरकार अधिग्रहण करती है तो क्लॉज 9 अधिग्रहण की प्रक्रिया को सोशल इम्पैक्ट असैसमेंट से मुक्त रखेगा। अब बताइए, गांवों की यही असली समस्या है, सबसे बड़ा संकट यही है - अर्जेन्सी प्रोविजन। उसका सोशल इम्पैक्ट असैसमेंट नहीं होगा, इनवायरमेंटल इम्पैक्ट असैसमेंट नहीं होगा। मंत्री जी, इस समस्या का निराकरण कैसे किया जाएगा, मैं इस संबंध में भी आपसे क्लैरिफिकेशन चाहूंगा, क्योंकि मैं जानता हूं कि गांवों में अधिकांश विवादों का कारण अर्जेन्सी प्रोविजन ही है।

मेरा सुझाव है कि क्लॉज 9 का उपयोग यदि कोई बहुत आपात स्थिति पैदा हो जाए तभी किया जाना चाहिए। मैं तो कहना चाहूंगा कि इस क्लॉज़ 9 को ही समाप्त कर दिया जाए, इसका कोई औचित्य नहीं रह गया है। किसी भी प्रकार का अधिग्रहण हो, प्राइवेट कम्पनीज के लिए हो अथवा पब्लिक परपज़ के लिए हो, सोशल इम्पैक्ट असैसमेंट और इनवायरमेंटल इम्पैक्ट असैसमेंट निश्चित रूप से होना चाहिए।

मैं नए बिल के क्लॉज 10 की ओर ध्यान आकर्षित करना चाहता हूं। क्लॉज 10 कहता है कि कुछ परिस्थितियों को छोड़कर मल्टी क्रॉप लैंड का अधिग्रहण नहीं किया जाए। मगर सैक्शन 2 के सब सैक्शन्स में यह बात कही गई है कि नहीं, किया जा सकता है यानी फिर से एक अधिग्रहण का रास्ता यहां खोल दिया गया है। एक तरफ कहा गया है कि मल्टी क्रॉप लैंड अथवा इरीगेटेड लैंड का एक्वीज़िशन नहीं होना चाहिए, लेकिन दूसरी तरफ उसका रास्ता भी खोल दिया गया है। हमारा मानना है कि जब तक किसान सहमति न दे तब तक कृषि योग्य भूमि का किसी भी सूरत में अधिग्रहण नहीं होना चाहिए। इस सरकार ने अभी दो-तीन दिन पहले फूड सिक्युरिटी बिल इसी संसद में पारित किया है। इस देश में फूड सिक्युरिटी की इतनी बड़ी क्राइसेज पैदा हो जाएगी कि मैं इस सरकार को याद दिलाना चाहता हूं कि जिस समय फॉरैस्ट कवर डिप्लीट करने लगा था, कम होने लगा था, उस समय इस सरकार को ही फॉरैस्ट कन्जर्वेशन एक्ट बनाना पड़ा था। वैसे ही खेती योग्य ज़मीन जो धीरे-धीरे एक्वीज़िशन के कारण कम होती चली जाएगी, तो एग्रीकल्चरल लैंड कन्जर्वेशन बिल फिर इसी संसद में लाना होगा और उसे एक्ट बनाना होगा। इसलिए मैं बार-बार आग्रह कर रहा हूं कि इरीगेटेड लैंड अथवा जिस खेत में फसल पैदा होती है, उसे एक्वायर मत कीजिए। काम चलाना है तो बहुत सारी बंजर भूमि पड़ी हुई है, उससे काम चला लीजिए। लेकिन खेती योग्य भूमि का अधिग्रहण किसी भी सूरत में नहीं होना चाहिए, यह मैं आपसे अनुरोध करना चाहता हूं। इस संबंध में पार्लियामेंट की स्टैंडिंग कमेटी ने भी अपनी रिकमैंडेशन में इस बात की चर्चा की है और साफ-साफ कहा है कि किसी भी सूरत में ऐसा नहीं होना चाहिए।

मैडम, मैं इस बिल के सबसे चिन्ताजनक बिन्दु की ओर आपका ध्यान आकर्षित करना चाहता हूं। क्लॉज 16(3) - यदि किसान द्वारा भूमि अधिग्रहण के संबंध में कोई ऑब्जैक्शन किया गया और सरकार द्वारा कोई फैसला आ गया, तो वह अपील नहीं कर सकता। यह कहां का इंसाफ है? मैं समझता हूं कि हमारे न्याय का जो मान्य सिद्धान्त है, यह उसके सर्वथा खिलाफ है। ऐसा क्यों होना चाहिए? क्या किसान को यह हक नहीं है कि यदि सरकार द्वारा कोई फैसला आ जाता है और वह किसान को मंजूर नहीं है तो वह अदालत नहीं जा सकता? इसलिए मंत्री जी, मैं आपसे अनुरोध करना चाहूंगा कि इस संबंध में यह व्यवस्था की जानी चाहिए कि यदि किसान द्वारा कोई आपत्ति की जाती है, वह संतुष्ट नहीं है और किसी कोर्ट में जाना चाहता है, तो उसे कोर्ट में जाने का अवसर दिया जाना चाहिए।

मैं एक सुझाव यह देना चाहता हूं कि बिल को पूरी तरह रिट्रॉस्पैक्टिव इफैक्ट के साथ लागू कीजिए। जहां लोगों ने कम्पेनसेशन नहीं लिया, चाहे जानबूझकर न लिया हो अथवा सरकार द्वारा न दिया गया हो अथवा जहां लैंड एक्वीज़िशन का प्रोसेस पूरा

नहीं हुआ है, यह बिल विद रिट्रॉस्पेक्टिव इफैक्ट उन सब ज़मीनों पर भी लागू होगा। मैं चाहूंगा कि आप संसद को अभी यह आश्वासन दें।  क्योंकि बहुत सारे मामले अभी भी उलझे हुए हैं।

बिल का एक और खतरनाक क्लॉज 38 है, जिसमें अर्जेन्सी प्रोविजन्स के तहत जो डिस्ट्रिक्ट मजिस्ट्रेट, डिस्ट्रिक्ट कलेक्टर होता है, उनको एक शक्ति दी गयी है, पावर दी गयी है कि आप नोटिफिकेशन करके तीन  दिन के बाद किसी भी लैंड का एक्वीज़िशन कर सकते हैं। मैं समझता हूं कि इस बिल को लाने का फिर परपज़ ही क्या है ? जब इस बिल को लाने का परपज़ ही पूरी तरह से डिफीट हो जाता है, तो फायदा क्या है। सरकार जब चाहे क्लॉज 38 का प्रयोग करके उन्हें बेदखल कर दे। मैं संसद में यह मांग करना चाहता हूं कि क्लॉज 38 को ही समास किया जाना चाहिए, लेकिन यदि  कोई आपात परिस्थितियां पैदा होती हैं, तो उस पर हमें कोई आपत्ति नहीं है। मैं उसका स्वागत करता हूं।

अब मैं बिल के क्लॉज 45 की ओर ध्यान आकर्षित करना चाहता हूं कि लैंड एक्वीज़िशन रिहैबिलिटेशन एंड रीसैटलमैंट अथॉरिटी के गठन का प्रोविजन किया गया है। ये अथॉरिटीज कितनी गठित होंगी, यह बिल में मैंशन नहीं है। क्या केवल स्टेट लैवल पर ही ये अथॉरिटीज बनेंगी अथवा केवल सैंट्रल लैवल पर ही बनेंगी ? हमारा यह मानना है कि भूमि अधिग्रहण की समस्या लगभग इस देश के अधिकांश जिलों में है। इसलिए अध्यक्ष महोदया, मैं यह मांग करना चाहता हूं कि जो अथॉरिटी बनाने की बात है, यह डिस्ट्रिक्ट हैडक्वार्टर पर निश्चित रूप से बनायी जानी चाहिए। यदि किन्हीं कारणों से डिस्ट्रिक्ट अथॉरिटीज पर जहां पर एक्वीज़िशन न होता हो, कुछ ऐसी समस्या है तो कम से कम कमिश्नरी स्तर से यह निश्चित रूप से बनाई जानी चाहिए। अथॉरिटीज को यह भी अधिकार दिया जाना चाहिए कि जैसे केसेज का निस्तारण, डिस्पोजल फास्ट ट्रैक कोर्ट जल्दी करती है, वैसे ही चूंकि लैंड एक्वीज़िशन का इश्यू बहुत ही सैंसिटिव होता है, ऐसी जो अथॉरिटीज बनें, इनका फास्ट ट्रैक कोर्ट की तरह ही जल्दी से जल्दी डिस्पोजल हो, एक ऐसा भी अधिकार अथॉरिटीज को दिया जाना चाहिए।

अध्यक्ष महोदया, मैंने कई बार देखा है कि आवश्यकता से अधिक भी लैंड एक्वीज़िशन प्रोजैक्ट कर लेते हैं, तो लैंड पड़ी की पड़ी रह जाती है, खुली रहती है। उसका कोई मतलब नहीं है। वैसे ज़मीन एक सीमित संसाधन है, एक लिमिटेड रिसोर्स है। इसका अधिकतम उपयोग कैसे हो, संसद को ही नहीं, बल्कि सारे देश को इस बात की चिन्ता करनी चाहिए। इसलिए हमारा कहना है कि इसे रोकने के लिए कोई न कोई ऐसा मैकेनिज्म डेवलप करना चाहिए, ताकि जरूरत से ज्यादा किसी भी सूरत में लैंड एक्वीज़िशन न हो। यदि कोई लैंड एक्वीज़िशन जरूरत से ज्यादा

कर लेता है तो उसके लिए उसका कोई उपयोग नहीं है। उसे किसानों को वापिस किया जाये या क्या किया जाये, इसके संबंध में भी सरकार को गंभीरतापूर्वक विचार करना चाहिए।

अध्यक्ष महोदया, इसके अतिरिक्त दो–तीन बातों की ओर मैं आपका ध्यान आकर्षित करना चाहता हूं। मौजूदा बिल में क्लाज 94 में कहा गया है कि यदि अधिग्रहीत भूमि पांच वर्षों तक उपयोग में नहीं आती है, तो या तो वह किसानों को वापस लौटा दी जायेगी या फिर वह ज़मीन सरकार के लैंड बैंक में चली जायेगी। ...(व्यवधान) ज़मीन वापस कर दी जाये, यह बात तो हमारी समझ में आती है, लेकिन वहीं पर आप हमारी स्टैंडिंग कमेटी की रिकमैंडेशन्स देखिये। स्टैंडिंग कमेटी की रिकमैंडेशन्स कैसे इग्नोर होती है? जबकि स्टैंडिंग कमेटी ने अपनी रिपोर्ट में साफ तौर पर कहा है कि यदि किसान अपना कम्पेनसेशन लौटा देता है, तो लैंड के अनयूज्ड रहने की दशा में वह भूमि किसान को वापस सौंपी जाये। यदि मान लीजिए कि विशेष परिस्थितियों में लैंड बैंक में वह ज़मीन जाती है, मान लीजिए कि किसान अपना मुआवजा वापस नहीं करता है तब ऐसा किया जा सकता है, उस पर मुझे कोई आपत्ति नहीं है। मगर मौजूदा बिल में जो स्टैंडिंग कमेटी की रिकमैंडेशन है, उस संबंध में कोई क्लैरिटी नहीं है। इसलिए मैं मंत्री जी से यह भी जानना चाहता हूं कि क्या आप इससे सहमत हैं?

अध्यक्ष महोदया, मैं कम्पेनसेशन के बारे में थोड़ा ध्यान आकर्षित करना चाहूंगा। बिल का जो नया ड्राफ्ट है, नया बिल है, उसमें ग्रामीण क्षेत्रों में मार्केट वैल्यू का एक से दोगुना और शहरी क्षेत्रों में मार्केट वैल्यू के बराबर ही मूल्य निर्धारित होगा। इसमें सोलेशियम भी शामिल हैं। जब सोलेशियम शामिल हो जायेगा, तो शहरी क्षेत्रों को दोगुना और ग्रामीण क्षेत्रों को चार गुना, लेकिन उसके लिए सीमा निर्धारित की गयी है कि इतने किलोमीटर के बाद इतना और इतने किलोमीटर के बाद इतने टाइम कम्पेनसेशन दिया जायेगा। वन टाइम, 1.25 टाइम, 1.50 टाइम, ऐसा किया गया है। यह निर्धारित कर पाना, क्योंकि मैं जानता हूं, यह काम बहुत ही कठिन होता है। शहर से गांव कितनी दूर है, कहां से आप नापेंगे? पहले यह भी तो तय होना चाहिए। गांव की दूरी आप कहां से मानेंगे, इसके बारे में भी कुछ क्लैरिफिकेशन होना चाहिए। कम्पेनसेशन के बारे में मैं संसद में अपनी आपत्ति दर्ज करना चाहता हूं। कम्पेनसेशन के बारे में जो भी नार्म्स निर्धारित किये गये हैं, वे कम हैं। यहां पर मैं अपनी आपत्ति दर्ज करना चाहूंगा। क्यों कम है? क्योंकि जो लैंड की रजिस्ट्री होती है, वह अंडर वैल्यू होती है, मार्केट वैल्यू पर नहीं होती है। यदि मार्केट वैल्यू के आधार पर कम्पेनसेशन उपलब्ध कराया जाए, तो कम-से-कम किसी हद तक उन्हें राहत मिल सकती है। लेकिन जो कुछ भी रजिस्ट्री ऑफिस के द्वारा लैंड वैल्यूड है, उस आधार पर करेंगे,

तो किसानों को इसका खामियाजा भुगतना पड़ेगा। एक सुझाव और देना चाहता हूं कि हर गांव के चारों ओर कम-से-कम पांच सौ मीटर की एक चौहद्दी छोड़ी जानी चाहिए, एक क्षेत्र छोड़ा जाना चाहिए। ताकि लाल डोरा आबादी का दबाव बढ़ने पर इसे बढ़ाया जा सके। लेकिन इसमें इसका कोई उल्लेख नहीं है।

अध्यक्ष महोदया, मैं एक गंभीर बिन्दु की ओर ध्यान आकृष्ट कराना चाहूंगा। कभी-कभी किसानों का एक बार डिसप्लेसमेंट (विस्थापन) होता है, लेकिन कभी-कभी दुबारा भी उनके डिसप्लेसमेंट के हालात पैदा हो जाते हैं। वैसी परिस्थिति में यह सरकार क्या कदम उठाएगी? इसके बारे में भी मैं मंत्री जी से क्लैरिफिकेशन चाहूंगा। वैसे प्रिकॉशन यह लिया जाना चाहिए कि किसानों का डबल डिसप्लेसमेंट किसी भी सूरत में न हो।

अब मैं शहरों की ओर आता हूं। दिल्ली ही नहीं, बड़े-बड़े शहरों के किनारे चले जाइए, झुग्गी-झोपड़ियों में बसे हुए हमारे जो गरीब हैं, उनकी दयनीय हालत है। भारत की राजधानी दिल्ली की सड़कों पर निकलिए। आपने पतली-पतली टांगों वाले उन गरीब बच्चों को देखा होगा। वे सड़कों पर किस तरह की जिन्दगी बसर करते हैं? यदि म्यूनिसिपल कारपोरेशन बुलडोज़र लेकर उनकी झोपड़ी को गिराने चला जाता है, तो मैं समझता हूं, किसी भी संवेदनशील व्यक्ति की आंखें नम हो जाती होंगी, उसका कलेजा दहल उठता होगा। लेकिन यहां पर जो झुग्गी-झोपड़ी वाले बसे हैं, यह कहा जाता है कि यह अतिक्रमण किया गया है। निर्ममतापूर्वक इन्हें हटा सकते हो, तो हटा दो। लेकिन मैं जानता हूं कि झुग्गी-झोपड़ी वालों के लिए आप इस बिल में व्यवस्था नहीं कर सकते। हमने भी बिल तैयार कराया है, मुझे जानकारी है, आप ऐसा नहीं करा सकते। लेकिन ग्रामीण विकास मंत्रालय देखते हैं, भले ही शहरों के किनारे वे बसते हों, मंत्री जी उनके बारे में जरूर सोचिए। यदि आप इसके लिए अलग से बिल लाएंगे, तो हम लोग उस बिल को सर्वसम्मति से, जिसमें झुग्गी-झोपड़ी का इंसान रहता है, हम संसद में पास करेंगे।

अध्यक्ष महोदया, मैं अब स्टैंडिंग कमेटी की रिपोर्ट की ओर ध्यान आकर्षित कराना चाहता हूं। स्टैंडिंग कमेटी ने अपनी रिपोर्ट में एक बहुत ही गंभीर विषय की ओर ध्यान आकर्षित कराया है। इस देश में 90 प्रतिशत अधिग्रहण केंद्र और राज्य सरकारों द्वारा बनाये गये क़ानूनों के माध्यम से होता है। जिनकी एक अलग से सूची बनायी गयी है, उसमें उसे रखा गया है। हैरानी की यह बात है कि जो विधेयक इस सदन में भूमि अधिग्रहण की भावी रूपरेखा पर विचारार्थ रखा गया है, उसके प्रावधान इन कानूनों पर लागू नहीं होंगे, जिन्हें एक अलग सूची में चिह्नित किया गया है। मेरा कहना यह है कि इन कानूनों को इस विधेयक से बाहर रखने का क्या औचित्य है? यह मैं माननीय मंत्री जी से जानना चाहता हूं। हम लोगों ने माननीय मंत्री जी को एक

सुझाव दिया था कि ज़मीन का अधिग्रहण नहीं किया जाना चाहिए, बल्कि लीज़ का प्रोविज़न किया जाना चाहिए। मंत्री जी आपने इसे माना है, मैं आपका स्वागत करता हूं, लेकिन इसमें अभी आपने रास्ता खुला रखा है। यह मैंने देखा है। सरकार यदि चाहे, तो किसान कहता रहे कि हमारी ज़मीन लीज़ पर ले लीजिए और सरकार कहेगी कि नहीं-नहीं लीज़ पर नहीं लूंगा, मैं इसका एक्वीज़िशन करूंगा। मैं यह सुझाव देना चाहता हूं कि इस बिल में यह प्रोविज़न होना चाहिए कि ज़मीन लीज़ पर ली जाए अथवा इसका एक्वीज़िशन किया जाए, इसका फैसला किसानों की सहमति से होगा, बिना किसानों की सहमति के नहीं होगा। मैं यह एक विनम्र निवेदन करना चाहूंगा।

अध्यक्ष महोदया, बहुत से बिन्दु हैं जिन पर विचार किया जा सकता था, लेकिन पढ़ने के बाद मैंने सोचा कि यदि इन सभी बिन्दुओं पर मैं बोलूंगा, तो लगभग डेढ़-पौने दो घंटे का भाषण हो जाएगा, तो आपको घंटी बजानी पड़ेगी। उस घंटी से बचने के लिए मैं जितना शॉर्ट में बोल सकता था, उतना शॉर्ट करने की कोशिश की है।

अध्यक्ष महोदया, मैं आपके माध्यम से इस सरकार से विनम्र अनुरोध करना चाहता हूं कि भूमि अधिग्रहण बहुत ही संवेदनशील प्रश्न है, बहुत गंभीरतापूर्वक लिया जाए और अब भी मंत्री जी, आप अपने विवेक से जो भी संशोधन स्वीकार कर सकते हों, उनको स्वीकार कीजिए जिससे किसानों के लिए यह बिल हितैषी बन सके, उसके लिए आप भरपूर कोशिश कीजिए।

इसी निवेदन के साथ, अध्यक्ष महोदया, आपको बहुत-बहुत धन्यवाद देते हुए अपनी बात समाप्त करता हूं।

## [2] Mulayam Singh Yadav

**श्री मुलायम सिंह यादव (मैनपुरी):** सभापति महोदय, आपको बहुत-बहुत धन्यवाद। भूमि अधिग्रहण के संबंध में मैं अपनी बात कहना चाहता हूं कि किसानों की भूमि का अधिग्रहण करने की आवश्यकता नहीं है, क्योंकि लाखों एकड़ ऊसर और बंजर ज़मीन पड़ी है। मैं यह इसलिए कह रहा हूं क्योंकि मैंने यह कार्य करके दिखाया है, हमें जब ज़मीन की आवश्यकता पड़ी, आपको पता है आप उन दिनों सदन में थे, हमने हरदोई में ऊसर-बंजर ज़मीन का अधिग्रहण किया था। कानपुर में ऊसर-बंजर ज़मीन पड़ी थी, उसका अधिग्रहण किया था। इटावा में बीहड़ तुड़वा दिया और उस बीहड़ की ज़मीन का हमने अधिग्रहण किया। यह विचित्र मानसिकता वाले लोग हैं कि जब ज़मीन देखने जाते हैं तो किसान की उपजाऊ ज़मीन पर अंगुली रखते हैं। मैं यह जानना चाहता हूं कि आज देश की स्थिति क्या है? तीन फीसदी ज़मीन प्रति वर्ष कम हो रही है। कॉलेज बन रहे हैं, मेडिकल कॉलेज बन रहे हैं, सड़कें बन रही हैं और तमाम काम हो रहे हैं। जनसंख्या बढ़ रही है और ज़मीन घट रही है ज़मीन घटने पर

पैदावार घटेगी तो मंत्री जी आपने इसका विकल्प क्या सोचा है ? तीन फीसदी ज़मीन हिन्दुस्तान में प्रति वर्ष कम हो रही है। आप पता लगाइए। मेरे आंकड़े गलत नहीं हैं। हमने पता लगाया है कि तीन फीसदी ज़मीन हिन्दुस्तान में प्रति वर्ष कम हो रही है। आप जब जमीन अधिग्रहण करते हैं तो इसमें कोई आपत्ति नहीं है, लेकिन ज़मीन अधिग्रहण कीजिए आगरा से लेकर बांदा तक का जो बीहड़ पड़ा है, ऊसर-बंजर ज़मीन हर जिले में पड़ी है। उस ज़मीन को क्यों नहीं अधिग्रहित करते हैं ? जहां खेती-बाड़ी होती है, पैदावार होती है, उसी ज़मीन पर आप क्यों निशाना लगाते हैं ? मैं आपको सलाह दे रहा हूं, आपको सोचना चाहिए कि खेती के अलावा किसान के पास क्या है। अगर आपके पास कुछ है तो जवाब में बता दीजिए। किसान के पास खेती के अलावा क्या है ? क्या आपको इसके बारे में व्यावहारिक जानकारी है ? आप जानते हैं कि जिसके पास ज़मीन नहीं होगी उसके लड़के की शादी नहीं होगी।

**श्री मुलायम सिंह यादव:** क्या आपको यह अनुभव है ? यहां बहुत से लोगों को अनुभव होगा। राजनाथ सिंह जी, क्या आपको अनुभव है कि अगर गांव में किसी के पास खेती नहीं होती है तो उसके लड़के की शादी नहीं होती है ? अध्यक्ष जी, व्यावहारिक जीवन की बातों को भी सोचना होगा। मेरी साफ राय है कि किसान की ज़मीन छूने की बिल्कुल आवश्यकता नहीं है, उसका विकल्प है, बंजर-बीहड़ ज़मीन का अधिग्रहण कीजिए उस पर कारखाने लगवाइए। हम आपको लाखों एकड़ ज़मीन बताएंगे, आगरा, एटा से औरैया तक चले जाइए, कानपुर तक चले जाइए, नोएडा चले जाइए। सभी जगह बंजर ज़मीन पड़ी है।

**श्री मुलायम सिंह यादव:** अधिकारियों से सावधान हो जाना। आपको तो अनुभव है। आप स्वयं इस मामले को देखना, अधिकारियों पर मत छोड़ देना। अगर अधिकारियों पर छोड़ दिया तो जहां बढ़िया ज़मीन दिखी वहां निशाना लगा देंगे।

दूसरी बात किसानों की ज़मीन के अधिग्रहण के बारे में है। जहां परती ज़मीन है, और वह खेती योग्य है। यूपी सरकार ने परती भूमि पर इफैक्ट किया है, भूमि सेना गठित की है। आपको भूमि सेना गठित करनी होगी। इससे दो काम होंगे, बंजर-बीहड़ ज़मीन खेती लायक होगी और लोगों को रोजगार मिलेगा, बेरोजगार मजदूरों को काम मिलेगा। आप रिपोर्ट मंगा लीजिए यह हमने किया था, जो भूमिहीन थे उन्होंने खेती लायक ज़मीन बनाई, मैंने कहा कि जो ज़मीन खेती लायक बना देगा उसी के नाम कर देंगे। उन्होंने मन से काम किया और हमने ज़मीन उन्हीं को दी। आपको पता है कि ज़मीन उन्हीं को दे दी। आप भी इसी तरह से काम कीजिए। इससे ज़मीन खेती लायक बढ़ेगी, लोग मन से काम करेंगे, आपको समर्थन मिलेगा और सरकार की तारीफ होगी। यह बिल तो पूरी तरह से किसानों को बर्बाद करने के लिए है। आपको

ऐसा नहीं करना चाहिए। अगर बंजर-बीहड़ ज़मीन नहीं है और जरूरत है तो भी वह किसान की राय से ज़मीन लें। किसान की राय ही लेनी चाहिए जबकि सब लोग किसान को ज़मीन का मालिक नहीं मानते हैं। सब लोग अपनी संपत्ति बेचते हैं, उनसे बात होती है तो वे जितना रुपया मांगते हैं उचित दाम होता है तो वह ज़मीन दे देते हैं। इसी तरह किसान की जरूरत देखनी चाहिए और किसान से सीधी बात करनी चाहिए कि वह कितना रुपया मांग रहा है। अभी हमने एक हफ्ते पहले सैफई में मेडिकल कॉलेज के लिए ज़मीन ली है, 75,00,000 रुपए प्रति एकड़। उन्होंने मांग की कि 75,00,000 रुपए एक एकड़ के लेंगे। अगर वह एक करोड़ मांगते तो हम एक करोड़ दे देते। मैं जानता था कि उनके पास कुछ बचेगा नहीं, हमने दे दिया लेकिन आप कितना देंगे? अगर जरूरत पड़े तो ज़मीन लेना नहीं तो ज़मीन घटी तो पैदावार घटेगी, अन्न घटेगा। जनसंख्या तो बढ़ेगी, यह भी संकट देश के सामने है। आप को इस बात को भी ध्यान में रखना चाहिए।

**श्री मुलायम सिंह यादव:** मैं आपसे कह रहा था कि किसान की सहमति के बिना ज़मीन का अधिग्रहण नहीं होना चाहिए। किसान उसका मालिक है, हर मालिक अपनी सम्पत्ति को अपने आप बेचता है, भाव तय करता है। जहां तक मैंने आपको राय दी है और आपको अब भी राय दे रहा हूं, बहुत बड़ा कल्याण हो जायेगा। आगरा से लेकर बांदा तक का बीहड़ तुड़वा दीजिए, उसमें कारखाने लगा दीजिए, इससे देश का बहुत बड़ा कल्याण हो जायेगा। आप डकैतों से बच जायेंगे और सब बातों से बच जायेंगे और लाखों एकड़ ज़मीन बच जायेगी। उससे किसानों का बहुत भला हो जाएगा और बीहड़ ज़मीन का उपयोग भी ।

**श्री शरद यादव:** बहुत उपजाऊ ज़मीन है।

**श्री मुलायम सिंह यादव:** वह उपजाऊ ज़मीन है, जहां हमने अपने इलाके में बीहड़ को ठीक कराया है, वहां सबसे अच्छी पैदावार हो रही है। मैं आपके सामने कह रहा हूं कि सरकार ऐसा करके दिखाये। मैं वह बात दोहराना नहीं चाहता कि जो परती ज़मीन पड़ी है, खाली ज़मीन पड़ी है, उसमें आप कल-कारखाने लगाइये। लेकिन हमने आपको यह बता दिया है कि जहां असली उर्वरा ज़मीन है, उपजाऊ ज़मीन है, उसका अधिग्रहण मत कीजिए।

**श्री शरद यादव:** आपके इलाके में कितनी ज़मीनें बेकार पड़ी हुई है।

**श्री मुलायम सिंह यादव:** हां बेकार पड़ी है, वही मैं कह रहा हूं कि मेरे इलाके में काफी ज़मीन बेकार पड़ी है।

**सभापति महोदय:** माननीय मुलायम सिंह जी को मालूम है।

**श्री मुलायम सिंह यादव:** आप इटावा, मैनपुरी में चले जाइये, औरैया, कानपुर, बांदा तक यमुना के किनारे लाखों एकड़ ज़मीन हो सकती है और बहुत उपजाऊ हो सकती है, आप उसे लीजिए। लेकिन मैं आपको सलाह दे रहा हूं कि किसान की ज़मीन को अधिग्रहित मत करना, उसके पास कुछ नहीं है। खेती के अलावा उसके पास कुछ नहीं है। परती, बेकार ज़मीन पर कोई भी फैक्टरी या कारखाना लगे तो आप लगायें। मैं बहुत ज्यादा लम्बा भाषण नहीं दूंगा। लेकिन जो खेती लायक ज़मीन है, उसे आप किसी कीमत पर मत लीजिए और मैंने जो सुझाव दिया है कि बीहड़ में ज़मीन की कमी नहीं है, आप उस पर फैक्टरी, कारखाने लगाइये, यही मेरी स्पष्ट राय है।

## [3] Surendra Singh Nagar

**श्री सुरेन्द्र सिंह नागर:** सभापति जी, आपने मुझे भूमि अर्जन, पुनर्वासन और पुनर्व्यवस्थापन विधेयक, 2011 पर बोलने का मौका दिया, मेरी बहन मायावती जी ने मुझे बोलने का मौका दिया, इसके लिए मैं आपका और उनका आभार व्यक्त करता हूं। जैसा इस बिल के बारे में बताया गया, मीनाक्षी जी कह रही थीं कि बड़ा ऐतिहासिक बिल है। लेकिन सभापति जी, अब आपका ध्यान इधर नहीं है...(व्यवधान) क्योंकि यह हमारा भी पहला मौका है और आपको भी मैं आसन पर देख रहा हूं, हालांकि हम चाहते थे कि आप कहीं और बैठें।

**श्री सुरेन्द्र सिंह नागर:** जब-जब चुनाव आते हैं, तब-तब कांग्रेस पार्टी को इस बिल की याद आती है। मुझे ध्यान है कि सन् 2008 में मेरे लोकसभा क्षेत्र गौतम बुद्ध नगर में कांग्रेस के एक बड़े नेता ने जाकर मीटिंग की थी और सन् 2009 के लोकसभा के चुनावों से पहले वादा किया था कि सन् 1894 का जो भूमि अधिग्रहण बिल है, उसमें हम संशोधन करेंगे। लोकसभा का चुनाव हो गया। सत्ता में आ गए। चार वर्ष से ज्यादा का समय भी निकल गया। अब चूंकि चुनाव नज़दीक हैं तो इनको किसानों की याद दोबारा से आई है। लेकिन जयराम रमेश जी, किसान अब इतना बेवकूफ़ नहीं रहा है। वह आपके झांसे में आने वाला नहीं है। वह इसलिए झांसे में आने वाला नहीं है क्योंकि आपने बार-बार वादा किया है। आपने सन् 2008 में वायदा किया। जिस भट्टा-परसौल का जिक्र मीनाक्षी जी ने किया, वह भी मेरे लोकसभा क्षेत्र में आता है। आपके एक बड़े नेता वहां गए और गांव-गांव जाकर किसानों से वादा किया कि सन् 1894 का जो भूमि अधिग्रहण बिल है, हम उसमें संशोधन करेंगे। वह बात सन् 2010 की है। मेरे क्षेत्र से किसानों का एक डेलिगेशन भी आया। जयराम जी, वह

इस देश के प्रधानमंत्री जी से मिला। प्रधानमंत्री जी ने वादा किया कि हम अगले सत्र में ही भूमि अधिग्रहण बिल में संशोधन लेकर आएंगे। ...(व्यवधान) हालांकि मुझे इतना कहना है, क्योंकि बहुत अपेक्षाएं थीं। सन् 2008 के बाद से देश का किसान इंतजार कर रहा था कि एक बिल आएगा, उनके लिए कुछ नई चीजें होंगी, उनका मुआवज़ा बढ़ेगा। लेकिन मैं इतना कहना चाहूंगा कि बिल तो आया, लोग कहते हैं कि देर से आए, दुरुस्त आए लेकिन मैं कहूंगा कि देर से भी आए और दुरुस्त भी नहीं आए। आपने नकल भी की लेकिन वह भी तरीके से नहीं की। उस समय उत्तर प्रदेश में बहुजन समाज पार्टी की जो सरकार थी, सन् 2010 में हम लोग एक नया लैंड एक्वीज़िशन बिल ले कर आए थे, जो राज्य सरकार की सीमाओं के भीतर होता है। उसमें हमने किसान को मुआवजा देने की बात नहीं की। वह बिल इस बिल से बहुत बेहतर था। उस बिल में हमने किसान को भागीदारी देने का वादा किया था और किसान से वादा किया था कि अगर हम आपकी ज़मीन लेंगे, दोनों ऑप्शन हमने दिये थे, बहन मायावती जी की सरकार की वह पॉलिसी थी कि हम या तो आपको 23 परसेंट विकसित ज़मीन देंगे या मुआवजा और 10 परसेंट विकसित ज़मीन देंगे। आप कहते हो कि हमने बेहतर मुआवजे की बात की है। अगर आप उस पुनर्वास नीति को ले आते, जिसकी आप बात करते हो, उसे तो ऑलरेडी वर्ष 2010 में हमारी बहुजन पार्टी की सरकार लेकर आ चुकी है। अगर आप बात करते हो कि प्राइवेट सेक्टर को 70 परसेंट सहमति जरूरी है, आपने कह दिया कि परिवारों की सहमति जरूरी है। जो हमारी उत्तर प्रदेश की बहुजन समाज पार्टी की उस समय की सरकार की नीति थी, उसमें यह है कि केवल परिवारों की सहमति नहीं, 70 प्रतिशत ज़मीन किसानों की पहले प्राइवेट बिल्डर को खरीदनी पड़ेगी, तब सरकार उसका अधिग्रहण कर सकती है। यह फर्क है हमारी नीति में और आपकी नीति में। आपने उसकी नकल कर ली, आपने बहुत बड़ा मुद्दा बनाया। इस प्रदेश में किसानों को उकसाने का काम किया और यहां तक नौबत आयी कि किसानों पर गोली चलवाने का काम भी किया क्योंकि आपका काम है कि कह जाओ, कर जाओ और चुनाव में वोट ले जाओ, उसके बाद भगवान भरोसे छोड़ जाओ। अब फिर वोट का मौसम आ गया है। इसलिए मैं आपसे कहना चाहता हूं कि जो मुआवजे की बात आप कह रहे हैं, उसमें आपने जयराम रमेश जी सारे अधिकार कलेक्टर को दिये हैं, 1894 का भी जो कानून है, उसमें भी सारे अधिकार कलेक्टर को हैं। सोनिया जी यहां उपस्थित नहीं हैं, मैं उनके जल्दी स्वस्थ होने की कामना करता हूं। उनकी जो नेशनल एडवाइजरी काउंसिल है, उसकी भी बात जयराम जी आपने नहीं मानी है। उन्होंने कहा था कि ग्रामीण क्षेत्र में तीन गुणा और सोलेशीएम तीन गुणा, छह गुणा मुआवजा ग्रामीण क्षेत्र को दिया जायेगा और शहरी क्षेत्र में वह जो ड्रॉफ्ट है, नेशनल एडवाइजरी काउंसिल का, उसमें वादा किया था कि

शहरी क्षेत्र में दो गुणा और सोलेशीअम दो गुणा, चार गुणा मुआवजा आप देने का काम करेंगे। जब आपने यह बिल प्रस्तुत किया तो इस बिल में आपने उसको ग्रामीण क्षेत्र में दो गुणा प्लस सोलेशीअम दो गुणा चार गुणा और शहरी क्षेत्र में एक गुणा प्लस एक गुणा सोलेशीअम करके दो गुणा करने का काम किया। यह आपकी सोच है। जो सोनिया जी की अध्यक्षता वाली एन.ए.सी. की रिकमेंडेशंस हैं, वे भी आपने इसमें नहीं मानी हैं, उनकी बात को भी आपने नहीं माना है। उसके बावजूद आपने कह दिया कि मुआवजा कलेक्टर तय करेगा। जो संशोधन आप जयराम जी लेकर आये हैं, उसमें आपने कलेक्टर को अधिकार दिया है कि वह जो दो गुणा आपने राशि तय की थी, उस दो गुणा को घटाकर आपने एक से दो गुणा कर दिया है। अब यह कलेक्टर का अधिकार है कि वह एक गुणा मुआवजा दे, वह दो गुणा मुआवजा दे और दूरी वह तय करेगा। मैं जिस क्षेत्र से आता हूं, हर 10 से 20 किलोमीटर पर कस्बा है, शहरी क्षेत्र है। आप बताइये कि आप कैसे पे करेंगे? मेरा इसमें एक सुझाव है कि यह तय होना चाहिए कि जो ग्रामसभा है, जो उसकी ज़मीन है, उसे ग्रामीण क्षेत्र की ज़मीन माना जाना चाहिए और जो नगर पालिका की सीमा है, उसको नगरीय क्षेत्र की ज़मीन माना जाना चाहिए। यह मेरा सुझाव है और ऐसा होने पर ही उस क्षेत्र के किसान को न्याय मिल सकेगा। इसके अलावा आप जब मुआवजा तय करते हैं, सबसे बड़ा फेर इसमें एक है कि लैंड यूज का बड़ा खेल है। मेरा इसमें आपसे एक अनुरोध है कि जब आप ज़मीन का मुआवजा तय करें तो पहले उसका जो उद्देश्य है कि आप किसके लिए उसको एक्वायर कर रहे हैं, वह स्पष्ट होना चाहिए। उसके बाद जो उसकी कीमत हो, उससे किसान को मुआवजा मिलना चाहिए, तब किसान को बाजार मूल्य का मुआवजा मिल पायेगा, नहीं तो किसान को बाजार मूल्य का मुआवजा नहीं मिल पायेगा। किसान तो वैसे ही रजिस्ट्री कम में करा लेता है। उससे भी अच्छी बात यह होती कि आप किसान को विकास में भागीदार बना देते तो बहुत अच्छा होता। आपने प्राधिकरण को जो पब्लिक परपज़ में प्राधिकरण को अधिकार दे दिया है, कोई बात नहीं शहर विकसित होने हैं।

आदरणीय सभापति जी, जब रक्षा के लिए, रक्षा मंत्रालय के लिए भूमि की जरूरत पड़ी है तो इस देश के किसान ने कभी मना नहीं किया है। अगर हमें सड़क बनानी है तो इस देश का किसान कभी विरोध नहीं करता है, उस पर गलत आरोप लगाया जाता है। अगर रेल ट्रैक बनता है तो किसान कभी मना नहीं करता है। अगर पोस्ट ऑफिस बनता है तो किसान कभी मना नहीं करता है। अगर स्कूल बनता है तो किसान कभी ज़मीन देने से मना नहीं करता है। लेकिन उसको परेशानी तब होती है जब ज़बरन उसकी ज़मीन का अधिग्रहण करके लैंड यूज़ चेन्ज करके महंगे दाम पर बेचा जाता है। किसान की मुसीबत यहाँ तक हो जाती है कि अपने घर में रहने की जगह उसको

नहीं बच पाती है क्योंकि सारी ज़मीन उसकी अधिग्रहीत कर ली जाती है। एक मैंने जो विकसित भूमि देने की बात की है, आपने 20 परसेंट भूमि देने की बात कही है जबकि बहुजन समाज पार्टी की हमारी सरकार की जो नीति है, उसमें 23 प्रतिशत की बात की है। अगर आज आपने जो भूमि का दुगना और चौगुना मुआवज़ा देने की बात की है, अगर आपकी नीति लागू होगी तो मैं जिस नोएडा-ग्रेटर नोएडा क्षेत्र से मैं आता हूँ, आज वहाँ 75 लाख रुपये एकड़ का रेट आता है। अगर आप 23 परसेंट की जो बहुजन समाज पार्टी की सरकार की नीति है, उससे लेने का काम करेंगे तो साढ़े चार करोड़ रुपये एकड़ किसान को ज़मीन मिलेगी। आप इसमें संशोधन करिये। इसके अलावा आपने बार-बार कहा कि पब्लिक परपज़ को हम डिफाइन करेंगे, उसे परिभाषित करेंगे। जयराम रमेश जी से मैं कहना चाहता हूँ कि पब्लिक परपज़ में तो आपने कुछ ओरिजिनल बिल ही नहीं छोड़ा, सारी चीजें आपने डाल दी हैं। प्राइवेट सैक्टर की बात आपने की है। जो प्राधिकरण क्षेत्र होते हैं, जयराम रमेश जी को पता नहीं जानकारी हो या न हो, लेकिन मेरे क्षेत्र में बड़ी समस्या रहती है। वे पहले नोटिफाई कर देते हैं। एरिया पहले नोटिफाई हो जाता है, उसके 20 साल बाद तक उसका विकास नहीं होता है। किसान को यह अधिकार नहीं होता है कि अगर उसे जानवर पालने के लिए एक मकान बनाना हो या उसे पशुचारा खिलाने के लिए कुछ बनाना हो तो उसकी परमीशन भी उसे प्राधिकरण से लेनी होती है। इसको ध्यान में रखा जाए, इसे खत्म किया जाए कि जितनी लैंड को डेवलप करना हो, उतनी ज़मीन नोटिफाई होनी चाहिए, उससे ज़्यादा ज़मीन नोटिफाई नहीं होनी चाहिए। इससे बहुत बड़ी परेशानी किसान को आती है। मैं बहुत ज़्यादा टैक्निकल बातों में नहीं जाना चाहता हूँ।

**श्री सुरेन्द्र सिंह नागर:** महोदय, पहली बार स्वर्गीय इंदिरा गांधी जी ने जो 1894 का भूमि अधिग्रहण अधिनियम था, उसमें संशोधन किया। आपको उनकी भी परवाह नहीं, उसे भी आप भूल गए। उसमें उन्होंने अधिकार दिया था कि 28ए के तहत अगर किसान मुआवज़े को लेकर संतुष्ट नहीं है तो वह हाई कोर्ट तक जा सकता था। हमारा संवैधानिक अधिकार है कि हम न्याय की लड़ाई के लिए कोर्ट जा सकते हैं, उस अधिकार को भी आपने इस बिल में छीन लिया। आप वह अधिकार वापस दें। मैं मीनाक्षी जी से कहना चाहता हूँ कि वह संशोधन किसी और ने नहीं दिया था, स्वर्गीय इंदिरा गांधी जी की सरकार के समय में वह संशोधन हुआ था। अंत में मैं आपका बहुत ज़्यादा समय नहीं लूँगा।

**श्री सुरेन्द्र सिंह नागर:** मैं क्षमा भी चाहूंगा, लेकिन चूंकि आज इस लोकसभा में जिधर भी देखें, तो मैडम ही मैडम हैं, ऊपर चेयर से देखें या इधर से देखें या उधर से देखें। यह अच्छी बात है।

अंत में मैं कहना चाहता हूँ कि आपने एसईजेड को इससे बाहर रखा है। आपने एक तरीका निकाला है। देश के बड़े-बड़े पूंजीपतियों को आपने ज़मीन देने का एक रास्ता निकाला है। मैं इसका विरोध करता हूं। जिस लोकसभा क्षेत्र से मैं आता हूं, वहां पिछले सात-आठ साल से देश के एक बड़े घराने को 2500 एकड़ ज़मीन दी गई। वह 2500 एकड़ ज़मीन तीन सौ रुपये प्रति वर्ग मीटर पर एक्वायर की गई। उस 2500 एकड़ ज़मीन पर आज तक एसईजेड नहीं बन पाया है।...(व्यवधान) बहुत समझदार लोग हैं।...(व्यवधान) उस 2500 एकड़ ज़मीन की कीमत आज 40 से 50 हजार रुपये प्रति वर्ग मीटर है। जयराम जी, आप एसईजेड को इसमें शामिल कीजिए, एसईजेड को बाहर मत कीजिए, नहीं तो किसानों को बहुत बड़ा नुकसान होगा। अब एक और चक्कर हो गया है कि एक डर दिखाया जा रहा है।...(व्यवधान) मुरादाबाद नहीं मुम्बई है। मुरादाबाद नहीं है।...(व्यवधान) एक डर दिखाया जा रहा है और पूरे देश में एक माहौल बनाया जा रहा है कि अगर यह भूमि अधिग्रहण बिल पास हो गया तो इस देश में इंडस्ट्री नहीं लग पाएगी, विकास का कोई काम नहीं हो पाएगा। यह झूठा डर है। इंडस्ट्री क्यों नहीं लग पाएगी? आप किसान को उसकी ज़मीन की सही कीमत दे दो, बाजार मूल्य दे दो, किसान इस देश के विकास में कभी न आढ़े आया है और न आढ़े आएगा। लेकिन एक बात जरूर है कि उसकी ज़मीन की कीमत आप तय करेंगे, उसकी फसल का मूल्य आप तय करेंगे, सारी चीजें सरकार तय करेगी।

**श्री सुरेन्द्र सिंह नागर:** सारी चीजें तय करने का अधिकार सरकार को मिलना चाहिए। आपने कहा कि प्राइवेट सेक्टर को 70 परसेंट ज़मीन सहमति से ली जानी चाहिए। हमारे यूपी में हाईटेक पॉलिसी है, जिसमें 70 प्रतिशत ज़मीन सहमति से नहीं, बल्कि प्राइवेट बिल्डर को किसानों से खरीदनी पड़ेगी। उसके बाद 30 परसेंट ज़मीन एक्वायर की जा सकती है। आप कर दीजिए, इसमें कोई परेशानी नहीं है। लेकिन इसमें एक परेशानी जयराम जी यह है कि आप नोटीफाइड कर देते हैं कि पांच गांवों की ज़मीन हमने इस बिल्डर के नाम कर दी। इससे कॉम्पटीशन खत्म हो जाता है और वह अपनी मर्जी पर, अपने रेट पर किसानों से ज़मीन खरीद लेता है, जिससे किसान को बाजार का भाव नहीं मिल पाता है। ये सारी परेशानियां इसमें हैं। मुझे आशा है, हालांकि राजनाथ सिंह जी यहां नहीं हैं, उन्होंने भी कुछ सुझाव रखे थे। उनकी सरकार भी रही है, आपकी भी सरकार रही है, आपका खेल रहा है। मैं अंत में कहना चाहता हूं कि जो संशोधन मैंने रखे हैं, आप उन्हें इनकोरपोरेट करेंगे। अगर इन संशोधनों से सुधार कर लेते हैं, तो निश्चित रूप से मुझे लगेगा कि किसानों का भला होगा। मैं इस बिल का समर्थन इसलिए करता हूं कि अगर इसमें कुछ संशोधन कर लिए जाएं, तो इस बिल का मैं समर्थन भी करता हूं।

## [4] Rajiv Ranjan Singh (AKA Lallan Singh)

**श्री राजीव रंजन सिंह उर्फ ललन सिंह (मुंगेर):** महोदय, 1894 के भूमि अधिग्रहण बिल के बाद आजादी के पहले से जो बिल था, उसके बाद कई संशोधनों के साथ भूमि अधिग्रहण होता रहा और पिछले कई वर्षों से इसकी जरूरत महसूस की गई कि एक कन्सोलेडिटेड बिल आना चाहिए। वर्ष 2011 में मई के महीने में जब परसौल की घटना हुई, उसके बाद इस काम में थोड़ी तेजी आई। जब तेजी आयी तो माननीय मंत्री जी का उस समय का बयान और अखबारों में कई तरह की बातें छपीं, तो उससे पूरे देश में यह मैसेज गया कि इस बार वास्तव में इस बिल के माध्यम से किसानों के हितों की रक्षा होगी। मंत्री जी का स्वभाव है कि वे दबाव में नहीं झुकते हैं लेकिन जब चारों तरफ से घूम-फिर कर यह बिल सदन में आया तो ऐसा लगा कि यह दंतविहीन बिल हो गया। किसानों का हित कहीं से सुरक्षित नहीं रहा, दिखावे के लिए उसे सुरक्षित दिखाया गया लेकिन उसमें कई ऐसे छिद्र डाल दिए गए, जिनके माध्यम से सारे रास्ते खुले के खुले रह गए।

महोदय, आज पूरे देश में मात्र 47औ कृषि योग्य भूमि बच गयी है। किसानों का सबसे बड़ा हित सुरक्षित होता यदि आप ने इसमें प्रतिबंधित किया होता कि कृषि योग्य किसी भूमि का या बहुफसली किसी भूमि का अधिग्रहण नहीं होगा। अगर आप ने यह सुनिश्चित किया होता तो किसानों का हित सुरक्षित होता।

कहां बच गए हैं अब किसान? वर्ष 2001 में जो कृषक थे, उनकी संख्या करीब-करीब 20-21 लाख थी। आज किसानों की संख्या घटकर 17-18 लाख पर पहुंच गयी है। मज़दूरों की संख्या भी उसी रफ्तार में घटी है। कृषि मज़दूर जो खेतों में काम करने वाले मज़दूर हैं, उन की संख्या पन्द्रह लाख से घटकर बारह लाख हो गयी है। 76 लाख लोग कृषि पर निर्भर थे। आज वह घटकर 62 लाख हो गया है। किसान खेती छोड़ते जा रहे हैं। आप उसी किसान पर हमला कर रहे हैं, लगातार हमला कर रहे हैं। इसलिए आज अगर आपने यह फैसला किया होता कि हम कृषि योग्य भूमि का अधिग्रहण नहीं करेंगे तो हम समझते हैं कि किसानों का हित उसमें सुरक्षित होता। आपने 80 औ किसानों की सहमति की बात की है। अगर यह करना भी था और अगर आप ने यह कहा होता कि अगर 100 लाख किसानों की सहमति होगी, तभी कृषि योग्य भूमि अधिग्रहीत होगी तो यह बात समझ में आती कि उनका हित सुरक्षित है और वे सिक्योर्ड हैं।

सभापति महोदय, इस बिल के माध्यम से राजनाथ जी ने भी चर्चा की। बिल के माध्यम से कई सरकारी परियोजनाओं के लिए आपने छूट दे रखी है। हम भी यह मानते हैं। इस देश का जो नागरिक है, हर कोई यह मानेगा कि विकास के लिए

ज़मीन चाहिए। लेकिन क्या सरकार को यह मालूम नहीं है कि आज रेलवे के नाम पर पूरे देश में हज़ारों एकड़ ज़मीन अधिग्रहीत करके छोड़ी हुई है जिसका 25-30 वर्षों से कोई उपयोग नहीं हो रहा है। आज उन ज़मीनों के उपयोग के लिए यह किया जा रहा है कि गीगीगी गॉडल में उस ज़मीन का पूण षदल दिया जा रहा है। क्या उस ज़मीन को आप व्यावसायिक उपयोग के लिए ला रहे हैं? अगर किसानों से आप ने औने-पौने दाम पर सरकारी परियोजनाओं के लिए ज़मीन खरीदी तो आज उन ज़मीनों का व्यावसायिक उपयोग क्यों हो रहा है? वह ज़मीन सीधे किसानों को वापस होनी चाहिए। अगर यह फैसला आपने इस बिल में किया होता तो किसानों का हित सुरक्षित होता।

**श्री राजीव रंजन सिंह उर्फ ललन सिंह:** सभापति महोदय, आज इस बिल में यह प्रावधान होना चाहिए था कि सरकारी उपयोग के लिए जो ज़मीनें अधिग्रहित हुई हैं, उनका व्यावसायिक इस्तेमाल नहीं होगा, उन पर मॉल, होटल नहीं बनेंगे और किसानों को वे ज़मीनें वापस दी जाएंगी। अगर यह फैसला हुआ होता तो हम समझते हैं कि किसानों के हित सुरक्षित होते। आपने उसका पूरा लैंड यूज चेंज कर दिया। अब आप ने निजी परियोजनाओं के लिए भी ज़मीन अधिग्रहण का रास्ता खोल दिया। भट्टा परसौल की घटना सब को मालूम है। राजनाथ जी भी शायद किसानों से मिलने के लिए वहां गए थे। उस पूरे ज़मीन का अधिग्रहण औद्योगिक क्षेत्र को विकसित करने के लिए हुआ था, इंडस्ट्रिलाइजेशन के लिए। आज वहां क्या बन रहे हैं? आज वहां मॉल बन रहे हैं। वहां मल्टीकम्प्लेक्स बन रहे हैं। आज आपने इसके लिए कोई प्रावधान नहीं किया कि हम वैसे लैंड को निजी क्षेत्रों को उस तरह से उपयोग करने की अनुमति नहीं देंगे और अगर इस कानून को बनाकर आप इसे भूतलक्षी प्रभाव से लागू किए होते तो इसमें शायद किसानों का हित सुरक्षित हो जाता।

एसईजेड की चर्चा राजनाथ जी ने भी की। एसईजेड में क्या हो रहा है? सन् 2005 में एसईजेड की योजना आप लाए, जब आपकी यूपीए-वन की सरकार थी। आपने अब तक जो टोटल 590 एसईजेड स्वीकृत किए हैं, उनमें लगभग चार सौ एसईजेड नोटिफाइड हुए हैं और काम मात्र 170 एसईजेड परियोजनाओं पर अब तक शुरू हुआ है। बाकी ज़मीन कहां गई, बाकी ज़मीन क्यों पड़ी हुई है? क्यों ज़मीन खरीदते हैं, आपने लोगों से औने-पौने दाम में पूंजीपतियों के हवाले कर दिया और आज एसईजेड पर काम नहीं हो रहा। एसईजेड इस देश का सबसे बड़ा घोटाला है। मंत्री जी, अगर आप वास्तव में मानें, हम समझते हैं कि आपके जैसा इस विभाग का मंत्री अगर है तो उस पर जरूर हमला होना चाहिए। एसईजेड के नाम पर जिन लोगों ने ज़मीन लेकर छोड़ रखी है, उसको वापस होना चाहिए, उसको किसानों को वापस दिया जाना चाहिए।...(व्यवधान)

**ग्रामीण विकास मंत्री (श्री जयराम रमेश):** कई माननीय सदस्यों ने एसईजेड का जिक्र किया, मैं इसका स्पष्टीकरण करना चाहता हूं कि जब हमारे संशोधनों का वक्त आएगा, औपचारिक संशोधन जो हम ला रहे हैं, ये कानून एसईजेड को लागू होगा। यह बात सही है कि जब मसौदा तैयार किया गया था, एसईजेड को छूट दी गई थी। स्टैंडिंग कमेटी की सिफारिश भी आई थी, उसके बाद जीओएम में भी इसका जिक्र हुआ था। आज हम संशोधन ला रहे हैं, ये जो अभी अधिनियम बनेगा, ये एसईजेड पर भी लागू होगा।

**श्री राजीव रंजन सिंह उर्फ ललन सिंह:** माननीय मंत्री जी ने जो कहा, उसका हम स्वागत करते हैं। यह होना चाहिए और भूतलक्षी प्रभाव से होना चाहिए, यह हमारा सुझाव है। आपने जो कम्पेनसेशन और रिहैबिलिटेशन के लिए प्रक्रिया अपनाई है, आप सोशल इम्पैक्ट असैसमैंट करेंगे। उसके बाद एक्सपर्ट कमेटी उसका एनवायरनमेंटल असैसमैंट करेगी और फिर गवर्नमेंट सर्वे होगा। उसके बाद आप कम्पेनसेशन और रिहैबिलिटेशन की प्रक्रिया फाइनल करेंगे। इस पूरी प्रक्रिया के दौरान किसी को भी अदालत में जाने की छूट है। अब यह प्रक्रिया इतनी लम्बी होगी कि कोई भी किसान, जिसकी भूमि अधिग्रहीत हो रही है, उसकी आयु समाप्त हो जाएगी, तब तक यह प्रक्रिया पूरी नहीं होगी, उसको कम्पेनसेशन नहीं मिलने वाला है। इसलिए इस पूरी प्रक्रिया को आप सहज, सरल और पारदर्शी बनाइए और समय-सीमा के अंदर इसको निर्धारित करिए कि यह पूरी प्रक्रिया एक समय-सीमा के अंदर पूर्ण हो सके। ये हम आपसे आग्रह करना चाहेंगे और हम चाहेंगे कि आप ये सदन को आश्वस्त करें।

सभापति महोदय, अंत में हम आपके माध्यम से मंत्री जी को सिर्फ एक बात कहना चाहते हैं कि आप इन सारी चीजों को छोड़कर जो आपका पहले स्टैंड था, उस पर कायम हों और संशोधन लेकर आएं कि पूरा अधिग्रहण सिर्फ, जो हमारी 14 परसेंट बंजर भूमि है, उसका अधिग्रहण हम करेंगे। उस बंजर भूमि का अधिग्रहण करके उसको डेवलप करिए। हम ये नहीं कहते हैं कि उद्योगीकरण नहीं होना चाहिए, हम इसके खिलाफ नहीं हैं, लेकिन उद्योगीकरण अगर होना चाहिए, माननीय मुलायम सिंह जी ने भी कहा, हम सब लोग ये मानते हैं कि जो बंजर भूमि है, उसको विकसित करिए। उसमें आप जो भी खर्च कर सकते हैं, उसमें इंफ्रास्ट्रक्चर डेवलप करिए। सड़क, बिजली, हर चीज उसको दीजिए। उस बंजर भूमि का उपयोग आप उद्योगीकरण के लिए कीजिए, ये आश्वासन आज यह पूरा देश और सदन आपसे चाहता है, यही मेरा सुझाव है। इन्हीं सुझावों के साथ मैं अपनी बात समाप्त करता हूं।

## [5] Sudip Bandyopadhyay

SHRI SUDIP BANDYOPADHYAY: Sir, I attended two meetings which were convened by Shri Jairam Ramesh. I have no hesitation to say that he took all his efforts to make it a Bill acceptable to all. He circulated some notes of his own and few of his observations. The copies of them were also sent to us and we have gone through them. I will use his paper also.

In the context of this British-period Land Acquisition Act of 1894, Justice G.S. Singhvi of Supreme Court observed that 'the Act has become a fraud' and another Bench of Supreme Court has also observed by commenting on this 1894 Act that 'this Act does not provide for rehabilitation of persons displaced from their lands, although by such compulsory acquisition, their livelihood gets affected. To say the least, the Act has become outdated and needs to be replaced at the earliest by a fair, reasonable and rational enactment in tune with the constitutional provisions, particularly Article 300A of the Constitution.' So, it was a necessity to change that Act and it is good enough that the present Bill is now in front of us.

Sir, the Government needs land and the private companies and industrial houses also need land. Naturally, the Government needs land for construction of schools, roads, bridges, hospitals or even for some PPP-model projects while private companies and industrial houses need land for setting up industries, but the question is what the policy for acquiring lands would be. We have seen with our practical experience in West Bengal, where we succeeded to remove the 34-year old Left Front Government, how the farmers fight for their land when they are attacked. They feel helpless that there is nobody to guide them, to stand by them and to protect them while they are only politically exploited at the time of votes. It could have been better if this Bill had been introduced much earlier.

What we strongly feel is that we want an assurance from the Hon. Minister that the land of the farmers will never be acquired by force. We are totally opposed to the forceful acquisition and occupancy of land of the farmer and of the land owners. We want this assurance from the Hon. Minister that it will never be allowed to happen because normally, whenever acquisition is done, it is done by kicking on the stomach of the farmers, which we will never allow, and we will stand very firmly by them.

Sir, the Standing Committee had made 13 recommendations in regard to this Bill. Out of those 13 recommendations, 11 have been inducted into this Bill while two of them have not been included. We are for those two recommendations also, which the Government has excluded. We are 100 per cent in favour of those two recommendations. What are those two recommendations which the Government refused to take up? One of those two recommendations is about restriction on multi-crop land acquisition left to the State. In response to the recommendation made by the Standing Committee that since States better understand the peculiar and unique circumstances in their region, the fixation of the cap should be left to them, an amendment has been made to allow the State Governments to fix the limits on the acquisition of multi-crop land. Secondly, in response to the recommendation made by the Standing Committee that since States better understand the peculiar and unique circumstances in their region, the fixation of the cap should be left to them, an amendment has been made to allow the State Governments to fix the limits on the acquisition of agricultural land. We urge that let the total Report of the Standing Committee—by not excluding these two recommendations—be accepted by the hon. Minister by which it can be the most acceptable Bill for this Session.

I would like to further add that the Government has categorically said that 80 per cent land will be acquired by the private companies in case of their projects. In case of Government, it will be 70:30 and in case of private companies it will be 80:20. Why is it so? We are totally of the opinion that this deal should be between the private companies, land owners and farmers. Even the price should be fixed in consultation with both of them, and the Government should not play the role of the mediator. It should be very categorical, and it should be very positive. Once this system is adopted, then the Government can come all-out to help whatever projects anybody intends to make over there. Therefore, we firmly believe that 100 per cent land is to be purchased by the private group on their own.

Multi-crop land is to be protected. Industries can be set up on either mono-crop land or on the barren land. In many States, there is no continuity of land, which is, getting more than 100 acres of land at a stretch. Therefore, we propose that small and middle industries can be a very viable alternative over the big and giant industries as continuity of land is not available in every State. So, you will have to keep in your mind that land is the asset of the rural people, and it is the asset of the farmers. We should not acquire it by any means, which will cause them and send them to uncertainty.

We know that safeguards for the tribal communities and other disadvantaged groups have been mentioned. We want them to be protected with all steps. But what would be the compensation? The compensation mentioned is that the owner of the land/affected family be provided with job to the family; housing facilities; land for land, but normally, it is seen that whatever is mentioned with good intention is not properly implemented.

MR CHAIRMAN: How much time will you take?

SHRI SUDIP BANDYOPADHYAY: So, the State-level Monitoring Committees have to be activated. Certainly, some observations are to be kept from the Department for which I do not think that any National-level Monitoring Committee is at all necessary. But we totally support land bank, and there should be one land map also for every State. What do the land maps normally do? They demarcate that this is my State and this part of the State is demarcated as industry-proposed zones and these areas can be demarcated as agricultural-oriented zones.

MR CHAIRMAN: Kindly conclude your speech.

SHRI SUDIP BANDYOPADHYAY: If any person comes with a good motive, then the map can be placed before him to decide about his land. It can be shown that these are the areas that will make for industry and these are the farming areas, and multi-crop land will never be handed over to any private companies. So, the State Governments can take it if they feel it necessary. This should be a guide-map for the concerned State also.

Sir, we reaffirm our commitment to the principles to protect the interests of the farmers. We are also in favour of the industries. We believe that principles cannot be changed by debates or negotiations.

We firmly believe that if these changes are included, if these additions are taken care of, and if our proposals are accepted, certainly, this Bill could be acceptable to all in this House.

Sir, I began my speech by saluting the martyrs of Singur and Nandigram. They did their best, and the Government of India also keenly felt that this Bill, certainly, was the need of the hour.

We certainly believe that when, with an open mind, transparent outlook and foresightedness, Shri Jairam Ramesh is coming out with this Bill, let this Bill be acceptable to all.

We again reassure and reaffirm our stand that this ratio of 80:20 must be abolished. One hundred per cent means, it should be one hundred per cent. When 100 per cent of the land is to be acquired by a private company, how will the Government play the role of a mediator?

We support the Bill, if our amendments are accepted.

## [6]  T.K.S. ElanGovan

SHRI T.K.S. ELANGOVAN (CHENNAI NORTH): Mr Chairman, Sir, thank you for allowing me to speak on the Land Acquisition, Rehabilitation and Resettlement Bill, which has seen the light of the day after various changes. I am happy to say that many of the recommendations made by the DMK Party were accepted by the Hon. Minister, and I am thankful to the Hon. Minister.

Sir, the framers of the Constitution of India regarded the Right to Property as a Fundamental Right. Earlier, in the Constitution of India, this Right to Property was incorporated in Article 19(1)(f) of the Constitution. Right to Property is a Fundamental Right. But subsequently, it was deleted from that Article 19 and relegated to Article 300 (A), which merely says,

*No person shall be deprived of his property, save by authority of law.*

A Fundamental Right was taken away and a concession was given to a person, namely, he shall not be deprived of his property, save by authority of law. It means that Right was taken away by the Government.

Sir, there cannot be two views on the issue that the Land Acquisition Act, 1894 should be repealed. That Act has no purpose now. It is a very old Act, which will have no value now, and most of the problems relating to acquisition of land arose because of that Act. So, we welcome this Bill, but at the same time, we want to make certain suggestions, particularly about the price of the farmland.

The price of farmland differs from period to period. When there is drought for two consecutive years in an area, the cost of land will come down. The farmer wants to sell it away at a throw away price and go for another employment for his livelihood. If there is continuous rain, he will not be willing to sell the land. So, price of farmland varies, depending on the climatic conditions of a certain place.

So, the Government should protect the interests of the farmers. That should be the main aim of the Government. Sir, I want to read point no. 12 from the Statement of Objects and Reasons. It says:

> In Districts where net-sown area is less than 50 per cent of the total geographical area, no more than 10 per cent of the net-sown area of the District will be acquired.

Sir, this should be deleted. If, in a District the net-sown area is less than 50 per cent, there should not be any acquisition in that District because our population is growing, we need employment and we need food also. What is the use if we earn more and then, we do not have enough food? So, the Government should see that in every District, the sown area should not be less than 50 per cent of the geographical area of that district. We have such a system with regard to forests. There should be 33 per cent forest cover in this country. So, we should have such a stipulation that there shall be 50 per cent of arable land in this country. That should be divided in all the 600 odd districts of this country. So, if the land sown area of a District is less than 50 per cent, there should not be any acquisition from that District. The Government should keep this thing in mind which will help the people of that area.

Sir, when our leader Dr Kalaignar Karunanidhi was the Chief Minister, the Tamil Nadu Government had enacted the Tamil Nadu Acquisition of land for Industrial Purposes Act, 1997. The provision recognizes the legitimate right of the land owner and the need for consent and consensus in matters touching upon economic development. This Act further provided for the use of land only for the purpose for which it was acquired and not for any other purpose.

Impoverishing individual land owners in the guise of economic development was discountenanced by this legislation.

I am reading this because there is another point whose number is 19 in the Statement of Objects and Reasons. You have stated that:-

> Land that is not used within ten years in accordance with the purposes, for which it was acquired, shall be transferred to the State Government's land Bank. Upon every transfer of land without development, twenty per cent of the appreciated land value shall be shared with the original land owners.

This should not be there Sir.

SHRI T.K.S. ELANGOVAN: Further, there are certain State Acts like in Tamil Nadu, we have the Panchami Land Act where land is given to the Scheduled Castes. They innocently or ignorantly sell their land to others. In reality, this land cannot be saleable in the market. So, this land should not be acquired for any other purpose. It should be left only to the Scheduled Castes to whom the land was given by the Government. So, these things should be covered by this Act.

Now, I come to Section 98(1) and 98(2). Section 98(1) says: -

> Subject to sub-section 3, the provisions of this Act shall not apply to the enactments relating to land acquisition specified in Fourth Schedule.

But the other section says:

> Subject to sub-section (2) of the section 99, the Central Government may, by notification, omit or add to any of the enactments specified in the Fourth Schedule.

This is totally contradictory. You are saying that it shall not apply to enactments where the land acquisition is specified in the Fourth Schedule. Then, you took up the provision of adding or deleting anything in the Fourth Schedule which means 98(1) will lose its relevance in due course. You will add something. You have the power to add something and you still say that it shall not apply to the enactment related to Land Acquisition. You fix it. You fix the Fourth Schedule. You weed out whatever is not necessary. Otherwise, Section 98(2) contradicts Section 98(1). I want the Hon. Minister to note that.

There is one more thing. In Section 7, they talk about a Committee, an Expert Group consisting of people from various sections. It shall consist of two non-official social scientists. They have not clarified it; they have not defined a 'social scientist'. It is not clear whether a social scientist will be from elsewhere or from other State or from some other district and whether he will know what is happening in a particular district where the Government is going for land acquisition. So, the person who sits in the Committee should have some knowledge about the area in which land is acquired. So, it should be defined.

Otherwise, this is a welcome Bill. We were waiting for such a Bill which will repeal the century old Act. With these words, I support the Bill.

## [7] Basu Deb Acharia

SHRI BASU DEB ACHARIA (BANKURA): Mr Chairman, Sir, I never expected that such a situation will be created when we are discussing a very important Bill, Land Acquisition, Resettlement and Rehabilitation Bill. Now, the title has been changed with Right, Transparency, Resettlement and Rehabilitation Bill. The title is very good. He has chosen a very good title.

But all exercise is in deceit. Many good things, many good proposals are there in the new Bill, which were not there in the antique Act, which was enacted during the British regime like the social impact assessment, resettlement, rehabilitation, compensation, etc. All these things are there; and he has made such proposals in the Bill.

But when you go through the various provisions, like the exclusion that he has provided in the Bill, all these good proposals will yield no results and the peasants, the farmers will not be benefited out of this Bill. … (*Interruptions*)

SHRI BASU DEB ACHARIA: Sir, I want to thank the Hon. Minister. Out of 160 amendments that I have tabled, he has accepted only six amendments. These are very small amendments. He had agreed on one amendment when he had a meeting with us. He not only had All Party meeting but separately also he met us and tried to arrive at a consensus, but failed. The Minister has failed as there is no consensus on the Bill. The most affected persons are in West Bengal. On the floor of this House he said that only in the State of West Bengal share croppers' names are recorded. In none of the States except the State of West Bengal it is recorded. There are a large number of share-croppers recorded and unrecorded. He has included sharecroppers' names but a condition saying 'for the last three years from the date of acquisition' has been imposed. Why is this condition of three years? It is because the names of a large number of sharecroppers is not recorded. How will you be able to find out for how many years these sharecroppers are engaged in the cultivation of that land? So, there should be further amendment and three years condition should be removed. If this condition of three years is retained, a large number of sharecroppers and affected persons would be deprived of the benefits.

Now what are the exclusions? In all the meetings, I point out this exclusion. You are repealing an Act of 1894. Since long, we have been demanding that that Act should be repealed and a new legislation should be enacted. But when you are repealing this Act, we wanted that an all encompassing and a comprehensive Act should be brought forward. But you have excluded 13 Acts and these 13 Acts do not have any rehabilitation and resettlement package. You have kept one provision that within one year, they will have to implement the identical rehabilitation and resettlement packages. Why should it be after one year? Why should it not be immediately after the enactment of the Act? What is the problem in bringing all the Acts together to have a comprehensive Act or an all encompassing Act? What is the difficulty?

When Laluji was the Railway Minister, an Ordinance was promulgated because he was facing difficulty in Bihar in regard to acquisition of land. He promulgated an Ordinance and because an Ordinance was promulgated, it was not referred to the Standing Committee on Railways. I was the Chairman of that Committee. It was brought directly to the House. There is no provision of rehabilitation and resettlement. Now eastern Dedicated Freight Corridor is being constructed and the farmers are facing problem. What is the price of land in Etawah district? चले गये मुलायम सिंह जी, उन्हें सब पता है I There is a wide variation in the price of land in Etawah and Agra. These are the neighbouring districts. Nobody is there to listen to the problems of the farmers. Why is there wide price variation? What is the rehabilitation and resettlement package in those Acts? With this exclusion and with this condition, when this Bill will be converted into an Act, it will be a draconian Act.

MR CHAIRMAN: No comments please. Hon. Member, you may please continue. Please do not disturb him.

SHRI BASU DEB ACHARIA: The Collector is given arbitrary powers in case of emergency and exigency. Any land can be acquired in the name of exigency and urgency. After the acquisition, there would neither be social impact assessment, nor environment impact assessment, nor any rehabilitation and resettlement. Eighty per cent of land can be acquired through the provisions of the Act, particularly using urgency provisions in which case there are no rooms for providing any rehabilitation and resettlement. The Hon. Minister may clarify this point. The provision for rehabilitation and resettlement is there only in case of 20 per cent cases.

Sir, we have very recently passed the Food Security Bill. Our agricultural land is on gradual deceleration. We have not been able to achieve growth in agricultural production. During the Eleventh Five Year Plan, our target was 4 per cent but even in the first year of the Twelfth Five Year Plan, the achievement has been less than 4 per cent. It is something like 3.5 per cent. Unless there is growth in agricultural production, how will we be able to supply food grains under the provisions of the Food Security Act? There is also provision for acquiring five per cent of multi-cropping irrigated agricultural land which meant if one acquires 1,000 acres of land, five per cent of that could be multi-cropping irrigated agricultural land. How much does that come to? If one were to acquire 10,000 acres of land, five per cent of that could be multi-cropping irrigated agricultural land. How much does that come to? Only in rare cases when there is no other option … (*Interruptions*)

SHRI BASU DEB ACHARIA: Sir, I have many points to make.

My next point is about the provision of public purposes. So many things like infrastructure and all have been added in this provision. The Hon. Minister has brought in an amendment to exclude the SEZs where thousands and thousands of acres of land have been acquired. What has happened during the last 20 years? We have seen how thousands and thousands of acres of land were grabbed... (*Interruptions*) I will give you one example of that... (*Interruptions*)

MR CHAIRMAN: Please do not disturb now. Why are you disturbing?

... (*Interruptions*)

MR CHAIRMAN: It is not for you to say that.

SHRI BASU DEB ACHARIA: Sir, the Maharashtra Industrial Development Corporation acquired land. How much price was given to the farmers? They were given a sum of Rs. 1 lakh and Rs. 2 lakh per acre. Now those lands are being sold to a corporate house. At what price they are selling it now? It is at Rs. 1 crore per acre. How are these peasants being exploited for the last 20 years since the Government of India started following new liberal economic policies? Lands were liberally acquired and then sold to the corporate houses... (*Interruptions*)

MR CHAIRMAN: Hon. Member, please do not disturb him. Shri Acharia, please address the Chair.

... (*Interruptions*)

SHRI KALYAN BANERJEE: Sir, I am only pointing out to him that he is contradicting his own statements... (*Interruptions*)

MR CHAIRMAN: All right. You have said it once. Nothing, except what Shri Acharia is saying, will go on record.

(*Interruptions*) ... *

SHRI BASU DEB ACHARIA: Sir, my next point is about the quantum of compensation. What is the basis of deciding the quantum of compensation? The same methodology has been adopted which is there in the 1894 Act. What is there in the Indian Stamp Act, 1899? ... (*Interruptions*)

MR CHAIRMAN : Please wind up now. I gave you enough time. Two minutes more.

... (*Interruptions*)

SHRI BASU DEB ACHARIA: Sir, you know how the lands are sold. They are undervalued. Less price is shown for registration of the land so that stamp duty is less. So, why should not the current market price be the basis of deciding the value of the land? As a result of that, by adopting that methodology as it is there in the Indian Stamp Act, 1899, how much compensation farmers will get? Unless the land loser gets employment, how can there be resettlement and rehabilitation? If the entire land is acquired, on which the farmer is dependent, which is his only source of income, if employment in that project is not given, how can he be rehabilitated? ... (*Interruptions*)

MR CHAIRMAN: Hon. Members, please sit down.

... (*Interruptions*)

MR CHAIRMAN: Nothing will go on record.

(*Interruptions*) ... *

MR CHAIRMAN: This is very bad.

... (*Interruptions*)

MR CHAIRMAN: Shri Basu Deb Acharia, please wind up now.

... (*Interruptions*)

श्री बसुदेव आचार्य: माननीय सभापति महोदय, हम ऐसी उम्मीद कर रहे थे कि सदन में एक अच्छा विधेयक आएगा। यह हमारे देश की मांग थी कि एक अच्छा विधेयक आए। किसानों के साथ इतने दिनों से अन्याय हुआ है।...(व्यवधान)

MR CHAIRMAN: Nothing is going on record.

*(Interruptions) ...* \*

SHRI BASU DEB ACHARIA : Sir, I wanted that this Bill should be referred to the Standing Committee as 187 new amendments were moved by the Minister. This has never happened. This is unprecedented but he did not agree to refer it either to the Standing Committee or the Joint Select Committee. But there is a need for further modification and further amendment. In future, it will not protect the interests of the farmers. Rather it will go against the interests of the farmers. It will serve the interests of the corporate house and that is why there is a need for further modification of the Bill.

### [8] Tathagata Satpathy

SHRI TATHAGATA SATPATHY (DHENKANAL): Sir, I would thank you for giving me this opportunity to speak today.

   This is a Bill which actually affects a lot of people, innumerable people who are economically deprived. We are all sitting here to legislate a Bill that has come in as a replacement of an Act which is more than 100 years old. I will initially congratulate the Hon. Minister for trying out such a brave exercise although it is a bit late in the day.... *(Interruptions)*

MR CHAIRMAN: Hon. Members, please maintain the decorum in the House. Otherwise, I will request the Hon. Minister to start.

SHRI TATHAGATA SATPATHY: As we all know, for the average family in India, for the middle class and for the poorer sections of our people, land is the only sustainable asset that they have which they use for every kind of economic activity. When the father dies in the family, they sell a piece of the land to do the cremation and the ensuing activity. When the daughter gets married, they will sell a piece of their land and get the girl married. So, for everything, when the banks were not there in the country, our culture had ingrained into us—it is very much in our DNA—that land is the only asset with which families could survive.

   As you know, in Indian families, there may be many brothers and many components of the family living under the same roof but not necessarily with a united purpose or living as one family. They all may be doing different things; they all may be sharing the same roof but sometimes—and most often—they are not even sharing the kitchen. In such situations, when the land belonging to this kind of a family is taken over by the Government or by the private companies, the trouble that the families face cannot be imagined by most Members in this House now.

I come from a constituency Angul, Dhenkanal in the State of Odisha where a huge chunk of the land in blocks of Talcher, Chandipada, Ganiha and Pallora are coal-bearing areas, where the Mahanadi Coal Fields Limited, a very profit-making unit of Coal India, is operating. Under the CB Act which has somehow not been dealt with in this Bill, there is a lot of ambiguity. This is a populated country. In Odisha, most of the coal-bearing areas are also thickly populated. Now, you have given coal mining rights to a lot of private companies.

Their impact as well as Government companies like MCL come up with horrendous resettlement and rehabilitation activities which do not really reach the people. All of us are aware, resettlement of land oustees in most Government projects and also in mining and private industries have been a colossal failure all over India, including my State, Odisha. We have seen that the Land Acquisition Officers appointed by the Government, the LAOs, somehow when they work for a company, they become the puppets of the Collectors of the district and whichever company or body is taking over the land, they become puppets of that. The Collectors most often become puppets of these big companies. That is where the problem mostly arises.

It is unfortunate that we are in a country where during 1977, after a very dictatorial Government of the Congress was removed by the people through a democratic process, and the Government of Morarji Desai came to power, they removed the ownership of land from the Fundamental Rights list in the Constitution. Probably India is one of the few democratic nations where Fundamental Rights do not include ownership of land.

I would go from point to point and cover it up quickly. Land, I personally believe, should remain with the owners; lien to industry or Government should be given for 50 years; and monthly rent should be given to the land owners. Land should never be purchased from the owner. We have talked about Social Impact Assessment. One very critical thing is this. None of these Social Impact Asessments cover is that when a village is ousted, taken out of their old ancestral land, everybody lives with their neighbours, especially in rural areas. But Social Impact Assessment does not cover the aspect of the neighbour. You not only become a land oustee, you are also compelled to become an immigrant because the moment you move to a new village, or a new area, you do not know who your neighbours will be. This creates a huge amount of social unrest amongst the people who are moved out from their ancestral land. In a village, there are many people. For instance, barbers, farm labours, and many such people, who do not own land but they are an integral part of the cultural milieu of the village. What happens is, when land is taken over, these people do not get any compensation as we see in the case of Posco also. So, when the people are moved from one place to another, their whole social set up breaks down and this is never taken into account by any Social Impact Assessment that I have seen till now.

The other problem is that from the time of the notification till the time the actual acquisition takes place, and the resultant benefits accrue to the land oustees, that gap, that particular period of time, when the man cannot sell his land, he cannot buy anything nearby, he cannot even go to his field to sow paddy or anything, he cannot work, when there is virtually an embargo on any kind of economic activity, and that is the period when there is no income, no job, no work and we leave the people in a limbo. So, this is a period that is very important to create social unrest. Like we know, an idle mind is devil's workshop. Therefore, it is necessary that the Bill should also address this problem.

The other problem is, when compensation is paid to the land oustees, unfortunately, there is income levied on this compensation. As it is, you are taking away from a man his cremation ground, his *gochar*, his ancestral home and everything that he and his soul aligns with and then you are giving him some monetary compensation which gets devalued by the hour as we see what is happening today with the US dollar and Indian rupee and on top of that you tax him for the compensation you are paying him.

SHRI JAIRAM RAMESH: We are introducing an amendment a little later that all payments will be income tax free.

SHRI TATHAGATA SATPATHY: Thank you.

Sir, this Hon. Minister is very well read and a very conscious person. He goes to the rural areas himself and he sees things firsthand. So, I trust he knows all these problems. But there are certain ambiguities. For instance, I will cite one example. In the amendments brought by the Minister, on page 2, it is mentioned as follows:

*Manufacturing Zones as designated in the National Manufacturing Policy.*

This seems to be like just another name for a Special Economic Zone (SEZ). We will need clarifications on these issues.

As land is a State Subject, the new concept of a National Monitoring Committee, as it is mentioned in Chapter VII, should be deleted because it looks like there could be infringement on the federal structure that India has survived with. So also, Clauses 79 and 81, the punishment parts, are ambiguous and they could be erroneously interpreted.

As people may be aware, those who have ever gone to prison, 70 per cent of people imprisoned, life-term convicts, are in jails primarily because they have committed a crime which is directly related to land ownership. This is the situation in most jails of India. About 30 per cent would be crimes committed in passion concerning women or ownership or something else, but 70 per cent of the crime is connected with land. That means, land is a very emotional issue for most Indians and this Bill, somehow, does not, unfortunately, address the issue at that level.

I mentioned earlier that by giving the District Magistrate or the Collector this kind of immense responsibility, we have created a huge opening for corruption. At the district level, land acquisition has been concentrated in the district revenue officials. Therefore, there should be a system by which that authority can also be monitored by people's representatives.

MR CHAIRMAN: Please conclude.

SHRI TATHAGATA SATPATHY: Sir, I will conclude.

Sir, as far as agricultural land is concerned, you know, you have been a longtime politician, so also the Hon. Minister—politicians and other social activists go to villages and ensure that electricity reaches there, water reaches there, irrigation projects take place etc. Then, what is happening is, with the Indian industrial mindset, they want to go to such areas to put up their units where they already have electricity, road, water and everything available. So, we find in many instances projects of PMGSY have come within the boundary wall of many industrial units. This has happened many times. So, it is necessary that when land acquisition takes place, the law should be such that agricultural land and inhabited land where large groups of people are staying with progress and development having reached them over the years, we should try to avoid taking over such land.

Sir, conditions should be mandatory in the Act that industrial houses use at least one-third of the land that they take over for green activities. They should also take care not only to plant trees, which has become a sham nobody plant trees now, but they should put up water harvesting structure so that when they take out ground water they will also recharge the ground water and take care of the pollution.

MR CHAIRMAN: Kindly conclude now. I have given you more time.

SHRI TATHAGATA SATPATHY : Sir, I will need two more minutes and not much.

Sir, rehabilitation policy should itself be incorporated in the Statute Book under a separate Chapter so that it is not somebody's kindness that makes a difference, it should part of the law.

If industry does not come up, like the Tatas in Singur, then the original land losers or their successor in interest should be given preferential right to purchase the land back. Land losers and their successor in interest should be provided with similar facilities like that of industrial house employees in the field of health, education and community activities.

Lastly, in my constituency, there is the coal bearing area, MCL takes over a lot of land and now private companies are also moving in with huge tracks. Each unit takes around 2,000 to 3,000 acres of land. That is the general ownership or general preference of land for coal activities. What is happening is that they are not giving compensation to the people who are ousted and they are promising jobs; whereas if you see the records, MCL and also other units of Coal India Limited have actually come down in their total employment capacity.

## [9] Supriya Sule

SHRIMATI SUPRIYA SULE (BARAMATI): Mr Chairman, Sir, I stand here on behalf of my Party today in defence of this Bill. I congratulate the Minister for his relentless efforts to bring this Bill in this House finally today. I still remember the day when the Minister, Shri Vilasrao Deshmukh, who is unfortunately no more with us, had introduced this Bill for the first time. I think, he thought of it because the land acquisition from the State which I come from, which is Maharashtra, is probably one of the most developed and industrialized States in the country, and we are extremely proud of that.

I have been listening to all my colleagues' talk about acquisitions, all the exploitations that have happened there. I am very proud to say that my State, till today, which has the most industries in this nation, has never had any agitations or any issues regarding payments. So, actually, the Maharashtra model is probably one of the best models which should be included and a lot of interventions that we have made over the years should be considered in this Bill.

The district which I come from, which is the Pune district, has three exceptionally successful land acquisition issues. Hundreds of acres of land have been acquired by the Government. One is the Hinjewadi, which is the Rajiv Gandhi Infotech Park, where today, thousands or lakhs of software engineers work there. If you go there, you will probably feel that you are in some foreign country because the MIDC and SIDCO have done an exceptionally good job of acquisition. Sir, you will be surprised, and I would like to share this information with the House, that today the land price in the Rajiv Gandhi Infotech Park is not in lakhs but it is in crores, and Rs. Five crore an acre is the cost of that land today in the entire international park. I am proud to say that it is a part of my constituency. Today, most of my voters, who live in that area may not have been able to get good quality education, become a part of the success story. Unfortunately, the Bill does have rehabilitation and resettlement but

I would flag this point that the rehabilitation and the intention are very good but the growth story comes only when the money comes. I think, most of our members who have sold land to the Rajiv Gandhi Infotech Park have done good businesses; they have shops; they have restaurants but I do not think any of our children really have got the quality education to work in Infosys and that really will be our achievement. When one of my children from the locals who has given land for the park becomes the head of Infosys in Pune, that is really when our entire role will be complete.

The second project where again we have recently done land acquisition is the Chakan automobile hub. Today, the entire automobile industry revolves around the Chakan plants, and whether it is Mahindra, Tata Motors, Mercedes Benz, Baja Auto or you name them, all those industries are there. It is not just the acquisition of the industry because you all will realise that most people who are against this Bill today are people from the industry and have serious cause of concern. I think, the whole atmosphere today in the country is also a serious cause of concern because I was listening to the Hon. Finance Minister the other day in his reply to the Discussion under Rule 193, and he also showed some reservations about the Land Acquisition Bill in his speech. So, I am myself alarmed. It is really not about supporting the Bill or against the Bill. I think, we all have to support it. I think, industry also must be supported. If we help the poor, yes we will feed them; we will educate them; we will give them health care but where are the jobs going to come from if we do not support industry. It is not the capitalist view. I think, the whole House must think about it that industry must also be supported. I am sure the Hon. Minister and the Hon. Prime Minister will make an intervention, advise the industry and build some confidence because you all would have noticed that day before yesterday in the House twice and in the Press Conference, the Hon. Finance Minister of this country made three statements on one day, and the next day the rupee went down to Rs. 68.80 per dollar, and we have all discussed it. When the Finance Minister makes three statements, still the rupee slips against the dollar, I think, it is a serious cause of concern and all of us need to really realize that we are getting all these Bills which are of very good intention but if there is a section of the society, which certainly has reservations about it, whether it is the market, whether it is the industry or whether it is the common man, I think, we need to build the confidence right now in the nation, and that is the biggest achievement, and if you ask me I would say that it is a challenge ahead of our Government.

I am a part of this Government. We have looked at acquisitions severally like I told you my Chakan story, where we have given industry; ancillary jobs have come up and all our local children are doing good business in this entire area, and we are very proud of Chakan story as well as our Hinjewadi story.

But another big success story in Maharashtra, which we are very, very proud of and I would like the Hon. Minister to even come and see the project, is the Magarpatta Project. It is a township by itself where 546 farmers have come together and made a township, which has created 60 lakh jobs in that entire area; and the ownership stays with the farmers. It is a partnership between the farmers. So, the way, you are talking about here giving money, you are talking about rehabilitation, you are talking about resettlement, I think, the Magarpatta model, makes not just my State proud but makes India proud, where we have inclusive growth. I think that is what really the nation needs right now. The way they are considered about poor, every section of the society must be included in the growth. And, I really feel that the social impact, the assessment and the monitoring systems are absolutely clear.

But I think we really need to see it. The States need to play a much bigger role. I am fortunate because I come from a very liberal State, which has always looked at inclusive growth. Yes, there are other States also doing very well; and we are happy about it. But I am proud to say that Maharashtra has done exceptionally well not only just in industry but also in inclusive growth and bringing more investments. We have very good hospitals; we have got very good education systems; and we have got very good infrastructures.

There is one big point that I really need to make. I think they were talking about returning of land before my Shiv Sena colleague was talking about it. I am proud to say that in my own State, in my own Constituency, there is a place called Jejuri, which acquired land for MIDC; and there was a section of farmers came to me and said that 'there has been no investment made in this area. So, why don't you help us in returning our land?' They cannot even go and get education loans. So, I requested one of our colleagues in Maharashtra Government, Mr Narayan Rane, the Industry Minister who was very kind enough to take back and give back the entire land to those farmers. So, I am proud to say, the MIDC was not using that land, and the Maharashtra Government has shown a new path to this entire change of programme. So, return of land is possible; and Maharashtra has done it, as usual, for the first time.

There is just one last point, Sir, which I would like to address. Maharashtra has done all this way ahead of time. But we are having one major issue, right now, in Maharashtra with regard to land acquisition. It is about the Navi Mumbai Airport. I am only flagging this as an example because our State has done and contributed so much. Whenever you acquire land through City and Industrial Development Corporation of Maharashtra (CIDCO) for a development project, if you are acquiring 100 acres of land, 12.5 per cent of that land is developed and given back to the farmers. That is the policy of our State. When Navi Mumbai Airport started—it started years ago and as you are all aware, and to my disappointment I must say—the entire environmental clearance almost took a lifetime; and we have lost a lot of time. It is also a lot of infrastructure loss to Mumbai, which is the Financial Capital of this country. After the environmental clearance came, the acquisition started and we realized that the people had asked us to give much more compensation over and above 12.5 per cent. So, the Government of Maharashtra through CIDCO, which is our vehicle for acquisition, decided to give 22.5 per cent of land back, which was over and above the compensation. Today, the negotiations are struck; and they are demanding 35 per cent of land. So, every 100 acres of land that we acquire, 35 per cent will be given back to them; and they want compensation also. Is that really a fair deal? How will development happen? Mumbai can never have an airport like this. The per acre cost of that land in Navi Mumbai is Rs. 1 crore. The CIDCO, after negotiations, has decided to pay Rs. 5 crore. But the people over there, today are asking for Rs. 20 crore per acre. So, they are asking for Rs. 20 crore per acre and 35 per cent of the land to be returned back. This way how do we do development in this country?

So, I think, these are all issues in our developed States, which are there. They are slightly different than most of my other friends have been talking. We are looking at 1,100 acres of land for our Mumbai

Airport, which I think is just going to be a dream at the rate we are going. And, we cannot afford it. If Mumbai Airport does not happen, we realize that Chennai Airport had a problem with land acquisition, Bangalore Airport had an issue on land acquisition. So, I think, there are a lot of States where, maybe, injustice has been done like my colleague Sudip Bandyopadhyay talked about it. We have all seen Singur closely; and our hearts go out to everybody in West Bengal. I do not think any of us wants ugly scenes like this.

But let me assure the House that today, market sentiments and people's views, all matter. India is one of the fastest growing economies; and if we want to grow and make it inclusive for everybody in this country, I think, the land acquisition has to be done transparently. But at the same time, we have to take every section of our society together. You cannot just say that for one section you are doing. I am sure, the farmers will also agree that if we make extreme stringent laws and make the whole situation difficult, nobody is going to acquire land and nobody is going to invest in our country. So, given the situation of the country, I think this is time for all the seniors in our Government to step in, build in confidence and make sure that we grow fast by providing a much stronger and a better economy which is important not only for us but also for our next generation.

### [10]  M. Thambidurai (Karur)

DR M. THAMBIDURAI (KARUR): Sir, you know very well that land is the real wealth of every person. Our farmers are fully dependent on the land. They are cultivating the land for their livelihood. For centuries if you take, the farmers have been fully dependent on the land that they are cultivating and making their livelihood. The land is so precious. At the same time the Government wants to regulate it to protect the farmers. That is the issue. For example, the Government of India is making an attempt to replace the colonial era of Land Acquisition Act, 1894 with the Land Acquisition, Rehabilitation and Resettlement Bill, 2011.

In this connection, I want to say that even though the Government say that the Bill is to protect the farmers' interest and the land owners' interest but what the Hon. Minister had mentioned in Clause 38 is this. That is, if you go through page No.17, in the 'urgency' clause what they are telling is that under urgency clause, the Government can acquire the land for any purpose. At the same time, it is without following any procedure. That is what the urgency clause says. If they apply the urgency clause like that, the real farmers will be affected. By using this Clause 38, the poor farmers are going to lose their property rights which they are having legally for many years. The farmers cannot even go for appeal.

For that what I am requesting you is to give protection to the farmer in ensuring his legal rights. His legal right must not be taken away. This is what I am demanding. In this connection only, our Hon. Chief Minister of Tamil Nadu has written letters to the Prime Minister and others concerned. Also, she has expressed her concern about this Bill because in this Bill in the present form, even though the Central Government is claiming that it is going to protect the farmers and other land owners, actually there are so many clauses which affect the land owners and the poor farmers. Therefore, we have to take adequate precaution and include certain clauses which are necessary to protect the rights of the farmers.

First of all, I want to say that land is a State subject. You have to give some guidelines if you feel that let the State Government make the legislation according to the requirements of the Act. But you are entering the domain of the State Government. Already, you brought the Food Security Bill. Many State Governments are implementing the food security scheme successfully like Tamil Nadu. Now, in the same way, in your own interest and for including it in your own election manifesto of Lok Sabha, somehow you want to bring this kind of legislation which is the domain of the State Government. Therefore, we are objecting in that context only.

Second is regarding appropriate authority. Whenever you are telling 'appropriate authority' at many places, it means you are telling about the Central Government. When you are acquiring land, you have to get the consent of the State Government. The State Government will definitely do whatever the Central Government requires at that time to acquire the land. But, for example, if the Union Government is acquiring land for anything, it is all right but even for PP projects and even if certain private companies want land, at that time also you are going to interfere in that process.

Also, when you are acquiring land and two States are involved, at that time you cannot use the appropriate authority as the Central Government. You approach both the State Governments. Not only two States, even if three States are involved, you have to respect them and see that you get the consent of those States.

You have to get the consent of the State Government. Then, only it will be appropriate. That is what I am insisting.

The second thing is regarding the statutory body. Clause 2 currently mentions about appropriate Government, private companies and PPP projects. There is no clarity as to whether local bodies, statutory boards, public sector companies, universities, etc. would be covered within the definition 'Appropriate Government' or not. This needs to be clearly provided for the prevention of litigation.

In respect of acquiring the land, the Parliamentary Standing Committee has made some observation. For acquiring the land, you cannot apply everything as equivalent to Government. If the Central Government or the State Government acquires a land for public purpose, that is all right. But, if it acquires the land for private companies or some other purposes, it is not correct. Therefore, the principle of Eminent Domain should not be invoked for the land purchase for private companies. So, the same clause you cannot use for private companies. The public purpose is different. You cannot acquire it for private companies and equate it with public purpose. Therefore, Clause 3 (za) is bound to become fertile ground for unnecessary litigation and the deemed public purpose under sub-clauses (i), (ii), (iii), (iv) and (v) is also likely to be needlessly questioned as to whether they amount to public purpose or not. Therefore, we object to Clause 3 (za) of the Bill.

My next point is about Social Impact Assessment. It is all right that 50 acres may be prescribed for the appraisal of the SIA. Suppose, the State Government acquires some land for public purpose, at that time this Clause must not be applied, otherwise it will take long time to implement certain projects.

Clause 24 provides for lapsing of the land acquisition proceedings initiated under the earlier Land Acqusition Act where awards have not been passed and require fresh initiation of Land Acqusition proceedings. This could cause considerable delay in the process and stall the State Government projects. Therefore, we object to Clause 24.

The very restricted definition of 'urgency' in Clause 38—which I have already explained to you—to 'defence of India or national security or for any emergencies arising out of natural calamities' appears to be very restrictive. The urgency provisions can be extended to some critical infrastructure State Government projects also.

Then, I come to Clause 98 and the Fourth Schedule Protection. Under Clause 98, 16 Central Acts, which allow for acquisition of land, have been placed in the Fourth Schedule and the acquisition of land under these provisions have been made exempt from the application of the LARR Bill. Although, based on the Parliamentary Standing Committee's observations, a provision has been made to extend the provision of compensation and R&R packages under the LARR Bill to acquire under the exempted Acts by specific notification.

One thing that I want to say is that we had a bitter experience in Tamil Nadu with Petroleum Minister. For GAIL under the Ministry of Petroleum, you included it in the clause for acquiring the land laying gas pipelines. For it there was a lot of agitation in Tamil Nadu. But, the Minister for Petroleum wanted to acquire the land for laying the gas pipeline. Though the surface rights are returned to the land owner, the utilization of the land got restricted. Therefore, we are asking you to exempt that Clause and this can be deleted from this schedule. It is because of it that farmers are affected and they are agitating. The State Government has to face a lot of problems. Therefore, we request the Hon. Minister to see to it that it is deleted from the Act.

I would also like to say that the State Acts that provide for acquisition of the land like the Tamil Nadu Highway Act, 2001 and the Tamil Nadu Acquisition of Land for Industrial Purposes Act, 1999, should also be given protection of Clause 98 and included in the Fourth Schedule.

Regarding National Monitoring Committee, I would say that Clauses 43 and 44 provide for the establishment of a National Monitoring Committee. National Monitoring Committee can look at the things which are pertaining to the Central Government. At the same time, State must be given power to monitor other projects. You cannot apply the same thing for the State purpose. That has to be deleted. Regarding the compensation, Hon. Minister mentioned that under the rules, they can be given land or money. We are requesting that they may be given land for land because farmers are interested to have the land. Then, they are telling about the land bank. I do not know how it is going to help. If you are having land bank, the land will be kept in the land bank and then may not be utilized for some time. Therefore, what we are suggesting is that whenever you have acquired the land and you are not utilising the land for a long time, then the land must be given back to farmers immediately, within a short period. It must not be kept for a long period.

When you are paying compensation, you are paying interest at the rate of 12 per cent. I would request that the interest to be paid should be enhanced to 15 per cent. Then only it will be helpful to the farmers.

Then, there are certain amendments which we have already given. First of all, I request the Hon. Minister to look into the apprehensions that we have raised as well as the concerns raised by our State Government. They have to be addressed properly. Then only, it would be useful. When you are replacing such an old Act and bringing a new Bill, the new law must be more beneficial to the farmers. Some of the Hon. Members have already asked that when we are protecting the irrigated land, what about the dry land? Now-a-days, the dry land is costlier because the farmer is not able to do cultivation and they are suffering a lot due to the policies adopted by the Central Government which are not giving more attention to the agriculturists. At times, due to failure of the monsoon, most of the farmers are suffering in India. When several other calamities are also taking place and our State Government is requesting for help from the Central Government to provide compensation to the farmers, the Central Government is not coming forward and the farmers are suffering. So, most of the farmers, though they are having the wet land, are not in a position to cultivate that land. They are suffering a lot. Therefore, when you really want to protect the Food Security Bill, which you have already got passed in Lok Sabha, you should also see to it that more food is produced. In order to ensure that, we have to give more incentives to the farmers of the irrigated land. Only by doing so, you can protect the Food Security Bill. Otherwise, simply putting a clause that you want to protect irrigated land for the purpose of extending food security to people, will not help. What are the incentives that you are giving? The farmers are suffering. Their sufferings have to be removed. For that, the Government has to come forward with a new scheme to help the farmers.

Once upon a time, nobody was interested to have the dry land. The dry lands were being sold at lower rates. Now, the cost of the dry land has increased because even the irrigated—land farmers are also tempted to sell their land. That kind of thing is there. Therefore, the Central Government should really come forward, if it really wants to protect the farmers, to give financial assistance and also increase the MSP. Then, the farmers will be able to come forward to cultivate their lands.

### [11] Nama Nageswara Rao

श्री नामा नागेश्वर राव (खम्माम): सभापति महोदय, देश में 120 साल बाद लैंड एक्वीज़िशन बिल आ रहा है जिसका हम स्वागत करते हैं। लैंड एक्वीज़िशन बिल लाने से पहले मंत्री जी ने आल लीडर्स के साथ मीटिंग की। तेलगु देशम की तरफ से महत्वपूर्ण 12 प्वाइंट्स रेज़ किए गए थे। Out of them, eight points the Hon. Minister has agreed to. In respect of certain points, the Minister has readily agreed saying that 'This is an excellent suggestion.' I thank the Hon. Minister for accepting those suggestions.

Coming to the Bill, Sir, if you see, certain clarification and corrections are needed in it. Kindly see page no. 5 regarding *patta*. डेफिनेशन में जो पट्टा वर्ड लिखा है, उसमें स्टेट गवर्नमैंट, नहीं तो सैंट्रल गवर्नमैंट के रेगुलेशन के एक्ट की बात, उसकी लैंड का जो डाकूमैंट रहेगा, उसे पट्टा में मैंशन किया है। But this is the main problem. अभी स्टार्टिंग में आज के दिन देखें, तो बहुत जगह मेनली बैकवर्ड एरियाज में एससी, एसटी, ओबीसीज ने गवर्नमैंट लैंड आलरेडी दे दी है। हमारे एरिया में मेनली आंध्र प्रदेश में जो एसटीज, कोडबुमलु फॉरैस्ट लैंड को काटकर 30-40 साल से इरीगेट कर रहे हैं। इस तरह से बहुत जगह पट्टा लैंड नहीं है, मगर पोजैशन है, पोजैशन सर्टिफिकेट्स हैं।

मैं आपके माध्यम से मंत्री जी से यह कहना चाहता हूं कि जो भी पोजैशन में रहेगा, उसे पट्टा मानकर उसमें यह सब कुछ कवर करना चाहिए, अदरवाइज नहीं तो शुरू से ही बहुत से डिस्प्यूट में जाने की जरूरत पड़ेगी। उसी तरह से बिल में कम्पेनसेशन के लिए कलेक्टर को पावर दे रहे हैं। एक तरह से उसमें मार्केट वैल्यू को फोर टाइम्स मैंशन किया है। उसमें थोड़ा-सा कन्फ्यूजन है। It states that either the Collector may assess it or the market value, whichever is higher is to be considered for it. This is a very important point, which should be considered. उसी तरह से special power in case of urgency. अर्जेन्सी की डेफिनेशन कहीं भी नहीं है। When this is not mentioned in this Bill, then tomorrow, with that Clause, they can acquire any land. उसके लिए भी क्लैरिफिकेशन चाहिए। What is the meaning of urgency? उस प्वाइंट को भी क्लैरिफाई करने के लिए हम मिनिस्टर से रिक्वैस्ट कर रहे हैं। इसके साथ-साथ हम लोगों का भी रीसेन्टली फालो-अप प्रोजैक्ट नैशनल प्रोजैक्ट में डिक्लेयर किया गया है। एक फालो-अप प्रोजैक्ट के लिए आलमोस्ट एक लाख एकड़ लैंड एक्वीज़िशन के लिए जरूरत है। उसमें अराउंड 400 विलेजर्स आ जाते हैं। जब स्पेसिफिक प्रोजैक्ट रहेगा, उसके लिए गवर्नमैंट की तरफ से एक ही तरह का कम्पेनसेशन होना चाहिए। अभी एक प्रोजैक्ट के लिए डिफरेंट कम्पेनसेशन देकर जो एसटीज हैं, बैकवर्ड एरियाज हैं, उधर लैंड की कॉस्ट 1 लाख 15 हजार रुपये डिसाइड की गई है। उसी तरह से वैस्ट गोदावरी में जायें, तो सेम प्रोजैक्ट के लिए 3 लाख 50 हजार रुपये से लेकर 5 लाख रुपये तक डिसाइड किया गया है। इस बिल में यह प्रोविजन चाहिए कि जो भी प्रोजैक्ट के लिए स्पेसिफिक लैंड एक्वायर करेगा, उसके लिए एक ही कम्पेनसेशन कवर करना चाहिए। उसी तरह से वन ऑफ 17 एक्ट, जहां-जहां यह एक्ट है, उसके अंदर जो भी लैंड कम्पेनसेशन मिलेगा, उसमें भी एससी, एसटी, ओबीसी को मार्केट वैल्यू से कम्पेनसेशन मिलना चाहिए। इसी के साथ हमारे आंध्र प्रदेश में यूपीए गवर्नमेंट आने के बाद एसईजेड के नाम से करीब दो लाख एकड़ लैंड एक्वायर की गयी है। उसके बाद उसमें अभी कोई प्रोजैक्ट नहीं आया है। इस तरह की लैंड जो स्पेसिफिक प्रोजैक्ट के लिए एक्वायर की गयी है और जिस पर प्रोजैक्ट स्टार्ट नहीं हुआ है, उस लैंड को इसमें कवर करके फार्मर्स को रिटर्न करनी चाहिए। उसके साथ-साथ इन सब डिस्प्यूट्स को मेनली, उदाहरण के लिए अभी हमारा श्रीराम सागर प्रोजैक्ट है। करीब 30 साल पहले वह प्रोजैक्ट कंस्ट्रक्शन में आया है। It is an irrigational project. उस समय से अभी तक बहुत जगह हम लैंड कम्पेनसेशन के इश्यूज को सॉल्व नहीं कर पाये। इसलिए स्पेसिफिक प्रोजैक्ट के लिए लैंड एक्वीज़िशन के लिए स्पेशल कोर्ट विद टाइम बाउंड मैनर्स से लगानी चाहिए। इस प्रोविजन को भी इस बिल में प्रोवाइड करना चाहिए। एक बहुत इम्पोर्टैंट बात है कि पब्लिक परपज़ पर इसे देखें तो उसमें थोड़ा कन्फ्यूजन है। एक तरफ प्राइवेट परपज़ में पब्लिक अंडरटेकिंग्स को भी लिया है और प्राइवेट कम्पनीज को भी लिया है। On the one side, in private purpose public undertaking is included and private companies are also included. For example, if you want to put one steel plant of SAIL, then that is Government, and at the same time if the private people put the same near that steel plant, then either you are allowing the same thing to the private people also or it is only public company.

इसी तरह से स्टील प्लांट हो, पावर प्लांट हो, इन सभी के लिए फर्दर क्लैरिफिकेशन चाहिए। उसी के साथ-साथ हमारे खम्माम जिला संसदीय क्षेत्र में, जो सिंगरैनी कोलरीज़ है, उसमें जब भी लैंड एक्वीज़िशन होता है, तो प्रॉपर्ली कम्पेनसेशन नहीं मिल रहा है। जो लैंड एक्वायर कर रहा है, उसमें माइनिंग स्टार्ट करने के बाद योजना के प्रभावित होने के कारण लैंड बहुत खराब हो रहा है। जैसे, जब माइनिंग होता है, तो 50 फीट, 100 फीट तथा 200 फीट की गहराई तक कोयला खदान चला जाता है, तो उसके कारण आसपास के अधिकांश क्षेत्रों में इरिगेशन नहीं हो रहा है। इस बिल में उसके लिए भी प्रोविज़न होना चाहिए। लैंड एक्वायर करके, यदि माइनिंग का प्रोजैक्ट हो, उसी तरह से पावर प्लांट की वजह से लैंड प्रभावित हो रहा है, उसके कारण जो खेती-किसानी नहीं कर पा रहे हैं, उसे भी इसमें कवर करना चाहिए।

अंत में, मैं यह बोलना चाहता हूं कि ours is a developing country और सर्टेन प्वाइंट्स पर मैं एग्री करता हूं, जिनका उल्लेख सुप्रिया जी ने भी किया है। हम लोगों के विकासशील देश के लिए उद्योगों के लिए भी निश्चित रूप से स्पेशल परपज़ के लिए लैंड एक्वीज़िशन होना चाहिए।

**सभापति महोदय:** ठीक है।

SHRI NAMA NAGESWARA RAO: When our Leader Shri Nara Chandrababu Naidu was the Chief Minister, हम लोगों का जो वेस्ट लैंड है, जहां पत्थर वगैरह पड़ा हुआ है, पहले वहां हैदराबाद-सिकंदराबाद दो सिटीज़ थे, तेलगु देशम के समय में हमारे नेता जी created one Cyberabad City. It is the latest, world-class city. वहां हाईटेक सिटी डेवलप कर दिया है, इसी के वज़ह से काफी रोज़गार आया है। इसलिए जो वेस्ट लैंड होगा, जो सरकारी ज़मीन होगी, वहां इंडस्ट्री डेवलप करके, देश में इंडस्ट्रियल ग्रोथ करने की भी जरूरत है।

## [12] Jayant Choudhury

**श्री जयंत चौधरी (मथुरा):** धन्यवाद सभापति महोदय, मैं समझता हूं कि आज के दिन देश के किसानों की नज़र और हर वर्ग की नज़र इस सदन की तरफ है। एक लम्बे इंतजार और लम्बी यात्रा के बाद अंग्रेजों द्वारा बनाये गये क़ानून को आज हम बदलने जा रहे हैं। सम्मानित सदस्यों ने अपनी बातें रखी हैं। मैं समझता हूं कि अच्छी चर्चा

हुई है। जो बातें सामने आयी हैं और उसके पीछे जो भावना है, उसका मैं आदर करता हूं और अपने-आप को उससे जोड़ता हूं। वह भावना मूल रूप से क्या है? वह यह है कि आज जो ज़मीन का मालिक है, हमें देखना होगा कि उसके हितों को हम कैसे सुरक्षित रख सकते हैं। हमें संतुलन की भी आवश्यकता है। माननीय सांसदों ने इस बात को भी उठाया। देश के गांव में रहने वाला व्यक्ति, देश का गरीब व्यक्ति विकास की उम्मीद रखता है। वह मुख्यधारा में आना चाहता है। विकास की बड़ी-बड़ी परियोजनाएं उसके क्षेत्र में लगें, यह इच्छा भी वह रखता है। लेकिन यह संभव नहीं है कि विकास के नाम पर जो उनके अधिकार हैं, जो उनकी सम्पति है, जिस पर उनका जीवन आधारित है, उनके उस रिश्ते को हम पूरी तरह से नज़रअंदाज कर दें। यह उनके अधिकारों का हनन है। यह भी संभव नहीं है। मैं यह कहना चाहूंगा कि यह कोई नयी लड़ाई नहीं है। लगभग सभी माननीय सांसदों ने अपने-अपने क्षेत्र में देखा होगा, शायद ही कोई ऐसा ग्रामीण क्षेत्र हो, कोई ऐसा जिला हो, जहां पिछले एक-दो दशकों में यह तनाव हमने नहीं देखा हो। एक तरफ शहरीकरण है, जहां विकास के नाम पर परियोजनाएं बनती हैं, अधिग्रहण की कार्रवाई चालू होती है और जो लोग उस ज़मीन पर आधारित होते हैं, जो किसानी करते हैं, मज़दूरी करते हैं, उनके अंदर तूफान आता है, वे संगठित होते हैं, अपनी बात रखते हैं और आंदोलन-प्रदर्शन होता है। शायद ही ऐसे कोई जनप्रतिनिधि यहां बैठे होंगे, जो ऐसे आंदोलनों-प्रदर्शनों में न गये हों, अपनी बात न रखी हो, समर्थन न किया हो। तो यह ऐसा मुद्दा है, जिससे पूरा देश प्रभावित है। इसकी एक लम्बी लड़ाई रही है। "बॉल ब्रास" ने एक किताब लिखी है, स्व. चौधरी चरण सिंह जी के बारे में। उसमें उन्होंने उल्लेख किया है, 1950 और 1960 के दशक का उन्होंने उदाहरण दिया है कि भूमि अधिग्रहण के संबंध में चौधरी साहब की क्या राय थी। 1950 और 1960 के दशक में गाज़ियाबाद में राजनगर एक्सटेंशन के नाम पर एक कॉलोनी विकसित की जा रही थी, वहां उस समय जो जीडीए प्राधिकरण था, 62 पैसे प्रति वर्गमीटर की दर पर ज़मीन खरीद रहा था। जब आंदोलन हुआ, तो प्राधिकरण ने बढ़ाकर एक रुपये 62 पैसे प्रति वर्गमीटर की दर से मुआवजा दिया। उसी दशक में तीन-चार साल के पश्चात् वह ज़मीन अर्थाटी ने 35 से 45 रुपये प्रति वर्गमीटर की दर से बेची थी। स्वाभाविक है उस समय भी उत्तेजनाएं थीं। बहुत समय से लोगों की इच्छा रही है कि इस कानून में परिवर्तन होना चाहिए और आज एक महत्वपूर्ण कदम यह सदन लेने जा रहा है। चौधरी साहब के उस ऐतिहासिक कदम, जिसमें उन्होंने उत्तर प्रदेश में जमींदारी उन्मूलन का कार्य किया था, के पीछे उनकी मूल भावना यही थी कि ज़मीन पर जो लोग आधारित हैं, ज़मीन पर उनका अधिकार बना रहे, भूमिहीनों को भूमि का अधिकार दिलाने में उस कदम का एक बहुत बड़ा योगदान था। पिछले दो-तीन दशकों में हम देख रहे हैं कि

दुबारा वही संघर्ष देश के हर क्षेत्र में उठ रहा है। यहां कानून के संबंध में मैं यही कहूंगा कि एक बहुत अच्छा प्रयास किया गया है। इस विषय पर एक निजी विधेयक मैंने वर्ष 2009 में इस सदन में पेश किया था। यह बहुत काम्पलेक्स इश्यू है। मुझे खुशी है इस बात को लेकर कि काफी चर्चा इस विषय पर हुई, दो बार सर्वदलीय बैठक हुई, कमेटी के विचारों को भी सरकार ने रखा, बहुत सी चीजें जिनका मैंने प्रस्ताव किया था, इस कानून का हिस्सा बनी हैं। बहुत सी चीजें जो मैं नहीं सोच पाया, उनको भी इसमें शामिल किया गया है क्योंकि मंत्री जी संवेदनशील हैं, सबकी राय को लेकर उन्होंने इस कानून को बनाया है। मुआवजे को लेकर उन्होंने जो सुझाव दिए, अच्छे हैं। लेकिन मैं यह चाहूंगा कि समय के साथ, अनुभवों के साथ हम तैयार रहें कि अगर इस कानून को बदलना हो, तो बदलें। मुआवजे को एक तरह से हमने सर्किल रेट पर पैक कर दिया है, हो सकता है कि आने वाले समय में इसे बदलना पड़े क्योंकि अलग-अलग क्षेत्रों में अलग-अलग स्थिति है। मैं यह भी कहना चाहता हूं कि जब सर्किल रेट पर हमने इसे आधारित किया है, तो प्रदेश सरकारों के लिए लम्बे समय में यह एक इन्सेंटिव बन जाएगा कि वे सर्किल रेट न बढ़ाएं।...(व्यवधान)

**सभापति महोदय:** अब समाप्त कीजिए। आपको बोलते हुए दस मिनट हो गए हैं।

**श्री जयंत चौधरी:** महोदय, मैंने अभी बोलना शुरू किया है।

**सभापति महोदय:** आपको बोलते हुए दस मिनट हो गए हैं।

**श्री जयंत चौधरी:** महोदय, मैं मंत्री जी का ध्यान इस तरफ भी आकर्षित करना चाहूंगा कि एसईजेड के संबंध में उन्होंने स्पष्टीकरण दिया है कि एसईजेड एक्ट को भी इस बिल के दायरे में लाएंगे। लेकिन वहीं नेशनल हाइवेज के लिए ज़मीन का जो अधिग्रहण होता है, वह किस रेट पर हो रहा है, किस तरह से हो रही है, उसकी क्या प्रक्रिया है, अगर उसमें भी सुधार की आवश्यकता हो, तो सरकार उस पर भी नजर रखे और सदन में प्रस्ताव लाए। कई विषय हैं जिन पर चर्चा होनी चाहिए। मैं आखिर में कहूंगा कि एक बड़ा सवाल विचारधारा और व्यवस्था का है। हममें से बहुत से लोग हैं और अब सरकार की भी एक मुख्य राय रही है कि जो आदिवासी क्षेत्र हैं, जहां बहुत गरीब हैं, छोटे और मध्यम वर्ग के किसान हैं, वहां यह आशंका जताई जा रही थी कि अगर हमने इसे मार्केट पर छोड़ दिया और सरकार की नजर एवं दखल उन क्षेत्रों में न रही, तो हो सकता है कि बहुत सस्ती दरों पर वे अपनी ज़मीन बेच दें। लेकिन मेरा अनुभव यह है कि जहां सरकार की दखल रहती है, जहां हम किसी सरकारी अफसर को नियुक्त करते हैं कि वह ख्याल रखेगा, वहीं करप्शन शुरू होता है। लैंड माफिया

सांठ-गांठ से, किसी अधिकारी को साथ में लेकर या किसी जनप्रतिनिधि के समर्थन से जो करना चाहते हैं, करा लेते हैं। इसलिए हमारा लॉन्ग-टर्म गोल यही रहना चाहिए कि हम एफिशिएंट लैंड मार्केट बनाएं, हम ज़मीन के मालिक को प्राथमिकता दें, उसे सशक्त बनाएं, इसे आज़ाद करें कि वह स्वतंत्र निर्णय ले सके। सरकार का रोल सिर्फ लैंड यूज प्लानिंग तक सीमित रहे। अगर हम यह चाहें कि सरकार हर चीज में दखल करे और एक तरह से दलाली का काम करे क्योंकि आरोप फिर सरकारों पर लगता है। सुप्रीम कोर्ट भी इस बात पर टिप्पणी कर चुका है, कह चुका है कि जितने प्राधिकरण बनते हैं, विकास के नाम पर प्राधिकरण बनाए जाते हैं, लेकिन वे मुनाफा कमा रहे हैं। न तो जिस क्षेत्र का अधिग्रहण किया गया उस प्राधिकरण द्वारा, उसका विकास नहीं हुआ, न जिनकी ज़मीन एक्वायर हुई, न ही उन्हें विकास से जोड़ा गया। आप उनके एकाउंट खोलकर देख लें कि कितनी सस्ती ज़मीन उन्होंने खरीदी और कितनी महंगी वे बेच रहे हैं। ग्रेटर नोएडा का उदाहरण दे सकता हूं। यमुना एक्सप्रेस वे का उदाहरण दे सकता हूं। यमुना एक्सप्रेस वे औद्योगिक प्राधिकरण का उदाहरण दे सकता हूं। मेरी यह गुजारिश होगी कि लम्बे समय में चाहे वह लैंड टाइटल एक्ट, जिसकी चर्चा इस सदन में मंत्री जी कर चुके हैं और उनकी प्रतिबद्धता है, उसे लाएं। इसके अलावा इस प्रक्रिया में ज्यादा पारदर्शिता लाएं। प्रदेशों में जो कम्प्युटरीकरण हो रहा है, उसकी गति को बढ़ाएं। हमें एफिशिएंट लैंड मार्केट बनाने होंगे, यह हमारा अल्टीमेट गोल होना चाहिए और सरकार का इस प्रक्रिया में दखल कम से कम हो। यही किसान और ज़मीन के मालिक के हित में होगा।

## [13] Lalu Prasad Yadav

**श्री लालू प्रसाद यादव (सारण):** महोदय, मैं आपको धन्यवाद देता हूं कि आपने मुझे इस बिल पर बोलने का अवसर दिया। देश भर के किसानों ने जिस सवाल पर आंदोलन खड़ा किया, उनका और उद्योग लगाने वाले लोगों का ध्यान इस बिल की ओर है, जिसे पास करके हम कानून बनाने जा रहे हैं। हम ऐसे सवाल पर चर्चा कर रहे हैं जो कि अत्यंत महत्वपूर्ण है। हजारों वर्ष पुराने अतीत को अगर हम देखें तो ज़मीन का सवाल बड़ा संवेदनशील और गम्भीर रहा है। महाभारत की शुरूआत भी पांच गांव देने की बात को लेकर हुई थी, जब श्रीकृष्ण कौरवों से पांडवों के लिए मांगने गए थे, जो कि तैयार नहीं हुए और महाभारत हुआ, जिसमें हजारों लोग मारे गए। हमने कल ही श्रीकृष्ण का जन्मदिन मनाया है। उनके समय में राक्षसों का विनाश हुआ था।

हमारे बुजुर्गों ने हजारों वर्ष पहले ज़मीन को उपजाऊ बनाकर आने वाली पीढ़ियों को दिया। उस ज़मीन का विगत दिनों में जिस तरह से कौड़ियों के भाव पर अधिग्रहण किया गया, उससे देश के लोग, खासकर किसान आंदोलित हो गए। कोलकाता से

इस आंदोलन की आग समूचे देश में फैल गई। इस बात को आप भी अच्छी तरह से जानते हैं, क्योंकि आप भुगतभोगी रहे हैं। देश भर में किसानों की ज़मीन, जो खेती की ज़मीन है, जो उनकी जीविका का मूल आधार हुआ करती थी, जिस तरह से लूटा गया प्राइवेट लोगों द्वारा कम्पनीज बना-बनाकर, उससे सारा देश गर्म हो गया। इसे लेकर किसानों ने सभी जगह आंदोलन किया कि हम जान देंगे, लेकिन ज़मीन नहीं देंगे। आज भी जहां इस तरह की बात होती है तो जान भले ही चली जाए, ज़मीन नहीं जाने दी जाती।

इन्हीं सारे सवालों का समाधान करने के लिए सरकार ने सब दलों की मीटिंग बुलाई। उसमें राय बनी कि सरकार को बीच में नहीं आना चाहिए। देश की सारी ज़मीन का क्लासिफिकेशन हो। किसान सीधे निवेशकों से बातचीत करे। सरकार तब बीच में आए, जब किसान और उद्योगपति के बीच एग्रीमेंट हो जाए और फिर कोई इंडिविजुअली प्लाट वाला व्यक्ति खलल पैदा करके विशेष प्लाट को एक्वायर करने की कोशिश करे। इस मोटी-मोटी बात पर सबकी राय बनी कि सरकार को अलग-थलग रहना चाहिए और इसके अलावा किसानों को पैकेज मिलना चाहिए। जब उसकी ज़मीन जाती है तो उसे मार्केट रेट तो मिले ही, लेकिन जो उद्योग वहां लगे, उसमें भी उसका शेयर रहना चाहिए और उसके बच्चों को जॉब की गारंटी मिलनी चाहिए। यह राय सब की थी और यह जो बिल हम बना रहे हैं इससे सभी किसानों और सभी लोगों की संतुष्टि होगी और सब कहेंगे कि संसद ने, लोकसभा ने हमारे साथ इंसाफ किया। माननीय मुलायम सिंह जी बोल रहे थे कि इनका जो बीहड़ का इलाका है वहां इंडस्ट्री ले जाओ। बंजर भूमि, लो-लैंड, वाटर लॉगिंग हमारे बिहार में बहुत है। नार्थ बिहार में हजारों एकड़ भूमि लो-लैंड और वाटर लॉगिंग में फंसी हुई है। नदियां ही नदियां हैं और लोगों की जनसंख्या ज्यादा है, ज़मीन हमारे पास ज्यादा नहीं है। ज़मीन के टुकड़े-टुकड़े हो गये हैं और यह सवाल केवल बिहार का नहीं है क्योंकि यह बिल और नीति जो बन रही है इस पर हमें सोचना चाहिए कि इसमें सरकार बीच में नहीं आये। हम जानना चाहते हैं कि कहां कोई उद्योग-धंधा खोलने आ रहा है क्योंकि सारी इंडस्ट्री कोलकाता से लेकर मुम्बई में, कानपुर में, लाल-इमली से लेकर हरी-इमली की सब फैक्ट्रियाँ बंद हैं और एफडीआई को हमने इजाजत दी है तो उनके लिए भी हमें ज़मीन का इंतजाम उनके गोदामों के लिए करना पड़ेगा। मुम्बई में जाकर आप देखें कि मेन-सिटी में कितनी पुरानी फैक्ट्रियाँ बीमार हैं, सिक हैं। कोलकाता में, कानपुर में भी सिक-इंडस्ट्रीज हैं। ऐसी सिक इंडस्ट्रीज के लिए भी आपको प्रावधान करना चाहिए और उन्हें रिवाइव करके लोगों को देना चाहिए।

यूपीए(1) में जब हम रेल मंत्री थे तो इंफ्रास्ट्रक्चर के मामले में वैस्टर्न कोरीडोर और ईस्टर्न कोरीडोर पर कैबिनेट का फैसला है और उस पर रेल का खर्चा भी है,

इसलिए मैं माननीय मंत्री जी का ध्यान दिलाना चाहूंगा कि भारत सरकार की कैबिनेट द्वारा वैस्टर्न कोरिडोर पर, दिल्ली-लुधियाना-मुम्बई तक इंडस्ट्रियल हब बनाने की जो बात थी कि यहीं पर इंडस्ट्री का ध्यान केन्द्रित होगा। उस पर खर्चा भी हुआ और रेल मंत्रालय ने खर्चा भी किया। हमारी खेती और किसान को कोई ग्रीवेंस न रहे। बिहार में जहां वाटर-लॉगिंग है वहां कौन उद्योग-धंधा खोलने आ रहा है, सब अपार्टमेंट बनाने के लिए बिल्डर्स आ रहे हैं। नोएडा, हैदराबाद, मुम्बई, पटना के शहर में प्राइवेट कॉलिज और निजी संस्थान खोलने के लिए लोग आ रहे हैं। इसलिए किसान के हितों की रक्षा होनी चाहिए।

दूसरी तरफ जो आने वाली पीढ़ी है उसे भी काम मिले, ऐसा काम सरकार को करना चाहिए। इसलिए जो बिल आया है, वह क्रांतिकारी है और समय-समय पर इसमें सुधार संसद के द्वारा किया जाएगा। लेकिन कहीं भी किसानों की उपेक्षा नहीं होनी चाहिए। "जान देंगे, लेकिन ज़मीन नहीं देंगे" देश भर के किसानों की यह बात है। भारत सरकार को इंफ्रास्ट्रक्चर और जनहित के लिए उचित पैसा देकर किसानों की ज़मीन को लेना चाहिए ताकि कहीं खून-खराबा न हो। माननीय रमेश जी बहुत मेहनत करके इस बिल को लाए हैं, हम उन्हें धन्यवाद देते हैं और इस बिल का पुरजोर समर्थन करते हैं।

## [14] Sher Singh Ghubaya

SHRI SHER SINGH GHUBAYA (FEROZEPUR): Thank you, Chairman Sir, for giving me the opportunity to speak on Land Acquisition, Rehabilitation and Resettlement Bill, 2011. I thank the Hon. Minister for accepting the notice given by our leader Madam Harsimrat Kaur Badal a few days ago on land amendment.

Sir, this is an important Bill regarding acquisition of land of farmers. Several Hon. Members have mooted very good suggestions on this Bill. Sir, I would like to know from the Hon. Minister the amount of money the Central Government proposes to contribute towards the implementation of this programme. Sir the Bill proposes to provide compensation to the rural farmer for the land acquired at four times the existing rate whereas in urban areas, the compensation will be paid at thrice the rate. However, it is to be noted that it is the State Government that has to deal directly with matters pertaining to land acquisition in that state. It is in a far better position to know the ground realities. The local administration and the local people have better information about the nature and price of the land that is to be acquired.

Also, sir, our leader and Chief Minister of Punjab, Sardar Parkash Singh Badal has acquired thousands of acres of land for industrial purpose, etc.. However, he has provided just and fair compensation to the affected persons. So, not a single displaced person has ever complained or protested against our land acquisition policy. We have taken full care of the interest of the oustees. In fact, more and more people want the State Government to acquire their land due to the remunerative compensation package provided by the State Government. So, I urge upon the Central Government to emulate the flawless land acquisition policy of Punjab Government.

Sir, a lot of Special Economic Zones (SEZs) have been carried out in recent times. Land ranging from five lakh acres to two lakh acres has been acquired for this purpose. However, I am sorry to say that the land acquired for this purpose is not being utilized properly. The work undertaken at these places in not up to the mark.

Sir, the land mafia becomes very active when it comes to know that land is about to be acquired at a particular place for some purpose. It works overtime and pro-actively purchases land from their owners at very cheap rates. Then, the land-mafia sells the same land at exorbitant rates and makes illegal profits. The real owners of land suffer in the process. The Central Government has thrust the entire responsibility in this matter on the State Government. If this is the case, the power to decide the usage of land should also be vested in the State Government. The Chief Minister of the state, the Deputy Commissioner of the area and the local administration like Tehsildar will be able to fix a much better rate of the local land to be acquired. The centre should not dictate terms in this matter. Hence, relevant amendments should be made in this Bill.

MR CHAIRMAN: Please conclude.

SHRI SHER SINGH GHUBAYA: Sir, in India, we have created about 550 SEZs in recent time. This is a very high number. Nowhere in the world have this many numbers of SEZs been created. It seems as if bungling, malpractices and irregularities at a large scale are going on in the creation of SEZs. Land mafia is indulging in loot and plunder in collusion with powerful and corrupt elements, whereas the original land owners have been left in the lurch.

Sir, the Bill also talks about rehabilitation measures. Sir, ever since we attained independence, the hard-working farmers made even barren land fertile by the dint of their sweat and blood. However, in some states like Haryana, these farmers are being displaced from their land. Sir, in Punjab, our Chief Minister Sardar Parkash Singh Badal had in fact allotted land in the border areas to the poor and the needy at cheap rates. I urge upon the Central Government not to displace these land – owners.

MR CHAIRMAN: Please conclude.

SHRI SHER SINGH GHUBAYA: Sir, I have just begun my speech.

MR CHAIRMAN: Please wind up in one minute.

SHRI SHER SINGH GHUBAYA: Sir, Punjab provides maximum amount of food-grains in the central pool.

Sir, the recent floods in Punjab have wreaked havoc in the state. Half the districts of Punjab have been devastated. The standing crop of paddy has been destroyed. People have been rendered homeless.

Sir, there has been a great loss of lives and property due to floods. The State Government has provided a compensation of 1.5 lakhs per head to the affected families. But more needs to be done. The Central Government should also provide a compensation of Rs. 5 lakh per head to the affected families. A sum of Rs. 50,000 should also be provided to people whose cattle have been washed away.

School buildings that have been destroyed should also be reconstructed. The Central Government should provide aid in this matter.

MR CHAIRMAN: Please conclude. The allotted time is over.
Now, Shri Prabodh Panda ji.
SHRI SHER SINGH GHUBAYA: Sir, there is a fear of the outbreak of epidemics due to floods. I urge upon the centre to send a team of health—experts to assess the situation in the flood-affected areas. An economic package should be granted for the affected people at the earliest. New houses should be constructed for those who have lost their homes. Health-care system in the flood affected areas should be

streamlined. New school buildings should be constructed. New roads should be constructed where these have been washed away in floods.

## [15] Prabodh Panda

SHRI PRABODH PANDA (MIDNAPORE): Madam Chairperson, I am very grateful to you for giving me this opportunity to speak. You are not only chairing this House but you are also the Chairman of the Standing Committee. All the reports of your Standing Committee are very much encouraging and I fully endorse all the reports that have been prepared by your Standing Committee.

Madam, at the very outset, I must welcome this Bill and particularly I congratulate the Minister who is very energetic and dynamic. He has tried his level best but I would mention one thing. On the one side, when we are discussing the Land Acquisition (Rehabilitation and Resettlement) Bill in the Parliament House, on the other side, across the country, the land acquisition process is going on and it is not being stopped. So, these two things are going on. During Special Mention in this Parliament, I said several times that as this is the matter under discussion, let the State Government be requested to stop all the land acquisition processes right now. But still it is going on and it is quite unfortunate.

I am just going to touch the points. I would not make a long speech. Please allow me to complete all the points. Firstly, it should have a retrospective effect. The retrospective effect does not mean where the land has not been acquired or the compensation has not yet been awarded. My point is that the people who are agitating across the country in lakhs and lakhs of numbers, they will be deprived of if you do not give it a retrospective effect since 1990s. So, you think over it.

Secondly, my proposal is that the Government should set up a Price Commission. You are assessing the compensation based on the value of the land. How is the value of land determined? There are two systems for that. Number one is market value, but it is known to everybody that in the deed itself, it is undervalued. Secondly, as regards the Indian Stamp Act, it was also enacted under the British rule. It was enacted in 1899. As we are going to replace the Land Acquisition Act, 1894, we should also replace the Act which was enacted in 1899, namely, the Indian Stamp Act. Still you are working according to that Act. So, my proposal is that, let the Government come out with a proposal for setting up a Price Commission at the State level and the district level. I am thankful to the Standing Committee as it also recommended It but the Government did not agree to it.

Thirdly, as regards Fourth Schedule, there are 18 Acts in it but the Acts are not the same in regard to land acquisition. If you see the States' Acts, the Act of West Bengal, it is offering a solatium of 30 per cent. In Railways, the solatium is 60 per cent and as per the proposal in this Bill, the solatium is 100 per cent but in case of national highways, there is no solatium. Around 80 per cent of land acquisition is governed by other Acts and not by the Land Acquisition Act. So uniformity should be there. All the Acts which have been mentioned in the Fourth.

Madam, the next point that I would like to make is that provisions should be clearly made about the unused land. If for any purpose land has been acquired and it remains idle, then that should be returned to the original farmer. To this extent, there was an assurance given by the Hon. Minister himself in this House. He now should not deviate from that assurance. It will help a lot of farmers.

Madam, I do not agree with the proposal of 80–20 consent in relation to acquisition of land. Many Hon. Members of this august House have talked about article 300(a) of the Constitution. It is the Fundamental Right of every citizen to have his or her consent and how the Government is proposing to go in for acquiring land based on the consent of 80 per cent? It should be 100 per cent for acquisition of land. There is also another point with regard to 80–20 or 70–30 consent in case of PPP cases. What will be the fate of the farmers in that case? In case of 80 per cent procurement or purchase of land by an investor, a farmer will get only the value of the land but when 20 per cent is being offered by State Governments in that case a farmer will get the value of the land, compensation, solatium, rehabilitation and resettlement and all those things. Why is such discrimination being made? But that does not mean an investor should be allowed to acquire land limitlessly, without any ceiling from the farmers. There should be a ceiling on it. The Land Ceiling Act should not be deleted. If an investor needs more land, then he should approach the Government and the Government should examine it and then give a special ceiling for acquiring land. That condition should be imposed. There cannot be any differentiation between land being acquired by Government and procurement of land by private investors or private entrepreneurs.

Madam, I completely agree with the recommendations made by the Standing Committee on Rural Development, particularly the recommendation which says that public purpose should not mean private purpose. The old Act of 1894 is a draconian British law but even now the, according to the provisions of the Bill, Government is moving away from the spirit of public purpose to that of private purpose. That should be deleted. Government should be a facilitator in case of industrialization and not an agent of the industrialists. The Government should not be the agent of the investors. Why should the Government come in the way? Special ceiling can be offered to the investors with a condition in this matter.

Madam, I do agree with the Hon. Members who have suggested that a Land Conservation Act should be enacted just as it is there in case of Forests. The same kind of an enactment should be made for agricultural land also. I am not going into the details of it. Thousands and thousands of acres of agricultural land has been encroached upon. This should be taken care of.

I would like to congratulate the Hon. Minister for his assurance in this House for agreeing to the proposals of the Hon. Members in regard to the SEZ. I am sure he will think over it. Moreover, land use map is very much necessary and it should serve as a guideline to all the States. The last point that I would like to make is that Hon. Minister, though this subject does not come under the purview of this Bill, is very much interested in land reforms.

More than 50,000 farmers started route march from Porbandar to Gwalior and he gave the assurances. Even today thousands of farmers are organising movements to occupy the excess land in Bihar. I congratulate those who are organising these movements, particularly those in the Begusarai area. ... (*Interruptions*)

## [16] Sharifuddin Shariq

श्री शरीफुद्दीन शारिक (बारामुला): मैडम, आपका बहुत शुक्रिया। इस बात में कोई दो राय नहीं है कि ज़मीन किसान की रीढ़ की हड्डी ही नहीं, बल्कि हमारे देश की रीढ़

की हड्डी है। इस पर जितना कम बोझ डाला जाए, उतना देश के लिए और देश के लोगों के लिए बेहतर है। ज़मीन हासिल करना जरूरी है गवर्नमेंट के लिए, क्योंकि आसमान पर चीजें नहीं बनेंगी, हवा में नहीं बनेंगी, जो कुछ भी बनेगा ज़मीन पर ही बनेगा। सड़क हो, इंडस्ट्री हो, तामीर हो, तरक्की हो, बिल्डिंग हो, होटल हो, अन्य कोई भी चीज हो, उसे ज़मीन पर ही बनना है। लिहाजा एक्वीज़िशन लाज़िमी है मुल्क की तरक्की के लिए। लेकिन इस बारे में मेरी गुजारिश यह होगी कि जब आप ज़मीन हासिल करते हैं तो आप एक किसान की जान लेते हैं। उसका सारा गुजारा उस पर है, सारी उसकी जिंदगी का दारोमदार आईंदा नस्लों पर भी है, तो कम्पेनसेशन मुकर्रर करते वक्त जो चार गुना आपने कहा है, इसको आईंदा तीस साल का कैलकुलेशन करना चाहिए। आईंदा 30वें साल के बाद क्या कीमत होगी, उसका ख्याल रखना होगा। वह हमेशा के लिए उससे छिन जाती है, इस बात का ख्याल रखना चाहिए क्योंकि यही उसकी पूंजी है और यही सब कुछ उसका है। उसका मुआवजा देने के लिए इस बात को ठीक तरह से देखना चाहिए कि इसका मुआवजा आईंदा तीस साल, पचास साल तक कैलकुलेट होना चाहिए। अगर मुमकिन हो, नॉन टैक्निकल काम जो बाद में हों, वह उसी खानदान के लोगों से कराया जाए, ताकि वे कुछ रोजी-रोटी उससे कमा सकें। उसी खानदान के बच्चों को, जिससे यह ज़मीन ली जाती है, उनको यकीनी रोजगार देना चाहिए। इस सिलसिले में मैं एक गुजारिश करूंगा कि हमारी रेलवे लाइन जो कश्मीर में आयी, रेलवे डिपार्टमेंट ने एक ज़मीन का मुआवजा भी दे दिया और हर खानदान को जो मुतास्सिर हुआ, उनके बच्चों को एक घर से एक को नौकरी दे दी।

इसी तरह जिनके पास कम ज़मीन होगी, यह देखा जाए कि उनसे ज़मीन न ली जाये, बल्कि उसके मुकाबले में उन लोगों से ज़मीन ली जाये, जिनके पास खातिर ख्वाह ज़मीन है। अगर जबरदस्त हालात ऐसे पड़ें कि कम ज़मीन वाले से भी ज़मीन ली जाये तो फिर सरकार किसी दूसरी जगह, जहां बैरन लैंड हो, उसे मुआवजे में ज़मीन दे दे ताकि वह उसे आबाद कर सके। दूसरी बात यह है कि मुआवजा देने में सालों लग जाते हैं और उन बेचारों को सालों-साल दफ्तरों के चक्कर काटने पड़ते हैं। लिहाजा एक्वीज़िशन का फैसला होने के बाद, ज़मीन का कब्जा लेने से पहले उसे मुआवजा अदा किया जाना चाहिए। पहले उसे मुआवजा देना चाहिए और फिर उसकी ज़मीन लेनी चाहिए और ऐसी ज़मीन को एक्वायर करने के लिए तरजीह देनी चाहिए जो कम से कम नाकारा हो, जिसमें पैदावारी, सलाहियत कम हो और जिसमें इरीगेशन फैसिलिटीज कम हो, पैदावारी, सलाहियत कम हो। दूसरी मेरी छोटी-सी एक और गुजारिश है कि ज़मीन लेते वक्त कोलोनीअल जमाने में दबदबा होता था, लोग पुलिस लेकर आते थे और डरा-धमकाकर ज़मीन लेते थे। इसमें इंतेहाई प्यार,

मुहब्बत से उन लोगों को समझाना चाहिए। उनको इसकी इफ़ादियत से आगाह करना चाहिए। सरकारी दबदबा और कानून का खौफ़-व-हरास इसमें नहीं होना चाहिए। जिन रियासतों में ज़रई ज़मीनें बहुत कम हैं, वहाँ खुसूसी तौर ज्यादा मुआवज़े की ज़रूरत है। पैसा देते वक्त रुपये की सेहत का भी ख्याल रखना चाहिए क्योंकि हमारा रुपया अब बिल्कुल नाकारा हो गया है, इस चीज़ का भी ख्याल रखना चाहिए।

ज़मीन की पैदावारी सलाहियत को उसकी जगह की मुनासिबत को, उसके फाइनैंशियल वैल्यू को और इलाकायी हालत को मद्देनज़र रखकर ही ज़मीन ली जाए और मुआवज़ा उसी हिसाब से हो। किसी जगह की ज़मीन ज्यादा कीमती है, किसी जगह की ज़मीन उतनी कीमती नहीं है। मुआवज़ा तआय्युन करके मुकर्रर करने के वक्त इन बातों का ख्याल रहना चाहिए और उसके लिए गवर्नमेंट ऑफ इंडिया से बाकायदा रियासतों को भी हिदायत देनी चाहिए। ज़रई मज़दूर जिनकी अपनी ज़मीन नहीं है, वे आपकी ज़मीन पर मज़दूरी करते हैं, लेकिन आपकी ज़मीन चली गई तो वह ज़रई मज़दूर बेकार हो जाता है। उसके रोज़गार का भी कुछ न कुछ ख्याल रखना चाहिए। साथ ही में, जहाँ ग्रेजिंग लैन्ड्ज़ हैं, काश्त-चराई की ज़मीन है, अगर वह ज़मीन हम अक्वायर कर लें तो उससे किसान के माल-मवेशी खराब हो जाते हैं, दूध की पैदावार कम हो जाएगी, ऊन कम बनेगी, गोश्त कम होगा और इस तरह दूसरा नुकसान होगा। इन सब बातों को पेशे-नज़र रखते हुए इन बातों का ख्याल रखना चाहिए। इन बातों के साथ मैं इस बिल की हिमायत करता हूँ।

## [17] Prem Das Rai

SHRI PREM DAS RAI (SIKKIM): I support this long awaited bill on behalf of my party, but even as we support it, there are certain issues that must be pointed out. Previous speakers have already raised many important issues. I will like to emphasize some pressing issues that the Government must take into consideration.

The valuation of land in the mountain areas will necessarily have to be different from the rest of the country. In this regard, there is no mention of mountain lands where there are other forms of constraints. How will the same mechanism work?

We therefore will have to bring further amendment in the rules for this.

When it comes to acquisition of land for public purpose, the most basic question that arises is: What is a just acquisition price? As acquisition is not always a desired transaction, it is necessary to pay something more a 'solatium' for the sufferings caused therein.

The provisions of this Bill assumes, for example, rural land in Punjab and rural land in Sikkim are the same. But, in reality, Punjab and Sikkim have very different landholding sizes, very different traditions about the meaning of individual ownership of land, and radically different demand patterns. Considering the diversity within our vast country, I urge the government to consider how a uniform multiplier of two can be used to determine the solatium.

The government should also reconsider the bill's provision stipulating different consent requirements based on ownership, that is, consent by 80 per cent of land owners if acquired for use by a private company; 70 per cent if acquired for use by a PPP; and no consent if land is for use by government or a PSU. It is not clear why should a landowner who is about to lose his land care whether the intended use is to be executed by the government or a private company?

With these words, which may even be considered a form of caveat, I support this Bill and hope that the Hon'ble Minister will take note of the points mentioned by me.

## [18] Mohammed E.T. Basheer

SHRI MOHAMMED E.T. BASHEER (PONNANI): Madam, this is really opening of a horizon of development with a human face. We all know that we were facing hurdles in the land acquisition process and that is why several ambitious projects were forced to stall. There was a lot of bitter experience to the thrown out families. They were made landless and homeless. Along with this, getting adequate compensation was also a cumbersome process. This legislation marks an end to all such miseries and paves the way for infrastructure development in our country. In addition to this, this legislation ensures participation of victims in the development process and that is a good signal and message in the way of participatory development.

Coming to various provisions of the Bill, I wish to point out that the process envisaged in Chapter 2 on determination of social impact and public purpose is highly appreciable.

The Bill says that whenever the appropriate Government intends to acquire land for a public purpose, it shall carry out a social impact assessment study in consultation with the Gram Sabha at habitation level or equivalent body in urban areas. Involvement of local bodies in deciding the public purpose is really a welcome step in this legislation. I think, this is a most progressive part of this legislation.

As per Chapter 3(1), there is a special provision in this legislation to safeguard certain interests such as multi-crop irrigation land, which, of course, is the best interest of agriculture. Rehabilitation and Resettlement Scheme envisaged in this Bill is very comprehensive. The transparency ensured on rehabilitation and resettlement at all levels is really crystal clear. It is also a most welcome step.

With regard to the determination of amount of compensation and determination of value of things attached to land or building, it is stated in the Bill that the Collector may use the service of some 'Specialist' and 'Experienced persons'. It has not been clarified properly. It has to be clarified in detail. Otherwise, it may lead to many ambiguities and litigations.

I wish to say a word of appreciation to the definition to the 'affected families'. It is a broad definition. It protects the right of agricultural labours, tenants, share croppers, tribals and forest dwellers, etc.

Rehabilitation package as discussed in Chapter 5 of the Bill is also comprehensive. It includes land allotment, land cost, subsistence allowance, transportation, payment even for cattle shed and payment for artisans and small traders, mandatory employment, fishing right, etc. These are all excellent steps to meet the hardship of the victims. The time limit for payment of compensation is also specific in the Bill. That is also a highly appreciable step.

Formulation of a Rehabilitation and Resettlement Committee is narrated in Chapter 6 and it is having a judicious combination (officers plus people representatives and representatives of the local bodies). That also is very good.

Madam, the national level monitoring committee as specified in Chapter 7 is also a highly appreciable step.

MADAM CHAIRMAN: Please conclude now.

SHRI MOHAMMED E.T. BASHEER: Madam, I am concluding now.

I wish to add one more point. It has been stated that for certain private institutions, we have acquired land. Some institutions have really abandoned their function. I would like to give my own example. I was working with the Grasim Industries which is the biggest private industry in Kerala, owned by Birlas. That factory was closed after 30 years. Even now, thousands of acres of land are still remaining with Birlas. There must be a provision on the effective utilization of such land for some public purpose.

Madam, I would like to make one more point that enough lands are available with the Government unutilized. For that also, there must be some provision. Even to transfer land from one Department to another Department and that also is a very difficult process now. There must be a provision to simplify that process also.

I would like to conclude by saying that this Bill is a progressive legislation and this Bill can be called as a tribute to those innocent peasants killed at Nandigram in West Bengal.

With these words, I conclude my speech.

## [19] S.K. Saidul Haque

SHRI S.K. SAIDUL HAQUE (BARDHMAN-DURGAPUR): The present Bill seeks to replace the Land Acquisition Act, 1894. The 1894 Act does not provide for rehabilitation and resettlement (R&R) for those affected by land acquisition. Currently, the R&R process is governed by the National Rehabilitation and Resettlement Policy, 2007.

The present Bill combines the provisions of land acquisition and R&R with a single Bill. In September 2011, the Government introduced the Land Acquisition and Rehabilitation and Resettlement Bill in the Lok Sabha.

Some of the major issues of the Bill are (a) the process of land acquisition, (b) rights of the people displaced by the acquisition, (c) method of calculating compensation, and (d) requirement of Rehabilitation and Resettlement for all acquisitions.

I have submitted a number of amendments to this Bill. I like that Government will consider all those amendments. I admit that 1894 Act should be amended. I also admit that for public purpose lands needs to be acquisitional. But that should be done from a humanistic attitude so that land looses get proper compensation, resettlement and rehabilitation. Proper benefits should go to the *kisans*. As such, I like to make few points.

First, the provisions of this Act relating to land use, consent, land acquisition, livelihood guarantee, compensation, rehabilitation and resettlement, shall apply in all cases where the appropriate Government acquires land for its own use including for public sector undertakings and for stated public purpose subject to the following that the Government or public sector undertakings shall have full ownership and operational control of the project. Free and prior informed consent from the affected families shall be obtained at the time of social impact assessment in the form of a written resolution passed by 70 per cent of all affected families before Declaration under Section 18. Land acquired for public purpose under this Act shall not be transferred to private companies or public private partnerships through any instrument such as sale, lease etc.

No land shall be transferred by any kind of acquisition, in the Scheduled Areas in contravention of any law (including any order or judgement of a court which has been final) relating to land transfer prevailing in such Scheduled Areas.

In case of acquisition for Private companies for public purpose as defined in clauses (zaa) and (zab) of Section 3, provided that in case of acquisition under the sub-section, prior informed consent of at least 80 per cent of the affected families through a written resolution shall be obtained through a process as may be prescribed by the appropriate Government. The process of obtaining the consent shall be carried out long with the Social Impact Assessment referred to in Section 4. The acquisition of land under this sub-section shall require prior approval of the Government after proper enquiry. The acquisition of land under this sub section shall require a mandatory agreement between the company and the Government to ensure easy access of direct benefits to the general public and such mandatory agreement shall be executed prior to acquisition and strictly regulated subsequently.

The provision of this Bill shall also apply in case of purchase of land by private companies purchases or acquire land over and above the land ceiling prevalent in the respective State or above 10 acres (whichever is lower) in rural areas and 2 acres in urban areas (whichever is lower) through private negotiations with owners of the land after securing prior approval of the appropriate Government as per the provisions of Section 42.

No acquisition of land and forest rights shall be permitted in any area until computation of all proceedings for recognition of rights under the Scheduled Tribes and other traditional Forest Dwellers (Recognition of Forest Rights) Act, 2006 for restoration of land alienated from these persons in violation of revenue law and for settlement of rights under applicable revenue laws.

Without prejudice to any of the other provisions of this Act relating to consent of affected persons, no acquisition of rights shall be permitted in any area to which the provisions of the Scheduled Tribes and other Traditional Forest Dwellers (Recognition of Forest Rights) Act, 2006, or the Panchayats (Extension to Scheduled Area) Act, 1996 apply, except with the specific prior informed consent of the affected gram sabha and subject to any condition that these gram sabha may jointly or individually impose in exercise of their powers under the 2006 Forest Rights Act or Panchayat Act, 1996.

In case of land to be acquisitioned for infrastructure project like electricity, non-conventional energy, water supply and sanitation, tele-communication, roads and bridges, railways, small irrigation, storage, oil and gas pipeline networks, Government should ensure that such projects serve the large welfare of people and acquisition is made on the principle of 'quodest necessarium est licitum' implying only that much which is necessary is legal.

In case of compensation, among others as stated in Bill, a permanent farm servant or attached agricultural worker who has worked on the land for not less than one year prior to the notification and any person whose source of livelihood is likely to be adversely affected, including persons who are occupying Government, public, common or other land as well as those residing on such land for *bona fide* livelihood purposes.

The collector needs to take possession of the land only after ensuring that the compensation is paid and the rehabilitation and resettlement process is completed in all its aspects six months prior to displacement which shall be confirmed through a resolution of the displaced/affected persons.

There should be one comprehensive Act for such acquisition, Rehabilitation and Resettlement because like railways, defence, there are 13 organization who have their own Act of Land Acquisition. As a result, land loses acquired in their acts will not get the benefit of this Act.

Another important point is that a private company that acquires or purchases more than 50 acres of land in urban areas or 100 acres in rural areas is required to rehabilitate and resettle affected families. This threshold can be circumvented by a private company by purchasing multiple parcels of land, each under the prescribed limit, through other entities.

Provision should be there for an accurate estimation of the value of the land compensation shall be calculated four times on the basis of the market value and value of assets attached to the land.

## [20] Prasanta Kumar Majumdar

SHRI PRASANTA KUMAR MAJUMDAR (BALURGHAT): Respected Chairman Sir, I do not support this Land Acquisition, Rehabilitation and Resettlement Bill, 2011. The reason is that I believe that the scope and definition of 'public purpose' should be limited to infrastructure development, national security projects, economic infrastructure, social infrastructure like schools, colleges, hospitals, roads, etc. These infrastructures should be built with Government patronage. It has been said that consent of 80 per cent landowners is a must for acquisition of land. But I think that this provision is unacceptable because the Government must not have any role in acquisition at all.

There are 3 factors of production—land, capital and labour. The Government does not play any role in supplying capital and labour. Thus, land should also be acquired by the investors from the free market and Government must not interfere at all. In all the developed countries of the world *viz.* Europe, America, Canada, Japan, the Government does not acquire land and it is for the industrialists to purchase land on their own. Further, resettlement has been proposed where 100 acres of land is acquired in the rural areas and 50 acres in the urban areas. So if the quantum of acquired land is less than this, then the industrialists are not bound to offer rehabilitation packages to the land owners. This provision is utterly condemnable. If the investors acquire 99 acres in villages and 49 acres in the urban areas in order to bypass the provision of the Bill, then the farmers will be left to fend for themselves and they will not get any compensation whatsoever. Section 110 says that even fertile, multi-crop land can be acquired which I vehemently oppose. I believe that fertile land should not be acquired at all. If we intend to realize the dream of universal food security, it must be ensured that arable, cultivable multi-crop land are not acquired.

In clause 98, it has been mentioned that provisions of this Act not to apply in certain cases or to apply with certain modification. If that is accepted then SEZ has to be accepted too. It is surprising that this Bill is completely silent on mining land I can see that the land law of 1894 is still applicable and land is being acquired in the same fashion even today. We have huge natural resources in the country deep inside the earth. The tribal people, people living in hilly areas, in the forests, the SC and ST communities, they have been the custodian of these resources for years and now are being displaced from their land due to rampant industrialization. Even the land records are being changed. These people are not getting any compensation or rehabilitation. I request Hon. Minister that this practice must be stopped and adequate compensation packages should be paid with retrospective effect. Rehabilitation packages should also be offered to them.

I know that Hon. Minister of Rural Development is trying his level best to address all these issues but I urge upon him to sincerely look into the fall-out of such a momentous Bill and take corrective measures wherever required.

I thank you for allowing me to participate in this debate and with these words I conclude my speech.

## [21] Ajay Kumar

SHRI AJAY KUMAR (JAMSHEDPUR): Madam, I want to congratulate the Minister first for bringing this Bill. अच्छे प्वाइंट्स है जैसे नो प्राइवेट कम्पनीज के लिए एक्वीज़िशन है। रिहैबिलिटेशन एंड रीसेटलमेंट, सोशल इम्पैक्ट, में एक समस्या जरूर है कि इसमें टाइम बाउंड लिमिट नहीं है। मैं मंत्री महोदय से अनुरोध करूंगा कि रिपोर्ट को टाइम बाउंड करें।

अभी तक 500 एसईजेड हुए हैं। यह रिपोर्ट आयी थी कि उनमें से 300 एसईजेड जिस कारण स्थापित किये गये थे, उनके लिए इस्तेमाल नहीं किये जा रहे हैं। मेरा अनुरोध है कि अगर आप उन 300 एसईजेड को वापिस लेकर फिर से उद्योग के लिए दे देंगे, तो कम से कम आपको अगले पांच-दस साल के लिए लैंड एक्वीज़िशन

करने की आवश्यकता नहीं पड़ेगी। दूसरी बात यह है कि यह खेल एग्रीकल्चर और कमर्शियल लैंड के ट्रांसिशन पर ही है। आप किसान से एग्रीकल्चर लैंड लेते हैं। उसके बाद आप उसे कमर्शियल करने लगते हैं। मेरा यही अनुरोध होगा कि जैसे आप हर जगह देखते हैं, खेल वही है। कुछ हमारे साथियों ने कहा कि अब ज़मीन का दाम 5 करोड़ रुपये है। झगड़ा तो इसी बात का है कि किसान के लिए वह 5 करोड़ रुपया नहीं गया। वह तो किसान से दस रुपये में लिया गया है। इसलिए आपसे अनुरोध है कि अगर आप सब जगह मास्टर प्लान बनायेंगे तो उसे हर साल अपडेट करें और पहले से कमर्शियल यूज के लिए सुनिश्चित कर लें। आप रेलवे लाइन छोड़ दीजिए, रोड़ छोड़ दीजिए, तो आपको उसे कमर्शियल दर देनी ही पड़ेगी।

शैड्यूल पांच और छ: के बारे में काफी बातें कही गयी हैं। मैं मंत्री महोदय से यह अनुरोध करना चाहता हूं कि आपने कहा कि पीएसयूज के लिए यह लागू नहीं होगा। झारखंड में 65 लाख लोग अब तक विस्थापित हुए हैं। सरकारी कम्पनी पर कम से कम कुछ कंट्रोल रह सकता है। यदि आयरन ओर या कोल हो, तो वह सरकार के अधीनस्थ ही रह जायेगा। दूसरी बात है कि 20 प्रतिशत कोयले की चोरी होती है।

मैडम, एक छोटा-सा उदाहरण है कि अगर इंडिया गेट के नीचे आपको हीरे की खदान मिल जायेगी, तो आप इंडिया गेट को तो नहीं तोड़ेंगे। लेकिन आदिवासी की ज़मीन सबसे सस्ती पड़ती है। मैं आपसे यही अनुरोध करना चाहता हूं कि पहले 20 प्रतिशत चोरी रोक दीजिए और यह सुनिश्चित कर लें, तब आगे की ज़मीन के बारे में सोचें। इंफ्रास्ट्रक्चर के बारे में सरकार ने बहुत बड़ी परिभाषा दी है। हमने कहा कि यदि हाउसिंग डेवलपमैंट इंफ्रास्ट्रक्चर में है, तो यह कानून बना दिया जाये कि जिस किसान से आपने ज़मीन ली है, जैसे नोएडा, गुड़गांव, झारखंड आदि हर जगह हुआ है, तो आप कम से कम सुनिश्चित कर लें कि आपने जिसकी ज़मीन ली हैं और उस पर डेवलपमैंटल फ्लैट्स बना रहे हैं, वहां पर उसे भी फ्लैट मिल जाये, तो कम से कम उसे भी कुछ फायदा होगा।

जहां तक 16-17 लेजिस्लेशन्स...(व्यवधान) मैं एक मिनट में अपनी बात समाप्त कर रहा हूं। 16-17 लेजिस्लेशन्स जो रेलवे एक्ट, डिफैंस एक्ट वगैरह हैं, उसे भी इसके अधीनस्थ कर दें, तो कम से कम सेंसिबिलिटी आ जायेगी। अभी हुक्मदेव जी ने कहा कि मंत्री जी ने एकता परिषद् को आश्वासन दिया था जो भूमिहीन लोगों के बारे में है। गांव-गांव में जो सरकारी ज़मीन पर रहते हैं, ज़मीन एक्वायर करने से पहले उसका पट्टा दिया जाये। बिना पट्टा दिये उसे एक्वायर न करें। सबसे महत्वपूर्ण चीज है कि अगर आप बंजर ज़मीन को भारत के मैप में डालेंगे, वहां पर आप इंफ्रास्ट्रक्चर देंगे, तो प्राइवेट कम्पनियां वहां जायेंगी, हम लोगों को अच्छी ज़मीन देने की आवश्यकता नहीं है। अगर हम बंजर ज़मीन पर इंफ्रास्ट्रक्चर जैसे बिजली,

रोड़ की व्यवस्था कर लेंगे तो वहां पर एक्वीज़िशन भी हो जायेगा और नुकसान भी कम होगा।

मेरा मंत्री महोदय से यही अनुरोध है। इन्हीं बातों के साथ मैं इस बिल का समर्थन करता हूं।

## [22] Asaduddin Owaisi

SHRI ASADUDDIN OWAISI (HYDERABAD): Madam, at the outset I stand to support the Bill. I commend the Government and the Minister for bringing a comprehensive Bill. I have some few points to raise and that is in relation to this Act, the Land Acquisition, Rehabilitation and Resettlement Bill. How will it be used to acquire Wakf properties? It is because in my city in Hyderabad, more than 800 acres of Wakf land has been acquired illegally by the Government.

For example, wherein the India School of Business is working is a Wakf land; where WIPRO is working is a Wakf land. All these are part of Manikonda Jagir. In fact, the Shamshabad Air Port itself is on Wakf land. A masjid was demolished over there. All these things are there on the Wakf land. I want to know as to how this Act will apply in future acquisition of Wakf Act.

You take the example of Vizag. In Vizag, Hindujas were given more than 400 acres of Wakf land for construction of power project. All these cases are pending in Supreme Court. What will happen in future? How will you ensure that the Wakf lands are not used and are not acquired by the Government of the day? In fact, it was done for Lanco also. Unfortunately, it is owned by a Member from Congress Party, but you have never objected to it.

I want to know as to what happened to all these Wakf lands because there is no mention about it in the Act over there. In fact, the Chairman of the Joint Parliamentary Committee, who is now the Minister for Minorities, has clearly said that the Andhra Pradesh Government is the biggest Wakf land grabber. I will quote that in Andhra Pradesh from 2006 to 2011, 88,492 acres of land was given to 1,027 companies. Am I right in saying that the real reason behind this whole fight about Hyderabad being declared a Union Territory or second Capital, is that all these lands are there? I do not want to dispossess them. We do not want to dispossess them. But, we are asking as to how you will stop that. It is the land of the Wakf Board.

How do you bring it? My request to the Government, through you, is to tell to us, when you stand up to reply, as to how this Land Acquisition Bill will tackle the issue of acquisition of Wakf Land for public purpose. We are not against it. If you want to acquire it, you acquire it from the duly constituted Wakf Boards.

My last point is that in Hyderabad city, in the last 15 years not even a hundred houses have been given to weaker sections of Scheduled Castes or Muslims. Not even the hundred houses have been given. But, what we see is that hundreds of acres of land have been given to all companies. I was listening to the Hon. Member belonging to the Telugu Desam Party, who said that Chandrababu Naidu has done it. No. Whether Nizam was good or bad, he was a feudal. I do not agree with the feudalism but at least he had the common sense and he never gave jagirs around the city to anybody. But, Chandrababu Naidu or other Chief Ministers gave it away as if it was their jagir. Now, what is left around Hyderabad? We cannot construct houses for poor. Wakf properties have been given to all these companies. Indian School of Business is working there. WIPRO is working there. The airport has come there. I want to know as to where they would stop. So, my request to the Hon. Minister is that please ensure that Wakf properties are not taken for land acquisition purpose. If they have to be taken, they should be taken from a duly constituted Wakf Board.

About Special Economic Zone (SEZ), I would say that land under SEZ around Hyderabad is going to the real estate companies. On the one hand, you say that you do not appreciate SEZ, on the other, all SEZ land has gone to the real estate companies. Blatant abuses of land are happening around Hyderabad. This is why, my request to the Government of the day is to see that behind the demand of an UT or a permanent Capital there is this angle also. Anyway, we are opposed to the demand of making it a Union Territory.

## [23] Jairam Ramesh

श्री जयराम रमेश: अध्यक्ष महोदया, कुल पांच घंटे तक यह बहस चली है और 28 सदस्यों ने अपने विचार यहां व्यक्त किए हैं। मैं पहले तो स्टैंडिंग कमेटी की अध्यक्षा सुमित्रा महाजन जी को धन्यवाद देना चाहता हूं कि उन्होंने इस विधेयक पर बहुत गहराई से जाकर चर्चा की और कई सिफारिशें कीं। उनका जिक्र मैं बाद में करूंगा। उन्होंने अलग-अलग राज्यों और वर्गों के साथ बातचीत करके अपनी रिपोर्ट तैयार

की। मैं नेता प्रतिपक्ष को विशेष धन्यवाद देना चाहूंगा, क्योंकि दो सर्वदलीय बैठकों में ऐसा लग रहा था कि हम आगे नहीं बढ़ पाएंगे, लेकिन उन्होंने स्वयं रास्ता निकाला और आज हम इस बिल पर बहस कर रहे हैं।

मैं राजनाथ सिंह जी का शुक्रगुजार हूं कि पिछले दो साल से मेरी उनसे मुलाकातें हुई हैं और मुझे हर स्टेज पर उन्होंने सुझाव दिए। ज्यादातर सुझाव मैंने शामिल किए हैं और कुछ ऐसे हैं, जिन्हें नहीं कर सका। मेरी भी मजबूरियां हैं, जिनका मैं जिक्र करूंगा। शरद यादव जी और अन्य नेता भी सर्वदलीय बैठकों में शामिल हुए और अपने-अपने सुझाव दिए। मैं पश्चिम बंगाल की मुख्य मंत्री जी को विशेष धन्यवाद देना चाहता हूं। मैं खुद दो बार कोलकाता गया और उनसे बातचीत की। उन्होंने जो आशंकाएं जाहिर कीं, वे काफी हद तक जायज थीं और मैंने कोशिश की उन्हें हटाने के लिए काम करूं। मुझे खुशी है कि ज्यादातर सुझाव जो तृणमूल कांग्रेस की तरफ से आए, इस विधेयक में उन्हें संशोधन के रूप में शामिल किया गया है।

बहुत से राजनैतिक दलों ने मुझे लिखित में सुझाव दिए। हरेक दल को मैंने अपनी तरफ से टिप्पणियां की हैं और उन्हें सौंपा है। मैंने प्रयास किया है कि हर दल के साथ व्यक्तिगत रूप से बातचीत करूंऔर आम सहमति बनाऊं।

अध्यक्ष महोदया, इस विधेयक की कई आलोचनाएं हुई हैं। यह आवश्यक भी है और वास्तविक भी है, क्योंकि यह बीच का रास्ता हमने निकाला है। अलग-अलग वर्गों से, अलग-अलग मांगें आ रही थीं। हुक्मदेव जी, किसान संगठनों से मेरी लम्बी मुलाकात हुई है इसलिए यह कहना सही नहीं होगा कि मैंने बातचीत नहीं की। मैं विनम्रता से आपसे कहता हूं कि मैंने पिछले दो सालों से कई संगठनों के साथ कई बार बातचीत की है। उद्योग जगत के संगठनों से भी बातचीत हुई है। राजनैतिक दलों से भी बातचीत हुई है। सामाजिक कार्यकर्ताओं से भी मुझे सुझाव मिले हैं। सबको सुनकर हमने यह विधेयक तैयार किया है।

यह बात सही है राजनाथ सिंह जी कि जो मसौदा दो साल पहले सार्वजनिक रूप में रखा गया था, उसके और इस विधेयक में काफी अंतर है। आप जानते हैं, आप भी सरकार में मंत्री रह चुके हैं। हम सबको साथ लेकर चलने की प्रणाली में हमें कुछ समझौता करना पड़ता है। मैं इससे हटता नहीं हूं। जो मसौदा था और जो विधेयक है इसमें काफी अंतर है और अंतर इसलिए है कि मुझे राज्यों और मुख्यमंत्रियों की आवाज भी सुननी थी। एक ही मुद्दे पर अलग-अलग पार्टियों के अलग-अलग विचार हैं। मैंने सभी को साथ लेकर चलने का प्रयास किया है। हो सकता है कि सब लोग इससे असंतुष्ट हों क्योंकि सबकी कोई न कोई शिकायत होगी। बीच में चलने का खतरा यही है कि सभी को खुश करने के प्रयास में कोई खुश नहीं रहता। मैंने पहले भी कहा है कि मेरी आलोचना प्रगतिशील संगठनों की तरफ से हुई है कि यह विधेयक

प्रगतिशील नहीं है और उद्योग जगत से आलोचना आई है कि यह बहुत सख्त विधेयक है। अगर दोनों पक्षों से आलोचना हुई है तो मैंने कुछ सही ही किया होगा।

मैं माननीय राजनाथ सिंह जी का शुक्रगुजार हूं कि उन्होंने बहुत विस्तार से अलग-अलग क्लॉजों पर टिप्पणियां की हैं। मैं मुख्य रूप से कुछ का जवाब दूंगा। लीजिंग के बारे में उन्होंने जो कहा तो उसका प्रावधान हमने संशोधन में किया है। माननीया सुषमा जी ने सर्वदलीय बैठक में इसका जिक्र किया था और हमने तुरंत उसे माना है, पर लीजिंग का अधिकार इस संशोधन में हम राज्यों पर छोड़ रहे हैं। लीजिंग के टर्म्स एंड कंडीशन्स क्या होंगे, यह हम राज्यों पर छोड़ रहे हैं। हम इस संशोधन में नहीं कह रहे हैं कि लीजिंग किस प्रकार होगा, लीजिंग करते हुए किसानों की राय मांगी जाएगी या नहीं, यह सब हम राज्यों पर छोड़ रहे हैं। लेकिन लीजिंग का विकल्प जो आपने हमें दिया था उसका प्रावधान हमने संशोधन में किया है और यह एक बहुत ही महत्वपूर्ण बात है।

माननीय राजनाथ सिंह जी, आपने जो दूसरी बात उठाई है उसे देखकर मैं आश्चर्य चकित रह गया। आपने यह कहा कि कोई अपील का प्रावधान नहीं है। बहुत ही विनम्रता से मैं आपसे कहता हूं कि यह गलत है। सैक्शन 45 अगर आप देखें तो उसमें कहा गया है कि हरेक राज्य में एक प्राधिकरण का गठन किया जाएगा। लैंड एक्वीज़िशन, लार-अथॉरिटी उसका नाम दिया गया है और जो कलेक्टर का अवॉर्ड है वह फाइनल इसलिए कहा जाता है, वह लीगल भाषा है, कि प्रशासन की ओर से कोई सवाल नहीं उठा सकता। इसके यह मायने नहीं है कि अगर कोई शिकायत है तो वह अथॉरिटी में नहीं जाएगा और अथॉरिटी से अगर वह असंतुष्ट है तो वह हाई कोर्ट में भी जा सकता है। यह बात मैं आपसे कहना चाहता हूं कि सैक्शन 45 में यह प्रावधान किया गया है कि आर्डर अपीलेबल है, लार-अथॉरिटी में और लार-अथॉरिटी के बाद हाई कोर्ट में भी अपील कर सकता है।

तीसरी बात आपने अर्जेन्सी के बारे में कही। मैं आपसे बिल्कुल सहमत हूं कि 1894 के कानून का दुरुपयोग जो हुआ है फौरी-तौर पर यह अर्जेन्सी क्लॉज के नाग पर हुआ है। इसीलिए हमने अर्जेन्सी क्लॉज की परिभाषा की है कि दो ही ऐसे मौके हैं जब अर्जेन्सी क्लॉज का इस्तेमाल हो सकता है। एक तो नेशनल सिक्योरिटी और दूसरा डिफैंस। हो सकता है कि कभी-कभी प्राकृतिक विपदा आती हैं जैसे उत्तराखंड में हमें देखने को मिला है, उस वक्त कभी राज्य सरकारों को अर्जेन्सी क्लॉज का इस्तेमाल करना पड़ता है। मैं स्पष्ट करना चाहता हूं कि अर्जेन्सी क्लॉज की परिभाषा को हमने भारी मात्रा में सीमित किया है और राष्ट्रीय सुरक्षा और प्राकृतिक आपदा दो ही ऐसे मौके हैं जहां अर्जेन्सी क्लॉज का इस्तेमाल हो सकता है।

आपने रिट्रोस्पैक्टिव क्लॉज के बारे में सवाल उठाए हैं और माननीय राजीव रंजन जी ने भी यह सवाल उठाया था। यह सैक्शन 24 है, रिट्रोस्पैक्टिव क्लॉज है और मैं हंसी-मजाक में अपने सहयोगी मंत्री को कहता हूं कि अगर इस अमैंडमैंट का कोई नाम होता तो इसका नाम छिंदवाड़ा अमैंडमैंट होता, क्योंकि इसमें माननीय कमलनाथ जी का बहुत बड़ा योगदान रहा है। राजनाथ सिंह जी, यह सैक्शन 24 क्या कहता है ? यह कहता है कि अगर पुराने कानून के तहत अवार्ड पास नहीं हुआ है तो यह नया कानून लागू होगा। दूसरा, अगर अवार्ड पास हुआ है, लेकिन मुआवजा नहीं दिया गया है और भौतिक कब्जा नहीं किया गया है, तब यह नया कानून लागू होगा। तीसरी स्थिति है कि जहां अवार्ड दिया गया है, लेकिन पचास प्रतिशत से ऊपर किसान ने मुआवजा नहीं लिया है, तो यह नया कानून लागू होगा। रिट्रोस्पैक्टिव क्लॉज बिलकुल स्पष्ट तरीके से हमने किया है, इस बारे में राजनाथ सिंह जी बहुत लम्बा विचार किया गया है। मैंने कई सांसदों से भी राय ली है। जैसा कि मैंने कहा कि तीन स्थितियां ऐसी हैं, जहां कि रिट्रोस्पैक्टिव क्लॉज लागू होता है।...(व्यवधान) मैं आप सभी के प्रश्नों का उत्तर दूंगा।

राजनाथ सिंह जी, आपने एक बात और कही है और कई लोगों ने भी उस बात को उठाया है कि क्या यह विधेयक या अधिनियम नौकरशाही अधिनियम होगा ? क्या हम ब्यूरोक्रेसी को और अधिकार दे रहे हैं, मैं आपको कहना चाहता हूं कि हर स्तर पर हमने समय सीमा तय की है। अगर आप विधेयक देखें तो हर स्तर पर हमने समय सीमा निर्धारित की है और हमारा पूरा प्रयास होगा कि समय सीमा का उल्लंघन नहीं होना चाहिए। आपका तजुर्बा यही है और मेरा भी यही तजुर्बा भी यही है कि हम समय सीमा डालते हैं और उसका उल्लंघन होता है। मैं आपको स्पष्ट कहना चाहता हूं कि यह बात सही नहीं है कि हमने इसे ओपन एंडिड रखा है। प्रक्रिया के हर स्तर पर हमने समय सीमा लगाई है और मैं उम्मीद करता हूं कि राज्य इन समय सीमाओं का पालन करेगा।

राजनाथ सिंह जी, आपने दो बातें उठाई हैं, जिनका मैं विशेष जिक्र करना चाहता हूं और जो यह दर्शाएगा कि मेरे सामने कितनी कठिनाइयां इस विधेयक को लाने में थीं। आपने जिक्र किया कि बहुफसल सिंचित भूमि का अधिग्रहण नहीं होना चाहिए। मैं आपसे बिलकुल सहमत हूं और सितम्बर 2011 के मसौदा में यही प्रावधान रखा था। पंजाब, हरियाणा और केरल के मुख्यमंत्रियों से तुरंत खत आए कि हमारे राज्यों में सारी ज़मीन बहुफसल सिंचित ज़मीन है, आप क्या कर रहे हैं या आप पंजाब, हरियाणा और केरल का औद्योगीकरण चाहते ही नहीं हैं। इसलिए हम संशोधन ला रहे हैं कि कुछ सीमा होनी चाहिए, लेकिन वह सीमा राज्य सरकार तय करेगी। अगर पंजाब में और कोई ज़मीन नहीं है, तो हम वह पंजाब सरकार पर छोड़ते हैं। अगर हरियाणा में कोई ज़मीन नहीं है, तो हम हरियाणा सरकार पर छोड़ते हैं।

**श्री शरद यादव (मधेपुरा):** अध्यक्ष जी, मंत्री जी ने काफी मेहनत की है, इस बारे में कोई दो राय नहीं है। मेरा यह आग्रह ऑल पार्टी मीटिंग में भी था कि ये जितने नेशनल हाईवे बन रहे हैं और उनमें जितनी ज़मीन गई है, उतनी इंडस्ट्री में भी नहीं गई है। इस समय मान लीजिए यदि आधा किलोमीटर भी नेशनल हाई वे बन रहा है और उसमें यह प्रावधान कर दिया जाए कि सड़क के किनारे की ज़मीन कोई नहीं ले सकता है तो मैं आपको कहना चाहता हूं कि देश की जो सिंचित ज़मीन है, हरियाणा, पंजाब और वेस्टर्न यूपी का जो एतराज है, वह बहुत हद तक दूर होगा। दिल्ली में इतनी ज़मीन है, जिसके बारे में मेरी कोई सुनता ही नहीं है कि यह जो फार्म हाउसिज बने हुए हैं, सैनिक फार्महाउस बने हुए हैं, इन्हें हजार गज जगह दे दो, पांच सौ गज जगह दे दो। दिल्ली में इतनी आबादी है, वह कहां जाएगी? मैं सड़क वाले मामले में पर्टिकुलर हूं कि आधा किलोमीटर भी यदि आप रख देंगे, तो ज़मीन का बहुत बचाव होगा।

**श्री जयराम रमेश:** शरद जी, आपने सर्वदलीय बैठक में जो सुझाव दिए थे, उन पर मैं कुछ टिप्पणी करूंगा।...(व्यवधान)

**अध्यक्ष महोदया:** आप कृप्या चेयर को संबोधित कीजिए।

                    ...(व्यवधान)

**श्री जयराम रमेश:** अध्यक्ष महोदया, मैं कह रहा था कि बहुफसल सिंचित भूमि के बारे में अलग-अलग पार्टियों के अलग-अलग दृष्टिकोण हैं और यह बात सही है कि मसौदे में हमने कहा था कि किसी हालत में भी बहुफसल सिंचित भूमि का अधिग्रहण नहीं होना चाहिए, परंतु मुझे कहना पड़ेगा कि पंजाब, हरियाणा और केरल के मुख्यमंत्रियों के खत के कारण हम यह संशोधन ला रहे हैं और हम राज्यों पर छोड़ रहे हैं कि क्या सीमा होनी चाहिए, हर जिले में क्या सीमा होनी चाहिए या राज्य स्तर पर क्या सीमा होनी चाहिए, यह हम राज्यों पर छोड़ रहे हैं।...(व्यवधान)

PROF. SAUGATA ROY (DUM DUM): Have you brought this amendment?

SHRI JAIRAM RAMESH: Yes, I have brought this amendment. It is one of the amendments.

MADAM SPEAKER: Hon. Minister, are you yielding? We cannot have this kind of a discussion.

SHRI JAIRAM RAMESH: Let me just say in English what I was saying.

First we said no multi-crop irrigated land should be acquired.

PROF. SAUGATA ROY: That was the best thing. Why did you change it?

SHRI JAIRAM RAMESH: But we cannot make a policy which is not acceptable to some States—Punjab, Haryana, Kerala. ... (*Interruptions*) Please listen to me. ... (*Interruptions*)

So, what we said was that acquisition of multi-crop irrigated land will be acquisition of last resort; but if a State wants to impose some limits, we will leave it to the State Government. That is all we have said. So, if the West Bengal Government wants to say that no multi-crop irrigated land should be acquired, the West Bengal Government is free to say so.

माननीय अध्यक्ष महोदया, मैं आपके माध्यम से राजनाथ सिंह जी कहना चाहता हूं कि आपने लैंड बैंक के बारे में कहा था। मसौदा में लिखा गया था कि दस साल तक भूमि का इस्तेमाल नहीं होगा वह वापिस किसान को दी जाएगी। स्टैंडिंग कमेटी की सिफारिश आई कि दस साल को पांच साल कीजिए और हमने इसे स्वीकार किया। तब पश्चिम बंगाल के मुख्यमंत्री ने हमसे कहा कि आप लैंड बैंक को नजरअंदाज क्यों कर रहे हैं? महाराष्ट्र के मुख्यमंत्री ने मुझसे कहा कि लैंड बैंक को नजरअंदाज मत कीजिए, लैंड बैंक का विकल्प भी खोलकर रखिए। इसलिए हमने कहा कि अगर पांच साल तक भूमि का इस्तेमाल नहीं होता है, वह राज्य या लैंड बैंक को वापिस लौटाई जाएगी। यह राज्य तय करेगा कि किसानों को दी जाए या लैंड बैंक में रखी जाएगी।

मैं यह बात इसलिए उठा रहा हूं क्योंकि कई ऐसी बातें हैं जो हमें राज्यों पर छोड़नी चाहिए। यह राष्ट्रीय कानून है लेकिन कानून में कुछ फ्लेक्सिबिलिटी होनी चाहिए क्योंकि अलग-अलग राज्यों में परिस्थितियां अलग हैं। हम दिल्ली में बैठकर कानून बनाएं जो हर राज्य में शत-प्रतिशत लागू होगा, यह नामुमकिन है।

Madam Speaker, I just want to switch to English for two minutes because my good friend Mr Thambidurai has raised a very fundamental point as to the competence of the Central Government to come with this legislation on land acquisition. I want to draw the

Hon. Member's attention to the Concurrent List of the Constitution, Entry 42, which was introduced as a result of the 42$^{nd}$ Amendment which includes acquisition and requisitioning of property in the Concurrent List.

DR M. THAMBIDURAI (KARUR): Concurrent List is a provision. You should not take advantage of that provision to take away the powers of States.

SHRI JAIRAM RAMESH: We are not taking the State powers.

MR SPEAKER: Please, we cannot go on having discussion.

**श्री जयराम रमेश**: माननीय अध्यक्ष महोदया, सुषमा जी जानती हैं कि समवर्ती सूची में भूमि अधिग्रहण पर कानून बनाने का अधिकार केंद्र सरकार को दिया गया है। इसका एक ही मतलब है कि राज्य सरकार अपने कानून बना सकती है लेकिन केंद्रीय कानून की तुलना में घटा नहीं सकती है, इसे और ज्यादा कर सकती है।

That means, Mr Thambidurai, if the Tamil Nadu Government wants to have a legislation which improves on the compensation, which improves on the R&R, you are completely free to do so. You cannot have a provision for R&R and compensation which is lower than the Central legislation. That is all the matter. ... (*Interruptions*)

SHRI KALYAN BANERJEE (SREERAMPUR): Those are provisions that have been made in the amendment. ... (*Interruptions*)

SHRI JAIRAM RAMESH: Kalyan babu, I want to mention this to the Hon. Member. He is a lawyer, I am not a lawyer.

I have consulted all the legal officers of the Government of India. It is an established practice that when you pass a law in the Concurrent List, it does not mean that the State Governments are not free to pass their laws. They have full power to pass their laws. They cannot derogate from the Central law. They can improve on the Central law. If you need clarification for this, I am willing to provide this. ... (*Interruptions*)

अध्यक्ष महोदया, बार-बार यह बात आई है कि क्या हम जबरदस्ती भूमि अधिग्रहण कर रहे हैं। मैं सुदीप बाबू को आश्वस्त करना चाहता हूं कि इसमें ऐसा कोई प्रावधान नहीं है, जिससे जबरदस्ती भूमि अधिग्रहण होगा, कोई ऐसा प्रावधान नहीं हैं। हां यह बात सही है कि सिर्फ दो मामलों में स्टैंडिंग कमेटी की सिफारिशें नामंजूर की है। स्टैंडिंग कमेटी ने 13 सिफारिशें की थीं और उनमें से हमने 11 को स्वीकार किया है, परंतु दो ऐसी सिफारिशें थीं, उनका यह कहना था कि पीपीपी का और निजी प्रोजैक्ट्स का भूमि अधिग्रहण नहीं होना चाहिए। श्रीमती सुमित्रा महाजन से मेरी लम्बी बातचीत हुई, मैंने अपनी मजबूरी उन्हें बताई और मैंने कहा कि मैं इन्हें स्वीकार नहीं कर सकता हूं। मैं यह इसलिए कह रहा हूं कि अगर पश्चिम बंगाल चाहता है कि इस 80 प्रतिशत को सौ प्रतिशत करना है या 70 प्रतिशत को सौ प्रतिशत करना है तो आप ऐसा बिल्कुल कर सकते हैं, वह विकल्प आपके पास है। परंतु मैं यह बिल्कुल साफ कर देना चाहता हूं कि 80 प्रतिशत निजी प्रोजैक्ट्स के लिए और 70 प्रतिशत पीपीपी के लिए इसलिए रखा गया है, क्योंकि कुछ लोगों के मन में यह आशंका थी कि भूमि अधिग्रहण जबरदस्ती होगा, क्योंकि वह हमारा अनुभव रहा है। परंतु बिना लिखित अनुमति के भूमि अधिग्रहण होने की कोई गुंजाइश नहीं है।

महोदया, मैं सिर्फ दो-तीन मिनट और लूंगा। कई सदस्यों ने यह सवाल उठाया है, आप 158 औपचारिक संशोधन ला रहे हैं। लालू जी ने भी यही कहा था। मैं थोड़ा स्पष्टीकरण देना चाहता हूं कि इन 158 औपचारिक संशोधनों में से सिर्फ 28 मुख्य संशोधन हैं। 13 संशोधन स्टैंडिंग कमेटी की सिफारिशें हैं, 13 संशोधन हमारे ग्रुप ऑफ मिनिस्टर्स की सिफारिशें हैं, श्री शरद पवार जी उसके अध्यक्ष थे और दो संशोधन, अगर मैं नाम दे सकता हूं, सुषमा स्वराज संशोधन हैं तो 158 संशोधनों में से 28 मुख्य संशोधन हैं, बाकी सब संशोधन जैसा कि लालू जी अपने रंगीन तरीके से कहते हैं, कोमा, फुलस्टाप, पैराग्राफ चेंज, पैराग्राफ नम्बर, नीचे से ऊपर, ऊपर से नीचे सब कार्यवाही या प्रोसीजरल अमेन्डमैन्ट्स हैं, मुख्य अमेन्डमैन्ट्स, मुख्य संशोधन 28 हैं, जिनमें 13 स्टैंडिंग कमेटी के हैं, 13 जीओएम के और दो नेता प्रतिपक्ष के हैं।

आखिर में मैं यह कहना चाहता हूं कि कई माननीय सदस्यों ने संशोधन दिये हैं। कई लोगों के संशोधन हमारे औपचारिक संशोधनों में शामिल हैं, जैसे श्रीमती हरसिमरत कौर बादल ने संशोधन दिया है, वह संशोधन हम खुद सरकार की ओर से ला रहे हैं। वामपंथी पार्टियों ने जो संशोधन दिये हैं, मैं खुद बसुदेव बाबू के ऑफिस दो बार गया हूं और उनके छः महत्वपूर्ण संशोधन हम सरकार की ओर से ला रहे हैं। कई ऐसे संशोधन हैं, राजू शेट्टी जी के संशोधन, प्रशांत मजूमदार जी के संशोधन, शेख सैदुल हक के संशोधन, सभी संशोधनकर्ताओं से मेरी मुलाकात हुई है।

श्री निशिकांत दूबे वहां बैठे हुए हैं, वह अक्सर यहां बैठा करते हैं, आज अचानक पीछे चले गये हैं। ...(व्यवधान) उनके संशोधन पर भी मैंने टिप्पणी दी है। मेरी सबसे विनती है कि हमारे औपचारिक अमैन्डमैन्ट्स को स्वीकार करें, जो अपने-अपने अलग व्यक्तिगत अमैन्डमैन्ट्स हैं, उन्हें आप वापस ले लें और जितने तक हम संशोधन लाये हैं, आप देखेंगे कि ज्यादातर आपके संशोधन शामिल किये गये हैं। मैं हर एक सदस्य को जिन्होंने संशोधन दिया है, मैं उन्हें सबूत दूंगा कि किस तरीके से हम संशोधन लाये हैं और जब नियम बनाये जायेंगे, जब रुल्स बनाये जायेंगे, अगर ज्यादातर उसमें स्पष्टीकरण देने की जरूरत है तो उसे हम जरूर शामिल करेंगे।

अंत में मैं कहना चाहता हूं कि ओवैसी जी यहां बैठे हुए हैं। वह क्रिकेट के अच्छे खिलाड़ी रहे हैं, आज इन्होंने मुझ पर एक गुगली बॉल कर दी है और मैं स्वीकारता हूं कि इन्होंने जो मुद्दा उठाया है,. हमने उसके बारे में सोचा नहीं था। मुझे थोड़ा वक्त दीजिए, मैं हमारे सहयोगी मंत्री, श्री रहमान खान से भी मशविरा करूंगा। अगर किसी नए कानून की जरूरत पड़ेगी तो हम वापस सदन में आएंगे परंतु अभी आपने जो मुद्दा उठाया है, उसको मैंने नोट कर लिया है। यह बहुत गंभीर मामला है। मैं आपसे पूरी तरह सहमत हूँ कि इस कानून से वक़्फ़ की ज़मीन ज़बरदस्ती एक्वायर नहीं होनी चाहिए।

अध्यक्ष महोदया, इन्हीं शब्दों के साथ मैं आपसे और सभी सदस्यों से भी निवेदन करता हूँ कि औपचारिक संशोधनों को वे स्वीकार करें ताकि आज एक और ऐतिहासिक मौका है और 190 साल पुराने कानून को हम बदलेंगे और जैसा कि राजनाथ सिंह जी ने पहले ही अपने भाषण में स्वीकार किया है कि यह जो कानून का टाइटल है, यह हमने जानबूझ कर बदला है क्योंकि टाइटल लैंड एक्वीज़िशन एक्ट नहीं है। टाइटल है टू फेयर कम्पेनसेशन एंड आर एंड आर। ताकि किसानों का हक बनता है, जो आजीविका खोते हैं, उनका हक़ बनता है, दलितों और आदिवासियों का हक़ बनता है और वही हक़ यह कानून देता है। सरकार को भूमि अधिग्रहण का हक़ नहीं देता है।

**श्री राजनाथ सिंह:** अध्यक्ष महोदया, मैं मंत्री जी से एक क्लैरिफिकेशन चाहता था। मैंने सोशल इम्पैक्ट असैसमैंट के बारे में पूछा था कि इसको आप लैंड एक्वीज़िशन का प्रोसेस प्रारंभ होने के बाद करेंगे या पहले करेंगे?

**श्री जयराम रमेश:** सर, वह हम पहले ही करेंगे, जब नोटिफिकेशन आ जाएगा, पहले ही करेंगे।

**श्री मुलायम सिंह यादव:** मंत्री जी, मैंने आपको एक सुझाव दिया था कि तीन फ़ीसदी ज़मीन प्रति वर्ष कम हो रही है और देश की जनसंख्या बढ़ रही है। एक संकट पैदा होगा कि खाने के लिए कहां से आएगा? आपके पास उसका क्या विकल्प है? मैंने तो सुझाव दिया था। अब आप सहमत होंगे या नहीं होंगे वह अलग बात है। लेकिन आपके पास विकल्प क्या है?

**श्री जयराम रमेश:** मैडम स्पीकर, मुलायम सिंह जी ने जो सवाल उठाया है, वह इस विधेयक से बाहर जाता है। माननीय सदस्य ने जो सवाल उठाया है, हम इस पर जरूर विचार करेंगे। अगर हमें नीति में बदलाव लाना है तो लाएंगे। परंतु मुझे थोड़ा वक्त दीजिएगा क्योंकि प्रत्यक्ष रूप से हम इस विधेयक में उसको शामिल नहीं कर सकते हैं। परंतु आपका मुद्दा बिल्कुल सही है। ...(व्यवधान)

**अध्यक्ष महोदया:** इतने सारे सदस्य सवाल पूछेंगे तो ज्यादा समय लगेगा।

...(व्यवधान)

**अध्यक्ष महोदया:** सौगत राय जी, please be very brief.

...(व्यवधान)

**प्रो सौगत राय:** मैडम, मैं केवल स्पष्टीकरण के लिए माननीय मंत्री जी से यह सवाल फिर पूछता हूँ कि यह आपके कानून में है कि निजी क्षेत्र में ज़मीन लेने के लिए 80 प्रतिशत लोगों की सहमति होनी चाहिए। मैं यह स्पष्टीकरण चाहता हूँ कि अगर हम पश्चिम बंगाल में कहें कि सौ प्रतिशत कृषक को या ज़मीन के मालिक को सहमति नहीं होने से निजी क्षेत्र के लिए हम ज़मीन अधिग्रहण नहीं करेंगे। यह अधिकार पश्चिम बंगाल प्रांत का होगा कि नहीं होगा? इसके बारे में आप स्पष्टीकरण दीजिए।

**श्री जयराम रमेश:** मेरा स्पष्टीकरण है कि हाँ पश्चिम बंगाल को पूरा अधिकार है।

SHRI PRABODH PANDA: I have given a number of amendments. My suggestion particularly was that the Government should allow setting up of the Land Price Determining Commission. It has already been recommended by the Standing Committee. What is the attitude of the Government in this regard?

SHRI JAIRAM RAMESH: Madam, Speaker, I have assured Shri Panda that we will give it a very serious consideration. We do not want to have proliferation of too many bodies but let the rules be framed and I will certainly give his recommendation very serious consideration.

SHRI T.K.S. ELANGOVAN (CHENNAI NORTH): Madam, I have raised a pertinent question as to when the sown area of a district is 50 per cent or less than 50 per cent of the total geographical area, there should not be any acquisition because you have stated acquisition of 10 per cent of the net sown area. This is because if it continues, in due course, this 10 per cent will be reduced to very low sown area.

SHRI JAIRAM RAMESH: Madam, this matter has been considered and we have left this entirely to the discretion of the State Government.

चौधरी लाल सिंह (उधमपुर): मैडम, हम बड़े खुश हैं। मैं और मदन लाल बड़े खुश हैं। शारिक भी बड़े खुश होंगे। लेकिन मैं मंत्री जी से यह जानना चाहता हूँ क्या वे हमारे जम्मू कश्मीर स्टेट में क्या इस कानून को लागू करवा पाएंगे? ...(व्यवधान)

MADAM SPEAKER: Hon. Members, the discussion on the motion for consideration of the Land Acquisition, Rehabilitation and Resettlement Bill, 2011 is over. The House will now take up for voting the motion for consideration, the clause-by-clause consideration and the motion for passing of the Bill.

Hon. Members would appreciate that the Bill is an important piece of legislation and a number of amendments are to be moved by the Government as well as by private Members to the clauses of this Bill. I anticipate that on certain clauses or amendments to clauses, there may be a demand for voting by Division. Hon. Members are aware that before Division takes place, the Secretary-General informs the Members about the procedure of operating the Automatic Vote Recording Machine, which the Members are requested to listen to carefully.

I would also like to inform the House that several identical amendments to various clauses of the Bill have been tabled by the

Hon. Members. As per practice, moving of identical amendments is not in order. Therefore, in cases where identical amendments are tabled by Members, the practice is to call the Member who has tabled his notice of amendment first in point of time to move his amendment. If the Member is not present in the House or does not move his amendment, then the name of the second Member or the third Member and so on who may be present and wants to move his amendment is called. Therefore, when the relevant clauses are taken up, I will call the names of hon. Members accordingly.

I shall now put the motion for consideration of the Land Acquisition, Rehabilitation and Resettlement Bill, 2011 to the vote of the House.

## [24] Sushma Swaraj

**श्रीमती सुषमा स्वराज (विदिशा):** अध्यक्षा जी, मैं इस बिल की धारा 42 में संशोधन संख्या 109 जो मंत्री जी द्वारा प्रस्तुत किया गया है, पर बोलने के लिए खड़ी हुई हूं। बोलने से पहले मैं इस सच्चाई को स्वीकार करना चाहूंगी कि इस बिल पर आम सहमति बनाने के लिए जितना परिश्रम और सच्चे दिल से प्रयास ग्रामीण विकास मंत्री श्री जयराम रमेश जी ने किया है मैं उसकी सराहना करती हूं। शायद इसी कारण आज यह बिल इस सदन में पारित हो पा रहा है। अध्यक्ष जी, जहां तक इस संशोधन का सवाल है यह संशोधन मेरे ही सुझाव पर दिया गया है। यह विषय मैंने मंत्री जी के समक्ष रखा था और आपकी अनुमति से सदन के समक्ष रखना चाहती हूं। 5 अगस्त 2011 को इस बिल का प्रारूप लोकसभा में पेश किया गया था। जिसमें यह प्रावधान था कि यदि भूमि अधिग्रहीत की जाएगी तो चार गुना, छह गुना मुआवजा बाजार भाव से ज्यादा उस पर दिया जाएगा। जहां एक ओर किसान खुश हुए कि हमें भूमि अधिग्रहण के बाद पैसा ज्यादा मिलेगा, वहीं भू-माफिया भी सक्रिय हो गया और उन्हें यह लगने लगा कि जहां-जहां प्रोजैक्ट लगने हैं, अगर वहां पर हम आज सस्ते दाम पर ज़मीन किसान से खरीद लें तो कल जब यह भूमि अधिग्रहीत होगी तो इतना पैसा हमें मिल जाएगा कि रातों-रात हम अमीर हो जाएंगे। अपने आप यह गिरोह काम करने लगा और इन्होंने अलग-अलग जगहों पर हजारों एकड़ ज़मीन खरीद डाली। यह सब प्रभावशाली लोग थे और उन्हें लगा कि देर-सवेर यह बिल पारित होगा ही और उन्हें यह लगने लगा कि उसके बाद वे उस भूमि को अधिग्रहण करवा देंगे और इसकी मोटी रकम वसूल कर लेंगे। मैंने मंत्री जी से कहा कि हमें इस धोखे को ध्वस्त करना है और इसके लिए आप एक संशोधन लाइये कि अगर कोई भूमि 5 अगस्त 2011 के

बाद खरीदी गयी है और वह अगले पांच वर्ष के अंदर अधिग्रहीत की जा रही है तो उसके मुआवजे की राशि का 50 प्रतिशत उस किसान को दिया जाएगा, जिस किसान से वह भूमि खरीदी गयी है। मुझे खुशी है कि उन्होंने संशोधन स्वीकार किया, मगर एक कैंची चला दी। जो मैंने कहा था कि 5 वर्ष के भीतर अगर ज़मीन अधिग्रहीत की जाएगी, उसे घटाकर 3 वर्ष कर दिया और जो मैंने कहा था कि 50 परसेंट पैसा दिया जाएगा, उसे घटाकर 40 परसेंट कर दिया। इसलिए मैं यहां खड़ी हुई हूं यह कहने के लिए कि यह एक ऐसा सुझाव है जिसका पूरा सदन समर्थन करेगा, क्योंकि जो काम हम भूमि अधिग्रहण कानून के माध्यम से करने जा रहे हैं वह उस फ्रॉड को खत्म करेगा, जो फ्रॉड उनके साथ खेले जाने की साजिश कुछ लोगों ने रची है। मैं चाहूंगी कि माननीय मंत्री जी कैंची न चलाएं, 5 वर्ष को 5 वर्ष ही रखें और 50 परसेंट ही रखें तो वाकई एक बड़ा काम और बड़ी सेवा हम किसानों की कर सकेंगे।

**श्री जयराम रमेश:** अध्यक्ष महोदया, मैं नेता प्रतिपक्ष से यह कहना चाहता हूं कि जो उनका सुझाव है मैं उस पर जरूर गंभीर विचार करूंगा। मैं अभी इस वक्त आपको जवाब देने की स्थिति में नहीं हूं क्योंकि मुझे वित्त मंत्री, कानून मंत्री और प्रधानमंत्री जी से भी बात करनी है। मैं आपको पूरा यकीन दिलाता हूं कि मैं उनसे बात करके वापस आपके पास लौटकर आऊंगा।

**श्रीमती सुषमा स्वराज:** अध्यक्ष जी, यह मेरा दूसरा संशोधन है जो मंत्री जी ने स्वीकार किया है और मैं मंत्री जी को धन्यवाद देने के लिए खड़ी हुई हूं। यह नई धारा 97 (ए) मंत्री जी जोड़ रहे हैं। आप जानती हैं कि इसका जो पिछला प्रारूप था, उसमें भूमि को लेने का केवल एकमात्र विकल्प अधिग्रहण था। अधिग्रहण का मतलब था कि किसान का मालिकाना हक खत्म हो जाता था और हमेशा के लिए भूमि उससे छूट जाती थी। लेकिन मैंने मंत्री जी को कहा कि हमें एक विकल्प लीज़ का भी रखना चाहिए। जहां कहीं किसी भी प्रोजैक्ट में यह संभव हो कि हम किसान से लीज़ पर ज़मीन ले लें, तो इससे दो फायदे होंगे। एक तो भूमि से उसका जो भावनात्मक जुड़ाव है, वह बना रहेगा, क्योंकि भूमि के साथ वह सुरक्षित महसूस करता है। उसकी पीढ़ियां उस भूमि पर पली हैं और आगे कई पीढ़ियां पलेंगी और उसके साथ-साथ एक साथ पैसा न मिल कर के, क्योंकि जब एक साथ पैसा मिलता है तो उसे समझ नहीं आता है कि वह उस पैसे का प्रबंधन कैसे करे। भूमि का प्रबंधन तो वह जानता है, लेकिन पैसे का प्रबंधन करना वह नहीं जानता है और इसलिए उसके बेटे बड़ी-बड़ी गाड़ियां खरीद लेते हैं, होटलों में अय्याशी करने लगते हैं, बुरी संगत में पड़ जाते हैं और एक-आध साल में पैसा खुर्द-बुर्द हो जाता है। लेकिन अगर हम लीज़ का विकल्प

देते हैं, तो एक तो ज़मीन का उसका मालिकाना हक बना रहता है और दूसरा, एक निश्चित आमदनी उसे वर्ष भर मिलती रहती है। मुझे खुशी है कि मंत्री जी ने मेरे इस सुझाव को स्वीकार करके अब यह कहा है कि गवर्नमेंट लीज़ का आप्शन भी दे सकती हैं। केवल एक्वीज़िशन का नहीं और जहां कहीं किसान इस आप्शन को लेना चाहे वहां वह अपनी ज़मीन लीज़ पर दे सकेगा। इस चीज को मानने के लिए मैं आपका बहुत-बहुत आभार व्यक्त करती हूं।

**श्री जयराम रमेश**: इसमें कैंची का इस्तेमाल नहीं किया गया है।

**श्रीमती सुषमा स्वराज**: आपने कैंची नहीं चलायी, इसके लिए मैं धन्यवाद देती हूं।

# Selected Debates in the Rajya Sabha

## THE RIGHT TO FAIR COMPENSATION AND TRANSPARENCY IN LAND ACQUISITION, REHABILITATION AND RESETTLEMENT BILL, 2013 WAS PASSED BY THE RAJYA SABHA ON 4 SEPTEMBER 2013. THE FOLLOWING ARE THE MOTIONS PUT FORTH BY VARIOUS MEMBERS OF THE HOUSE.[3]

[1] P. Rajeev

SHRI P. RAJEEV (Kerala): Mr Vice-Chairman, Sir, I would like to congratulate the Minister for coming up with a new Bill to repeal the out-dated and draconian Land Acquisition Act of 1894.

Sir, we expect that the legislation should be a comprehensive legislation and it should be adopted in line with democratic principle of justice and fairness but with due respect, I would like to submit that our Hon. Minister, Mr Jairam Ramesh, actually destroyed a chance to move a historic legislation, which addresses all the concerns of the farmers and the society as a whole.

Sir, this is a shift from one extreme to another extreme, that is, colonial to a neo-liberal legislative framework, which is no less draconian, if not more. This is for addressing the concerns of the neo-liberal needs of the country which were stipulated after 1991.

---

[3] The full text is available at http://rsdebate.nic.in/bitstream/123456789/625823/2/PD_229_04092013_p25_p78_10.pdf#search=jairam ramesh and at http://rsdebate.nic.in/bitstream/123456789/625825/2/PD_229_04092013_p78_p155_12.pdf#search=jairam ramesh

Sir, actually the Government has taken this legislation as another gimmick for the coming elections. They are propagating several things like people will get more benefits. The urban people are waiting for passing of this Bill to give their land for construction of highways; they are waiting to give their land for construction of railways; they are waiting to give their land for construction of electric power generation projects; they are waiting to give their land for construction of metro stations and so on. But, Sir, will the people who are displaced for a national highway project get this benefit? Will the people who are displaced for a railway project get this benefit as per your new legislation? Will the people who are displaced for a metro rail project get the benefit as per this Act? Will the people who are displaced for electric power generation project get the benefit? Definitely not, Sir. As per Section 106(1), that is, the exclusion clause, there is Schedule IV. That enlists 13 legislations. As per the available statistics, 90 per cent of the acquisition of land in our country is as per these 13 legislations. That means, 90 per cent of the land acquisition will not come under the purview of this Act. This is actually a gimmick. This is actually a*[4] activity of the Government on the people of this country and this is an eyewash. Then, Sir, there is Clause 106 (2). It empowers the Central Government to make any changes in Schedule IV. That means, the Executive can decide in future whether any of these provisions is applicable to cess, whether any of these provisions is applicable to any other Act. This provision gives scope for the Executive to decide what they like on the land acquisition policy. It is totally * the people. This is a * activity of the Government.

It is true that the Government came with the legislation, LARR Bill. It was sent to the Standing Committee. The Standing Committee submitted a very detailed report, but the Minister is not ready to accept the major recommendations of the Standing Committee. It is true that there are some changes made to the former Bill and this is a new Bill. But the major recommendation was on Clause 106, that is, the exclusion clause. The Standing Committee, the mini Parliament,

[4] *means expunged from the official records as ordered by the Chair.

unanimously recommended to the Government that this clause should not be there. If Clauses 106(1) and 106(2) are there, then there is no relevance for this Bill. This is only for elections. If these two clauses are there, it will not be applicable to 90 per cent of the land acquisition of this country. So, we strongly demand to delete these two clauses from this Bill. It is true that a new clause is there in the new Bill, that is, Clause 106(3). That is actually a very clever exercise by the Minister to create a feeling. Yes, it accommodates some of your feelings. That is why he is very clever and very dynamic. It says, 'any of the provisions of this Act'. Why this 'any'? If you want to be genuine, if you are honest, you substitute this Clause 106(3). The Government should amend all the existing Acts in the Schedule IV in accordance with this new legislation. Why are you not ready for that? You are creating an atmosphere that you are trying to address the concern, you are accommodating the feelings of all sections, you are adopting this new Clause 106 (3). They can adopt any of the provisions. That is actually not a good activity, not an honest approach by the Minister. It is a very professional approach of a dynamic Minister. That is not the right way, Sir. Actually, he also tried to create an atmosphere that he is accommodating most of the submissions made by the CPI (M).

That is not true. You are trying to create an atmosphere, but most of our significant suggestions which are related to the exclusion clause, issue of proper definition of 'public purpose' and 'affected persons', binding nature of social impact assessment, land use plan, land use commission, provisions for safeguarding food security, enhanced compensation, fair and just rehabilitation and resettlement, prior informed consent and role of Panchayats as well as Grame Panchayats have been disregarded.

Sir, I would like to quote from the speech of H.W. Bliss who steered the Bill in 1894.

> *The Bill will not be used in furtherance of private speculations and that the Local Governments should not be subject to pressure, which it might possibly sometimes be difficult to resist, on behalf of enterprises in which the public have no direct interest.*

He stated that it was not the intention of the legislature that the Government should be made a property agent for companies to acquire land. This is 1894 speech by H.W. Bliss.

This is the first time in the world that a Government is ready to acquire land for corporates. Have you heard anywhere in the world Government acquiring land for corporates? Have you heard the Government of United States acquiring land for corporates? Is there any country in the European Union which does that? This is for the first time in the world that a Government is acquiring land for corporates and creating an atmosphere for corporates.

Sir, I have to make some suggestions on this Bill. We have already made several amendments to the existing Bill. One is relating to the definition of 'public purpose and infrastructure.' The Standing Committee gave a very detailed recommendation on this vague nature of the definition. Some changes have been made by the Minister in its definition. But still this definition of 'public purpose and infrastructure' is vague. It leaves scope for subjective interpretation of the Executive. They can implement this public purpose for any activities of the corporates and private enterprises. We demand that public purpose must be exhaustively and tightly defined, objectively determined, collectively approved, justiciable and strictly construed, limited to activities which are of direct benefit to the largest number of people and does not include the furtherance of private speculation and profit. This definition should be changed. It is very vague. It should be strict to this formulation.

Earlier the definition of 'infrastructure' was very vague and now some changes have been made as per the recommendations of the Standing Committee. (*Time-bell*) Sir, you are pressing the time-bell only now.

Sir, then there is urgency provision. That is another way for making vague interpretation and our demand is that special powers in cases of urgency should not be invoked for private companies and be restricted to national defence, and all other processes to seek consent, hear objections and undertake Social Impact Assessment. After passing the Bill in the Lok Sabha, the Minister came up with three or four amendments. That means it is trying to further dilute the objectives of the Bill.

For irrigation projects, land should be given to the displaced persons. As per new amendment land or compensation. That means de facto compensation will be practical. It should be only land. Compensation for displaced persons for irrigation projects is a dilution. I do not know what the compulsion was. I do not know after passing it in the Lok Sabha, the Minister came up with this amendment to please whom. What was the compulsion? There is a very famous phrase of the Prime Minister called 'coalition compulsion.' That is against the interest of the country.

Sir, social impact assessment study must be binding and should not be overruled. There should be some distinction between acquisition for PSUs and the Government and acquisition for private and PPP projects. The law prevailing in the Scheduled Areas should prevail over the proposed legislation. The Government proposal seems to indicate that rain-fed, dry-land and semi-arid land are unproductive and their acquisition does not affect food security. We did not believe that. It should be protected under this. SC, ST, small and marginal farmers should receive land for land. Tenants will not get compensation as per the definition. Tenants will only get the R&R package. But, they are working. Land distribution has not been implemented in major parts of the country. Tenants are the sufferers in the country. They are actually working in the land. Compensation should be given to tenants.

THE VICE-CHAIRMAN (SHRI BHUBANESWAR KALITA): Please conclude now.

SHRI P. RAJEEV: Sir, there should be no bar on jurisdiction of civil courts as this violates the principles of natural justice. I hope the Minister will actually take these points seriously and make proper amendments to the legislation. Thank you, Sir.

## [2] Derek O'Brien

SHRI DEREK O'BRIEN (West Bengal): Mr Vice-Chairman, Sir, the expression 'Ides of March' has come down to us from William Shakespeare in Julius Caesar. But for me, Sir, the 'Ides of March' is actually March 14, one day before March 15, 2007 because as a metaphor for a ruling order that had decayed beyond redemption and began to treat its citizens as subjects—in fact, began to treat its citizens like slaves just like the Roman Generals would take them captive. Sir, of course, my reference to March 14, 2007 is to the

firing on innocent householders and farmers in Nandigram....
(*Interruptions*)... A massacre that shook the conscience of our State.
...(*Interruptions*)...

SHRI DEREK O'BRIEN: I understand, Sir, sometimes the truth
hurts. Let me finish my speech. Because the Trinamool Congress
Party saw the absence of a well-defined modern land mechanism.
That is why, Sir, the issue here is not just about who should buy the
land, whether the State should buy, or, whether the industry should
buy. There is a broader context to it; and there are three parts of this
broader context: (a) Protecting farmers' rights; (b) concerns of food
security; (c) finding that talent between agriculture and industry to
flower together.

Sir, the Trinamool Congress Party's policy is based on what is
known as the doctrine of eminent domain. What is the doctrine of
eminent domain? When the State recognises the private party, the
private owner becomes the absolute title holder of that property. The
State still remains prior bound holder of that property. That is why
we understand and appreciate that a piece of land for any public
purpose, be it a bridge or whatever can be acquired by the State. The
Minister from 2009 ran the marathon but somehow we feel strongly
stopped half way through because in this Bill we have some serious
issues; and I will just touch three or four very serious issues. First,
no forcible acquisition of land at any cost. No, no, no. Second, you
are talking about 80 per cent farming families who have agreed, 70
per cent for public purpose who have agreed, our view on this is the
same just as what it was right through the land movement, no 80:20,
no 70:30, it is 100. Someone has to speak up in front of the farmer.
There are lots of people who are making speeches here about how
good this Bill is, how it could be improved. This is the very basic
issue that we have, 80:20 no, 70:30 no, it has to be 100:0. No multi-
crop land, because multi-crop land is an asset.

Sir, when they are talking about acquiring the land, industry, of
course, needs to acquire land. Industry acquires labour. Industry
acquires products. Industry acquires other inputs. In none of these
acquired by the industry, does the Government interfere.

So, why does the Government need to interfere for the purchase of this land? Now, I know, when I say this, that there will be

concerns whether farmers have necessary skills. Do farmers have necessary skills to negotiate directly with corporate buyers, or, with the Government? We believe, Sir, they do with little help, with little guidance. Of course, they do. Overall we believe, we should trust the sagacity of the Indian farmer. He knows what the best is for him. He knows what the best for India is. In all humility, Sir, the Trinamool Congress Party knows what the best is for the Indian farmer. We will not compromise on this.

We also know how to strike a balance between the industry and agriculture. Not one at the cost of the other. This Bill, overall, is better than what it was for the farmer three, four and five years ago. But this Bill is not good for the farmer. This Bill is not good for the conscience of the industry. This Bill is not good for the nation. We do not support this Bill. We have made a speech. Our button also will reflect that after we finish this debate.

Thank you, Sir. I have finished my speech on time because our second speaker is one of the most qualified eminent people from the world of land reforms, Mr D. Bandyopadhyay. I have also noticed that there are many people here who will come and speak on a variety of subjects. I am also looking forward to someone else here in the front Benches who will speak on the same subject on land reforms. Thank you, Sir.

SHRI N. BALAGANGA (Tamil Nadu): Thank you very much, Mr Deputy Chairman, Sir. Basically land is a State Subject. The details of land particulars, usage and the significant role it has in farmer's life are quite familiar to the State Government only. If the Central Government wants some guidelines to be followed by the State Government in the matter of acquisition, the State Government is ready to do so. Even according to this, the State Government will make legislation. Instead of doing that, the Union Government enters upon the domain of the State. I strongly oppose this tendency of the Union Government. Sir, after having found the provisions the 1894 Land Acquisition Act inadequate in addressing the vital issues, this Bill has been brought.

But this Bill also needs some amendments. Sir, there must be a provision in the Bill that without the consent of the land owners, land use and acquisition activities will not be taken through any of the existing laws, Sir. In Tamil Nadu, the Gas Authority of India carried out installation of pipelines in the cultivable land in the Western part of Tamil Nadu. The cultivators of this land rose in revolt and there was every inevitability of breakdown law and order. Thanks to the efforts of the Chief Minister of Tamil Nadu, Dr Puratchi Thalaivi, the trouble was prevented and she allayed the fears of the people by making a declaration that the projects are for the people and the people are not for the projects. She suggested that pipeline projects should be implemented along the highways.

The root cause for all this trouble was that the Central Government had not consulted the State Government in this matter. Sir, the Bill provides compensation, for the acquired land, to the rural farmers at four times the existing rates; whereas, in urban areas, the compensation will be thrice the existing rates. It is the State Government that has to directly deal with the matters pertaining to land acquisition in the States.

In the Statement of Objects and Reasons it is stated, I quote, 'Land that is not used within ten years in accordance with the purposes, for which it was acquired, shall be transferred to the State Government's Land Bank. Upon every transfer of land without development, twenty per cent of the appreciated land value shall be shared with the original land owners.' I would like to urge upon you that instead of sharing the appreciated land value, please give back the unused acquired land to the original owner. When the Government would pay compensation, as per the provision, 12 per cent interest per annum would be paid. I would like to urge that it should be enhanced to 15 per cent.

There is also a provision that any land can be acquired by using 'urgency' and 'exigency' clauses. There will be no social impact assessment, no environmental assessment, no rehabilitation and no resettlement. Eighty per cent of the land can be acquired through this Act. But one thing that causes concerns in our minds is the absence of the provision for rehabilitation and resettlement. I would like to urge upon the Hon. Minister to ensure that this facility is there for the land owner, whose land has been acquired.

I have come to understand through newspaper items that experts and analysts are of the opinion that it is a body-blow to the ambitious 'one trillion investment target' set for the infrastructure development in the Twelfth Five Year Plan, as the new rules envisage high compensation and near-total consent of the affected parties to acquire land. The Government should come forward to explain to the House the impact of the Bill on the infrastructure projects of the future. The economic situation in India, at present, is very worrying as the dollar is becoming more and more expensive and the rupee more and more weak. Unless large infrastructure projects come, our economy would not improve. I would, once again, like to know from the Government what the impact of this Bill would be on our future infrastructure projects. Provision for reservation and other facilities has also been made for the Scheduled Caste and the Scheduled Tribe people. I would like to urge upon the Hon. Minister to extend these facilities to the minority communities also.

With these reservations, I conclude my speech, Sir.

## [3] K.P. Ramalingam

DR K.P. RAMALINGAM (Tamil Nadu): Mr Deputy Chairman, Sir, I support this Bill on behalf of my party, Dravida Munnetra Kazhagam. First of all, I would like to appreciate the Hon. Minister who has brought forward this Bill after a very good study. Just like the Food Security Bill, this bill can proudly be called as Farmers' Security Bill.

Land is a scarce resource, but being a Welfare State, the Government is always in need of land for various welfare schemes. The power of Government to acquire private property for public use or public purposes is based on two well-established principles— one, regard for the public welfare, which is the prime object of any Government; and second, public necessity is greater than that of private necessity. The concept of Welfare State and these two important principals empower the State to acquire land for public purpose. With the acquisition of land, there comes a lot of issues and problems. How to tackle these issues and problems has always remained a concern for the Government. The three principal factors of production are land, labour and capital.

Often, a question was raised: Since there is no question of State acquisition of labour or capital, even at the margin, then, why should the State at all be involved in acquiring land—Mr Derek O'Brien also raised this point—which is the most precious and scarce of the three factors of production? And that too for private enterprises, PPP enterprises or even public enterprises! If we reduce the agricultural land lease, it will not only affect the production but also destroy cultivating practice for the next generation. If the farmers of India forget the farming activities, then, which country, other than India, will supply food to our nation, which has more than a 100 crore population. Then, the slogans, 'Garibi hatao', 'Hunger hatao' cannot be sought, only 'people hatao', without food, can be. While conceiving a project, all aspects are taken care of by private enterprises. Then, why is the Government coming into the picture for acquiring land alone? Maybe, in the past, some mistakes or errors might have occurred. They are all out of *bona fide* intention. To tide over the situation, the Government proposes that local bodies be engaged in the process of making Social Impact Assessment of the proposed project. This is mandated under Clause 4 which is a big leap. A cautious approach in the process of acquisition of land and including the representative body at the grassroot levels will, certainly, bring about a radical change. Sir, Clause 29 talks about how to calculate the market value. One method is by the provisions of the Indian Stamp Act, 1899 and the other method is by taking the average of the sale deed registered in that area or in and around that area.

Sir, I hope everybody knows that there is prevalence of a syndicate system in our country. As you can see, in our House, my friend, Dr. Maitreyan and our BJP Deputy Leader, Shri Ravi Shankar Prasad, cleft together. Sir, in this system, generally, people with a vested interest form a syndicate and they see that the market value is confined to a particular level and it is not taken beyond that level. ....(*Interruptions*)...

MR DEPUTY CHAIRMAN: It is a friendly remark.

DR K.P. RAMALINGAM: Sir, the same thing is happening in land acquisition also. There is still some scope for improvement in this regard. I request the Government to take necessary steps in this regard.

Sir, in addition to this, there is a provision for solatium under Clause 31. The solatium will be 100 per cent of the compensation arrived at by invoking clauses 27, 28 and 29. Sir, till now, solatium was awarded in motor accident cases to the relatives of the deceased. I hope not only me but the entire House will also join me in appreciating this new dimension.

Sir, the persons who lost their land in land acquisition process were made to run from pillar to post to have their genuine and legal compensation. The detailed procedures made out under Schedule-I ensure minimum compensation packages in a time-bound manner, which has been taken care of by Clause 26. In spite of all this, if any dispute arises, then comes into the picture the Land Acquisition, Rehabilitation and Resettlement Authority. There shall be a land acquisition, rehabilitation and resettlement authority. Section 17 of the Land Acquisition Act, 1894 empowered the Government to bypass the procedures for acquiring of land citing the urgency reasons as ground for acquisition of land. Sir, Clause 41 of the new Bill prescribes checks and balances—this is a very good sign—while invoking urgency clause. This is well defined.

Sir, now, I am coming to resettlement and rehabilitation aspect. I believe that for the first time in the history of our country, resettlement and rehabilitation has been given a statutory status. The ruler should frame the rules, not by brilliance but by heart. Here, this Bill has been framed by our Minister through his heart.

DR K.P. RAMALINGAM: Sir, instead of going to regular civil court, the people affected by the project will address their grievances to this Authority. This Authority will pass relevant order. If not satisfied, then the order can be challenged in the High Court. Thus, as per my knowledge, the burden of courts is removed by Clause 64. In addition to this, delay and time-consuming processes are also done away with this new system which will benefit the land owners.

Now, Sir, I am coming to the most controversial section. The most controversial section of the previous Act is 'Urgency Clause.' The Second Schedule to this Bill lists the elements of Rehabilitation and Resettlement that have to be included. While awarding Rehabilitation and Resettlement Award under Clause 32, the Schedule enumerates ten elements that are to be included in the award compulsorily while announcing Rehabilitation and Resettlement Award. Sir, this package has included all the elements that are required by an individual to start his life from beginning to end. ...(*Time-Bell*)...

Please give me two minutes more.

Sir, I wish to make one point more. While undertaking developmental activity, while executing a project, invariably, trees are chopped. The loss so happened should be suitably compensated and it has to be encouraged by 'Social Forestry' concept. The Hon. Minister may not have the portfolio of the Ministry of Environment and Forests now, but he must think about the forests.

Sir, I wish to urge upon the Government one more thing. He has to ensure that the extent of cultivable agricultural land should not be reduced. If this is allowed to happen, the loss cannot be compensated at any cost. Please take this point into consideration.

Sir, finally, land cannot be defined in a casual manner. Land is the real 'God' to the Indian people as it is the 'life' to the Indian farmers. After our Independence, our Central and State Governments distributed lands to poor and marginalized people. This land cannot be sold to others and it cannot be acquired too. This type of land is named 'Panchami' lands. But this type of land is looted by big powerful people. To avoid this type of land-grabbing, certain special section has to be included in this Bill. Sir, in this request, our friends from CPM will definitely join us because they have already undertaken more than twenty agitations and dharnaas to get back Panchami Land in Siruthavur in Tamil Nadu. .....(*Interruptions*)...

With these words, I once again say that this Bill is a Farmers Security Bill. So, I appreciate and support the Bill wholeheartedly. Thank you, Sir

## [4] Devender Goud T.

SHRI DEVENDER GOUD T. (Andhra Pradesh): Sir, I rise to support the Land Acquisition Bill moved by the Hon. Rural Development Minister. I support this Bill because no Government in the world, except a few, acquires land for private purpose. I support this because Andhra Pradesh is one such State which has suffered a lot. He belongs to Andhra Pradesh; he got elected from Andhra Pradesh Assembly. He knows how the Government there has acquired lakhs of acres of land, including fertile land, for private purposes. The land is lying unutilized. They have not even paid the compensation to the farmers. They are all suffering a lot. The State Government from 2004 onwards has been rampantly acquiring lakhs of acres of land, including multi-crop irrigated land, for private parties without giving adequate compensation and against the wishes of the land owners and farmers. So, I think, this Bill is in the right direction as this Bill will prevent the Government from acquiring land for private purposes. The land acquired by the Government of Andhra Pradesh, on behalf of private parties, should also be returned to land owners and farmers immediately because they have not yet started any activity there whether in the name of township or metros. They acquired lakhs of acres of land which is lying idle. For Jalayagnam they have spent more than Rs. 70,000 crore. I do not want to mention all those things because you have given me only six minutes. Even the CAG has pointed out that there are so many lapses in the Jalayagnam. They acquired the land but they have not utilized the land. The project is not coming in that area.

Secondly, the Bill allows acquisition of multi-crop irrigated land. If net-sown area is less than 50 per cent in a district, then it permits acquisition of ten per cent of the land. It is not acceptable. Sir, the agricultural production is less than four per cent in the country. And, the productivity of land in India is extremely low. By converting multi-crop irrigated land even as a last resort, we will not only lose productivity but also fertile land. The Bill permits to acquire 5 per cent of irrigated land for diversion to commercial purposes. It is recommended by the Mahajan Committee and the Government is taking shelter under this. It is not proper. I strongly demand that no irrigated land should be diverted to other purposes as we need to increase the production and productivity of foodgrains. This becomes more important after the passing of Food Security Bill.

Clause 95 of the Bill permits the Government to keep unutilized land for ten years in a Land Bank. I ask why that should be kept in Land Bank. I propose that either this should be returned to the land owners or period should be reduced to five years or it should be re-allotted to others for exactly similar purpose. It is only then the objective of such acquisition is fulfilled.

Third point I wish to make is relating to Social Impact Assessment (SIA) reports and mandatory rehabilitation and resettlement. Here, you are mandating SIA to be later reviewed by an expert committee, followed by Government survey. After that, any decision can be challenged in courts. Does such procedure not delay industrialization and urbanization and hamper the growth trajectory of the country? If so, I would like to know from the Hon. Minister how he is planning to reconcile both the things.

The next point I wish to raise is relating to jurisdiction of Parliament to make laws on transactions between private parties. I fail to understand how Parliament can make laws to oversee R&R on purchase of agricultural land through private negotiations. The Hon. Minister is saying that Union derives its power to make laws on 'acquisition and requisition of property' from Item No. 42 of the Concurrent List. Further, 'transfer of property, other than agricultural land, registration of documents and deeds' is included in Item No. 6 of the Concurrent List. However, 'transfer and alienation of agricultural land' is included in Item No. 18 of the State List. So, R&R arises out of transfer of agricultural land and the issue falls within the sole jurisdiction of State Legislatures. So, it does not fall under the residuary powers under Item No. 97 of the Union List.

Secondly, there is a possible circumvention of R&R requirements. For example, a private company can acquire or purchase multiple parcels of land below 50 acres in urban areas or 100 acres in rural areas to escape from rehabilitation and resettlement. In such a scenario, how will the Government protect the interests of affected parties? So, I suggest to the Hon. Minister to reconsider this.

The next point is relating to payment of compensation. The Bill says that four times compensation would be paid to land in rural areas and the compensation would be twice the value in urban areas. Sir, I was Revenue Minister in Andhra Pradesh. I know how the value is fixed in the area. In 1995, 20 years back, so many farmers used to come to my office. I know how these transactions take place. The House is also aware as to how it is done. They undervalue the land at the time of registration to escape payment of stamp duty. So, the current market price should be the basis in deciding the value of the land. You take current market price into consideration.

Sir, the Bill says that consent of 80 per cent people in the case of privately acquired land or 70 per cent people in the case of Government acquired land is required.

Hence, I draw the attention of the Hon. Minister to Article 300A of the Constitution which says that no citizen should be deprived of property. In view of this, I request the Hon. Minister to take appropriate decision on this issue.

With these words, I conclude my views on the Bill. Thank you very much

## [5] Chandan Mitra

DR CHANDAN MITRA (Madhya Pradesh): Mr Deputy Chairman, Sir, thank you very much for giving me an opportunity to express my views on this very, very important piece of legislation.

Sir, it is a well-intentioned Bill and I do not doubt the sincerity of the Minister because he has pursued this and other jholawala Bills for a long time and has been successful in getting through his agenda. So, he certainly deserves congratulations.

Sir, I have no serious issues with the Bill because frankly, it is an improvement on the 2007 Bill which actually was based on a Report of the Rural Development Committee of that time, of which I was a Member for six years. We had unanimously proposed a legislation, or rather the amended legislation that the Government had proposed, and the Bill was passed by the Lok Sabha, but it was presented to the Rajya Sabha on the very last day of the previous Lok Sabha when it could not get passed and, therefore, the Bill lapsed altogether. So, the entire legislation was sent back afresh and it has been improved upon considerably in terms of compensation in particular and I am glad about that.

Sir, if you look at the historical experience, I want to put on record that in India land has been grabbed and farmers have been duped for centuries. Pathos of the Indian farmer who is not only economically dependent on land but also emotionally and psychologically dependent on land, is something that we very often fail to appreciate.

Sir, Rabindranath Tagore wrote a poem entitled 'Dui Bigha Jami' which simply means 'Do Bigha Zamin' which is a famous film made under Mr Bimal Roy's direction. Balraj Sahini played a very memorable role. But I am talking of the poem written by Rabindranath Tagore. In [the poem], the poet talks about a very powerful landlord, feudal lord of the area, who fancies just two bigas of land, which belongs to a poor landless farmer. He had just those two bigas of land. The Zamindar decided to grab it. So, false cases were prepared that he had borrowed money and failed to return it. And pyadas of the landlord were sent; and the poor man was evicted from the land.

Bereft of livelihood, bereft of family and everything, the man leaves the village and wanders for many years. Then, one day he gets a strong urge to come back to his village and see what happened to those two bigas of his land that were seized from him. He finds that nothing has happened. It was just that landlord's desire that he should expand the area under his control and grab that land. Anyway, this man sits under a mango tree which he had planted many, many years ago when he was the owner of those two bigas of land. He sits under the shade. Two ripe mangoes fall at his feet in a while. Rabindranath expressing the man's emotions, says he felt as if the mango tree has recognized that he had planted the tree and was paying a tribute to him by offering him those two fruits. At that point, while he was just leaving with those two fruits, the guard of the landlord saw him moving out of the land, grabbed him, tied him with a rope and brought him to the court of the landlord. There he was mercilessly beaten black-and-blue. Then, he was told not to set foot on this land ever again. So, the concluding lines of the poem are: *Tumi Maharaj Sadhu holey aaj, Ami aaj chor batey.* That you oh Lord, have become a sadhu, you are being praised as a great man.

And I have become a thief because of the two mangoes that fell at my feet from the tree that I had once planted. Sir, the pathos of the Indian farmer is brought out in this where his land was grabbed. This, although has been written 100 years ago, by Rabindranath Tagore, is a reality even today. Anybody familiar with Munshi Premchand's writings will also testify to this reality. So, definitely, there is a prime need to reorganize the whole system, provide a mechanism so that land acquisition, if and when necessary, becomes fair and equitable, and just compensation is paid to the farmer.

Sir, my issue with this Bill is that while you have definitely tried to improve the conditions of the farmer so that he is not duped, not cheated, the Government's intervention. But, I think, there are other ways beyond working only on the compensation, rehabilitation and relief element.

Sir, I would like to point out to you that 16 per cent of the world's population resides in this country; and only 2 per cent of the land area is within the confines of the Indian Union. Sixteen per cent population and two per cent land! Very interestingly, Sir, 68.35 million hectares are designated as wasteland. And 50 per cent of designated wastelands are in non-forest areas. Even in the case of those in forest areas, we have to regenerate those forests. But 50 per cent are in non-forest areas. Since 1962, the Government of India has adopted a Wasteland Development Programme and further, if I am not mistaken, there is one more scheme, named after the Gandhi family, called the Rajiv Gandhi Wasteland Development Project or something like that.

SHRI JAIRAM RAMESH: There is no such programme.

DR CHANDAN MITRA: You may take it into account while you reply. Sir, I want to know from the Hon. Minister as to why this issue has not been brought forth in a significant way and why it has not been made mandatory. For the bulk of those seeking to acquire land for private industries or for public private partnership, why is it that they are not acquiring land in wastelands when nothing is happening there? But I will tell you the reasons why nobody wants to go there. Many of these places are remote areas. There is no road or rail connectivity. Industries are not being set up there because they say, 'What is the point? Production costs are very high. How will we transport our manufactured goods to ports or cities?' So, the Government should have focused on this issue. Ultimately, we have to balance the needs of agriculture and farmers along with the need to promote industries. The manufacturing industry in India is going down day by day. The share of agriculture in GDP is going down and down. It is just 13 per cent. We all know the state of the manufacturing industry, and we are dependent on the services sector alone for our GDP. This is not an acceptable situation. So, in order to promote the manufacturing industry, when you acquire land, I think, wasteland development is something that the Government needs to, seriously, look into. And, acquisition of land, whenever necessary, should first be done in wasteland areas. Allot the land to the industry, invite the industry to go there and provide the connectivity and infrastructure required. The Government is going to acquire land for infrastructure. Even in this Bill, it is very clear that land will be acquired for infrastructure.

But while creating the infrastructure which we, definitely, need, we should ask ourselves as to whether land will be used for infrastructure development alone. I am saying this in the context of what we have seen even in and around Delhi, that when a private organization was going to build an expressway, thousands of acres of land were acquired and handed over to the company. The Highway was built,—indeed, a very fine Highway—but along with that, a lot of agricultural land was acquired and farmers were displaced. They agitated, but nothing happened. What we see is a lot of multi-storey residential apartments coming along the way. The price of these apartments is phenomenal. With a fantastic infrastructure in terms of a highway, that company has been allowed to make hundreds and thousands of crores of profit by building residential complexes, malls, cinema halls and other things in that stretch.

And when a farmer sees that on his land, which was acquired at the circle rate, one square feet of built-up apartment is being sold at twenty or twenty five times more than the rate at which he was paid as compensation, don't you think that resentment is bound to occur? I would like to know whether there is any provision to prevent this kind of misuse of infrastructure building when in the name of infrastructure building, ultimately, you are enabling private profit, in large quantities, to individual property developers and industries. Sir, we have all seen what has happened,—I am just talking about the vicinity of Delhi—the kind of land mafia, the mall mafia and various other mafias which have come up and which have acquired farmers' land to the tune of hundreds and thousands of acres. I know that the Bill tries to prevent that. They say that there will be a social impact assessment for every 100 acres of rural land acquired and every 50 acres of urban land acquired to prevent any such kind of exploitation.

But, Sir, what is the guarantee that some developer is not going to start buying small pieces of land—three acres, four acres, five acres—which is exempt from SIA and would amount to private purchase? Under this Bill, actually from the time of initiating the process to completion of acquisition, it will take about three years' time. In that period somebody keeps on buying small plots of land in the same area, adjacent to one another and at the end of it, you suddenly find that 200 acres have been acquired. There is no SIA, no compensation because it is just two or three acres at a time. Sir, this is the kind of

misuse which is happening.[Continues in Hindi] … Naturally, new
towns are going to come up. Urbanization is happening. Populations
are going to shift. Now, how are you going to handle this because
there will be some understanding and there will be wanton misuse
of whatever law is brought about? I don't blame the Minister or
Government X or Government Y. I am saying as a country.

We have to try and confront this issue and devise appropriate measures so that the intention of the law makers—whether it
is the Congress Government, the BJP Government or any other
Government for that matter—can be actualized and the farmers are
ultimately benefited and not robbed of their compensation.

Sir, I have two more points to make. One, Sir, is I would need to
know whether it is possible to attach a value to the loss of livelihood
and I say this in the context of many small farmers in different parts
of the country, particularly in Eastern India—where I come from—
in Odisha, in Assam, in Bengal. There are small homesteads. Almost
every homestead in a village has a small pond and they also have
coconut trees… there are toddy tappers in the South. The Minister
is fully aware of it. There is an entire community of toddy tappers.

You will give them some other land. You will say, 'We are going
to retain your fishing rights.' The Bill says that if it is an irrigation
project, they will be given fishing rights in reservoir that is to come
up. But, Sir, it is not the same thing. I understand that it is not possible to recreate the same conditions somewhere else. But, we have to
workout some thing—whether in terms of monetary compensation
or in terms of finding an appropriate location in which lifestyle can
be maintained and there is no serious loss of livelihood and culture.

Sir, there is a film called Saudagar which the Hon. Minister might
have watched. It is on the life of a toddy-taper. What happened to his
livelihood when commercialization came in? We are witnessing this
all over the country. Commercialization is happening everywhere.
What is happening in Bengal is that coconut trees are being cut and
their stems are being used in brick kilns, because they burn slowly.
So, Sir, even before the Government pays any compensation, people
themselves are cutting off trees and using them in brick kilns, because
there is a demand for bricks as construction material. So, Sir, this
is something we have to look into. I think, the measurement of
livelihood and measurement of lifestyle is something that should be

incorporated in this Bill in some way…(time-bell rings)…Sir, don't hurry me up. You have always been good to me.

MR DEPUTY CHAIRMAN: I am good to everybody.

DR CHANDAN MITRA: Sir, I am raising issues and trying my best not to repeat anything what the Hon. Members have said before.

Sir, it has been said that there will be solatium. There is also a proposal that if there is any development and industry is set up one job per family must be assured at the minimum wage rate of that State. What happens if that thing does not happen, if no industry comes up? This has also been mentioned by my Hon. colleague from Odisha. We have seen what has happened in Kalinganagar. One company acquired land at a very low rate 12 years ago and has done nothing except building a boundary wall. Entire village in the surrounding areas has turned Maoist. They are threatening to take up arms, because they were cheated of their land and nothing has happened. No development took place. No industry has developed. Take Singur which is a classic case. You drive down NH2. You can see just some sheds. What happened to the farmers who willingly gave their land and you promised them jobs? You go and travel just beyond that highway. In every family, Sir, there is a tale of misery. They did not get jobs. They got land. They got compensation. Compensation money is over. This also referred here. Sir, again, just outside Delhi, what happened? People are buying Mercedes Benz and BMW cars from the compensation that they have got, going to pubs in Gurgaon and molesting women! It is a daily recurrence. All money has been blown up. Sir, therefore, I would urge the Hon. Minister that if industry is set up one job must be given. I would say that this Bill can be improved by saying, 'you pay a minimum salary per month to a family that has *vis-à-vis* been relocated or whose land has been taken and has been provided a house nearby.' Why do wait for industry to come up? Who knows when it will come up? And, by then, what kind of situation will prevail? Along with that, I think, there is a need to enforce on companies or Government organization that takes away land to ensure skill development to all the displaced people, so that they do not have to remain, idle and find better jobs, more paying jobs as times go on.

Sir, these are the two concrete suggestions I have to make.

Finally, I am glad that the Hon. Minister is bringing some amendments which take care of a few lacunae in the Bill and also I would like to stress again that leasing of land is a very good idea that has come up. Yes, I know. We have proposed it and the Hon. Minister has accepted it.

Sir, I would like to say that we are all together in this. This is in the interest of the country. We want to see our peasants happy. If they are happy, they will produce more. And, we must give them productive remuneration for this. And the country would again become a soney ki chidiya. Today, it is a dud chidiya. It should not become a dead chidiya. We would like to see our country about which again another

Bengali poet wrote:

*Dhana-dhanneye, pushpe bhara,*
*Amader ei basundhara, Tahar majhey achhey*
*Je desh, sakal desher shewa, Se je sapnon*
*Dije tairee shey desh, smriti diye gada.*
*Eman desh ti kothao khaje padey na koi*
*Tumi, Shakal desher vani sheyje amaar janambhumi*

## [6]  D. Bandyopadhyay

SHRI D. BANDYOPADHYAY (West Bengal): Thank you, Madam. I rise to oppose the Bill though I admit it has many notable features. With notable features, there are many concepts of the old draconian Bill which was totally inhuman, the Hon. Minister has tried to put a human face. For that I am grateful to him and I congratulate him. But our opposition is mainly on the whole concept of eminent domain. Eminent domain, Madam, was a royal prerogative. Notionally all land belongs to the king. Individual title holders are absolute owners but the King, now State, is the notional paramount owner of the land. Therefore, if the King, now the State, wants that land for his own purpose, then it can appropriate the land by paying compensation because it is the recognized right. One good point about this Bill which I oppose but I support the content. ....(*Interruptions*)... I am supporting the good point, but I am opposing the main point. ...(*Interruptions*)...

THE VICE-CHAIRMAN (SHRIMATI RENUKA CHOWDHURY):
Mr Bandyopadhyay, you are going to lose your time. …
(*Interruptions*)…

SHRI D. BANDYOPADHYAY: The concept of owner in original
Bill was not required. But for the loss of property and for the compulsory character of the acquisition, compensation is paid. Somehow
or the other, the owner always feels that since he cannot sell it in
the open market, he is being cheated. If 'cheated' is the wrong word
he is being betrayed. This comprehensive Bill is not the only law on
the land acquisition. There are 13 other laws as mentioned in the
Schedule IV of this Bill itself. Now my point is why there should be
such multiplicity of law on the same subject. I know the Minister of
Rural Development, in-charge of this Bill, cannot control all those 13
Ministries. But, at the time Government as a whole should take a view
that there are 13 Acts regarding the acquisition. Each Department
wants a Bill of its own. So, when you are having a comprehensive Bill
covering all aspects giving a human face to it, why should we have all
those Acts? I would request the Hon. Minister to take a view collectively in the Government so that you have only one Bill or maximum
another Bill if there is a specialized thing. I would like to commend
the Minister for inserting Chapter 3, entitled 'special Provisions to
Safeguard Food Security'. Large-scale acquisition involving large scale
displacement of the rural population creates a great adverse effect
on agriculture. Therefore, the point that you want to have the social
impact assessment is a very welcome feature. But I am afraid that
the limit suggested under clause 10 has not been properly defined.
(*Time-bell rings*) I am coming back. …(*Interruptions*)… Another good
feature of the Bill is the social audit which I have already talked about.
Now I come to the main thing. So far the acquiring authority never
thought of the policy of rehabilitation and resettlement. I congratulate
the Minister for bringing that in the statute book this concept to give
rehabilitation and resettlement. In spite of good features, we oppose
the Bill because this draconian law should not be used by profit making institutions, owners of such entities who believe in the efficiency
of market for efficient allocation of resources.

That applies to the principle: When they operate in the land market, as they are operating in the labour market, as they are operating

in the resource market, or, in whatever market they are, if there are imperfections in those markets and they operate and make money, why they should be given privilege under this Bill to acquire land forcefully.

Thank you very much, Madam.

SHRI JAIRAM RAMESH: Madam, I just want to say for record that Shri D. Bandyopadhyay had been a very distinguished Secretary in the Ministry of Rural Development. He has been a guru to the people of my generation. He was one of the main architects of Operation Barga, which was spearheaded by Hare Krishna Konar and Benoy Choudhury, which remains the single most important piece of land reform legislation in our country. He is also the person to whose house I went thrice in Salt Lake City and he has contributed much to the drafting of this legislation. And, I am very happy that he applauds me and opposes the Bill.

### [7] Sitaram Yechury

SHRI SITARAM YECHURY (West Bengal): Thank you very much, Madam. I am very happy that we are finally going to have a new law. I congratulate the Minister for all the painstaking homework that he has done. I am sure he would remember that ten years ago we sat together for drafting the Common Minimum Programme of the UPA-I. We had a lot of discussion on the new law that had to be acquired. And you would recollect, Mr Minister, there was an element that is missing in this law. But, I hope you would consider for future a better law that we can bring about that former landowners should have a share in the stake of the rise in the value of land after it has been acquired and not only compensation at the time of acquisition, and not only relief and rehabilitation. Most of the heartburn in the case of land acquisition comes because of the value of land that has multiplied after it has been acquired and a share of that does not come to the landowners. Now, this is a point that requires to be properly considered. I hope you will, in future discussions for improving this law, consider this aspect and, therefore, I want to draw this to your attention.

Sir, since my colleague has already spoken in detail about the point of view of my Party, I only want to give the plug points and say that these are the areas in which certain amendments for improving this law will have to be made. First is a proper definition of 'public purpose' and 'affected persons'. Second is the binding nature of social impact assessment. Third is a land use plan and land use commission. Fourth is, provisions for safeguarding food security. There I would like you to consider the point of arid and semi-arid lands which have now been excluded in terms of the concept of production of foodgrains. Now, that is not true. In many parts of the country, arid and semi-arid lands are also producing foodgrains and adding to our total foodgrains production. So, that cannot be completely excluded. That should also be taken into account. Next is the question of fair and just rehabilitation and resettlement. I have made my point on that. Then comes prior informed consent and role of Panchayats as well as Gram Sabhas. These are important. The role of Panchayats and Gram Sabhas will have to be properly brought into the Act and the question of protecting and safeguarding the rights of SCs and STs in terms of land acquisition, particularly STs in the Scheduled Areas. That is something that is not done unless Gram Sabhas are there. Madam, I have two more minutes. I just have to come to my basic points.

THE VICE-CHAIRMAN (SHRIMATI RENUKA CHOW-DHURY): Your total time was three minutes. You overshot it.

SHRI SITARAM YECHURY: I think these are the issues which need to be taken up for future consideration. We will move some amendments, particularly the amendment concerning Fourth Schedule. I know we have had these discussions outside and inside the Parliament and you said that within a period of one year, all these Acts will come under the purview of this Act. Even that one year is not necessary. Secondly, within that period of one year, through executive action, many of these laws can be amended. Now, you are aware of these problems. We have drawn your attention to them earlier. That must be taken on board. Further, there is the question of special powers of urgency. You must assure the House that it will never be invoked for the sake of private owners. That assurance has to come in that special powers of urgency will not be invoked for private owners. ... (*Interruptions*)...

THE VICE-CHAIRMAN (SHRIMATI RENUKA CHOW-DHURY): Please hurry up.

SHRI SITARAM YECHURY: Madam, I will just conclude. Land reforms is something, as the Minister himself mentioned, very dear to us, to the Communists. You have taken the names of some of the stalwarts of the Indian Communist who pioneered the entire move-ment of land reforms. Even today the State of West Bengal has the most comprehensive land reforms that ever have been implemented in the country. You have taken those names and you have also men-tioned the name of our colleague. It's a different matter that he is in a different party today. ...(*Interruptions*)... But, he would be better off where he was earlier. But, that's a different matter. ...(*Interruptions*)... I never claimed that. ...(*Interruptions*)...

THE VICE-CHAIRMAN (SHRIMATI RENUKA CHOW-DHURY): Please don't have cross-conversations.

SHRI SITARAM YECHURY: Madam, the point was that we have been arguing for a new law all these years and I am glad that a new law is coming, but not to our best satisfaction. Nevertheless, if such laws had been there, none of what happened in Singur or any other place would have happened. Even in Nandigram, not an inch of land was ever acquired or taken over, whatever be the forceful thing. Even after Nandigram, sixteen thousand acres of land was distributed through land reform laws in the State of West Bengal. Then, 14 lakh bargadars have been recorded for the first time in the history. Actually 13,00,000 families have received land through these land reforms. We are talking with a certain degree of experience and with a certain degree of commitment. Even in the national movement, whether it was Telangana, whether it was the issue of Surma Valley in Assam, whether it was the Tebhaga movement, whether it was the Worli trib-als struggle for land, all were led by the Communists and the passion for land to the tiller remains a slogan with us. Now, this Bill does not give land to the tiller. But we want to move in that direction. We want to move in the direction where finally the land will be owned by the tiller. If that needs to be done, Sir, I think this law will have to be strengthened further; and this is not an issue on which you will have to prove your credentials as is sought to be done. But this is an issue for building a better India that we will have to move forward. So, short-sighted and narrow people can't do it. You require a larger vision for this; and that larger vision is what is required in order to carry this forward to create a better Bill.

Finally, I want to appeal to the Minister, since you have accepted four of the amendments moved by the principal Opposition party, to accept the genuine concern, at least, two of the amendments that powers of urgency that will not be invoked for private companies. Secondly, accept the Schedule IV. What is your compulsion? I just really can't understand what your compulsion is. I think, Clause 4 should be .....(*Interruptions*)... Sir, I am actually intimidated.

MR DEPUTY CHAIRMAN: I did not say anything. You know that you are taking more time. I did not say anything.

SHRI SITARAM YECHURY: I thought when Madam Chairperson is in the Chair, I could revert back to Telugu and get an extra minute or so. But the moment you came and sat here…

MR DEPUTY CHAIRMAN: You can still speak in Telugu.

SHRI SITARAM YECHURY: You came and sat in the Chair and nodded your head. I was actually intimidated. Please don't ring the bell.

MR DEPUTY CHAIRMAN: I nodded my head because you were making a good speech.

SHRI SITARAM YECHURY: Thank you. But invariably after that nod your finger goes to the bell.

MR DEPUTY CHAIRMAN: I wanted to look at the display board also.

SHRI SITARAM YECHURY: Finally, the only point that I want to make is, you please take on board the concerns that I have listed out. I did not explain them because of lack of time. But accept some of these genuine amendments which I know, in heart of hearts, you also accept. You may be under your compulsion. As I said, what is required is not narrow vision, not bitter acrimony unnecessarily. What is required is to work collectively to build a better India. I think, we have to move towards building a better India through a better law which we can improve upon. I urge upon you to do that. Please consider seriously the points of giving a certain stake to the former land owner in the enhanced value of land after it has been acquired. Now, this is something very, very important I want to repeat because most of the heart-burn comes when you find that the land that you had owned after it has been acquired its value has gone up a number of times; and you get no share out of that. Now that is where a certain percentage should be fixed for the former land owners to get an enhanced value from that land. I would once again urge upon you to seriously consider these concrete amendments that we have put forward. Thank you.

## [8] D. Raja

SHRI D. RAJA (Tamil Nadu): Mr Deputy Chairman, Sir, thank you. In the past two decades, we witnessed farmers' resistance against forcible acquisition of their land by corporate houses and mining companies with the help of the State support. Farmers fought against police oppression and brutality in several parts of the country. It has become imperative to replace the 1894 Act which is a very obsolete one. In this regard,

I consider the present Bill is a step forward for which Mr Jairam Ramesh, the Minister deserves congratulations. Sir, the new Act should have been designed to ensure that rapid and indiscriminate transfer of agricultural land to non-agricultural uses is halted and regulated keeping in view the socially desirable use of land, and that poor farmers and tribals are not displaced from their meagre livelihood resource base. Instead, as the Title suggests, the focus of the Bill is limited to providing adequate compensation and rehabilitation and smoothen the transfer of agricultural land for mining purposes or industrial development or real estate development. Ideally speaking, there should be a moratorium for a considerable period of time on all transfers of agricultural land.

The Hon. Minister may kindly take note of it. The Government of India should produce a white paper on the land use, and there should be a thorough discussion on land use policy in totality in Parliament. Only then can every citizen be assured that the natural resources of this country belong to everyone and cannot be appropriated by a small elite population.

Sir, the term 'public purpose' is defined so loosely that the State can intervene to facilitate companies to acquire farm land for profit-making activities. In this regard, I refer to Chapter XIII, Clause 103. I think it is not sufficient to stop acquisition of land for speculative purposes. I would, therefore, request the Hon. Minister to consider that the resale of land is not allowed. If it cannot be used for the purpose for which it was acquired, it should be returned to their original owners or their heirs. If this is not possible, it can be acquired by the Government and used as agricultural land by distributing it to the landless and encouraging cooperative farming.

Sir, the agrarian scene in the country is a matter of great concern. Around 40 per cent of rural households do not possess any land other than homestead. Among those who have farm land, 80 per cent are marginal and small farmers. Farming is not a viable proposition with very small holdings. In such circumstances, these poor farmers can be persuaded to sell their land for a song. These sales are neither beneficial to them individually nor advisable from a macro point of view. There is no provision in the Bill which would intervene in exploitative deals concluded through economic pressures.

Sir, I would like to draw the attention of the Hon. Minister to one small important issue. The purposes which are recognized as 'public purpose' for which the appropriate Government may acquire land are listed at (a) to (f) of sub-clause (1) of Clause 2. There is no specific mention of the Scheduled Castes and the Scheduled Tribes in this important clause and sub-clause. Even if they are covered by items (d) or (f) under sub-clause (1) of Clause 2, this is limited to housing and residential purposes.

Sir, land acquisition will also be required for other purposes pertaining to the Scheduled Castes and the Scheduled Tribes. For example, it is essential to endow all rural landless SC and ST families with a viable extent of agricultural land. In the case of SCs, this is crucial because they are landless. Untouchability has been imposed on them, with all its ramifications, in all areas of life, occupational, economic, educational, health and child survival-related, etc., bonded labour, they constitute about two-thirds of all bonded labourers—and atrocities perpetrated on them are all known to everybody. Sir, in such a situation, I think, the Bill should protect the interests of landless agricultural workers, particularly, the Scheduled Castes people. Sir, we have been talking about land reforms. Radical land reforms have not been carried out in many parts of the country, even though since our freedom movement we have talking about land to the tiller, radical land reforms in the post-Independent India. But these land reforms have not been carried out in many parts of the country in true spirit. On the one hand, the feudal remnants still dominate our countryside.

MR DEPUTY CHAIRMAN: In spite of Communist Party of India? In spite of CPI and CPI (M)?

SHRI D. RAJA: I agree. In spite of the struggle conducted by the Communist Parties, we have feudal remnants dominating our countryside. Sir, this is one part. On the other side, the corporatization of agriculture is promoted. It is the paradox of the situation. So, this piece of legislation should not be an attempt to build the basis and super structure of neo-liberalism. That is where we question the sincerity of the Government. We want a new law. We always demanded that 1894 law should be replaced. We want a new law, but that law should be a better law in the interest of the country, in the interest of the toiling people of our country, particularly, small and marginal farmers, the Scheduled Caste and Scheduled Tribe people and I hope Mr Jairam Ramesh, a very sensitive and sensible Minister in the Government, will take note of all these things and concede some of our amendments when we move at the time of amendments. Thank you.

# Index

# About the Authors

**Jairam Ramesh** is Chair of the Future Earth Engagement Committee, a research platform on global sustainability. Formerly he was the Minister of Rural Development and Minister of State (Independent Charge) of Environment and Forests, Government of India. He is also a member of the Rajya Sabha, the Upper House of the Parliament of India. He has been Union Minister of State for Commerce and Power as well as Union Cabinet Minister of Rural Development, Drinking Water and Sanitation. He is a Visiting Fellow at various academic institutions in India and abroad and is a columnist and author. He has served on the UN Secretary General's High Level Panel on Global Sustainability.

**Muhammad Ali Khan** is an advocate practicing in the Supreme Court of India. He was formerly the Officer on Special Duty to the Minister for Rural Development in the Government of India. Prior to that he worked as an Aide to Jairam Ramesh in the Ministry of Environment and Forests. He began his career working with the litigation team of Amarchand and Mangaldas, a premier Indian law firm.